# IMPOSSIBLE JOY

The Good News for Lust and Sex Addicts

and Other Sinners

Ron J.

Libera

Scripture quotations, unless otherwise noted, are from the Revised Standard Version of the Bible (RSV), copyright © 1946, 1952, and 1971 by the Division of Christian Education of the National Council of the Churches of Christ in the United States of America, and are used by permission. All rights reserved.

Appendix 3, "The Remission of Sins," is reprinted from *Life Essential: The Hope of the Gospel*, by George MacDonald, edited by Rolland Hein, © 1974 by Harold Shaw Publishers. Used by permission of Harold Shaw Publishers, Wheaton, IL. 60189.

Copyright © 1999 by Libera Publishing.
All rights reserved
Published 1999 by Libera Publishing
Printed in the United States of America

Copies of this book may be purchased by writing to Libera Publishing, P O Box 31, Simi Valley, CA 93062 or e-mail ronjfile@aol.com. For other books, articles, and information, e-mail ronjfile@aol.com or write to Libera Publishing.

Cover by Howard Design

# CONTENTS

*Preface* page v

## INTRODUCTIONS

1        What It Was Like: The Boulevard Motel 1
2        What It's Like Now: Bus Stop 5
3        What Happened: The Fellowship of Recovery 7

## PART I ENCOUNTERING THE REAL JESUS

4        Jesus' Identification with My Sinful Human Nature—Introduction 13
5        Jesus' Identification with Our Sinful Human Nature—The Wilderness Temptation 25
6        Jesus' Identification with Our Sinful Human Nature—His Life 37
7        Jesus' Identification with Our Sinful Human Nature—His Death 51
8        The Gallery of God 63

## PART II ENCOUNTERING THE REAL ME

9        A Startling Discovery 73
10      The Woman in Line 79
11      The Sinfulness of the Believer—Romans 7 83
12      The Great Delusion 93
13      Religious Addiction—"Believism" as Unbelief 97
14      Idols out of the Id 105

*Contents*

## PART III  REAL VICTORY IN CHRIST

15  Jesus' Identification with Our Sinful Human Nature—His Present Saving Work 115
16  My Point of Contact with Jesus Now 133
17  The Real Connection 143
18  The "Obedience of Faith" 155
19  Victory over Temptation 171
20  Temptation Flagrante 187
21  Joy in the Impossible 191
22  The Personal Sacrament 199

## PART IV  REAL FELLOWSHIP

23  The Fellowship of Light 207
24  The Fellowship of Cleansing 211
25  The Fellowship of Harvest 221

*Appendixes* page 225

1  Notes on Jesus' Identification with Our Fallen Human Nature 227
2  Parable for a Lustaholic 235
3  "The Remission of Sins," George MacDonald 239
4  The Twelve Steps and Twelve Traditions 247
5  The Wrath Connection 251

*Acknowledgments* page 267

*Endnotes* page 269

Some Scripture passages reflect
a more literal translation of the
original and some a paraphrase.

## *Preface*

I am writing this book because sexual sobriety and victory over lust seem so difficult, if not impossible, for so many Christians, not to mention others. There's something wrong here. Also, so much of sobriety or attempted sobriety seems to be fear-driven and self-driven, which is doomed to failure. There is a better way. I want to bear witness to the fact that victory over lust can be energized by joy and love that come from a saving connection with the Son of man. This is the Good News for all, whether in or out of the church or Twelve Step recovery movement.

The heart of this book is a view of the One who is the source of my joy today. Looking back on my religious experience of a lifetime, my brief ministry in the church, and twenty three years of recovery and working with other lust-sex addicts, I suspect that many are unwittingly worshiping an unreal Jesus, as I was. That is, a Jesus who does not save from sin *now*. As I discovered in my own case, this is not only an impediment to recovery, it makes true recovery impossible. Not mere sobriety; sober is not well. Recovery. Recovery from sin—any attitude or action that shuts out the presence of God.

In recovery we come to see that "having the outward form of religion but denying its power" is a waste. Part of my bottoming-out was sensing that my having the form of Christ, my religious belief and practice, was not working for me. Years of belief, church-going, theological education, prayer, and all sorts of religious ministrations and exercises did not avail me of sobriety. I was going under. What was wrong? It wasn't the real Jesus that was wrong; it was my *mis*-conception and *mis*-connection with him that did not work. I had to have not form, but substance.

*Preface*

    I had to give up old ideas, keep it simple, and start living the basic Twelve Step principles of attitude change and action, with others. This would clear the way inside so I could then discover the One who could and actually did loose me from my lust and other temptations. In the actual encounter, time after time after time. Until I experienced *this* Jesus, I was secretly a cunning skeptic about his saving power.

    Perhaps every age and time has both its flight from and search for the real Jesus. Our time comes out of everything from the "Jesus-freak" subjectivism of the Sixties to the popular "believism" of the Eighties and Nineties. So who is the real Jesus for those of us living in the lust-driven addictive culture of our fast-moving and exceedingly complex time? And how do we actually connect with him in our moments of utter powerlessness?

    A psychologist, whose father went to AA, described what he saw in his father to be the prevailing practice of Twelve Step recovery. He wasn't impressed and called it "addiction to meetings and socialized spirituality." This could just as easily be applied to churchgoing, as was true in my case. Yes, people can feel better attending Twelve Step meetings and church. But what is recovery? The concept of recovery seems foreign to institutional religion today and is often shortchanged in the Twelve Step movement. In my case, I was supposed to be recovered after I "accepted Christ."

    From my own experience, I see that those of us addicted to sex, lust, and relationships eventually need a deeper sobriety, a deeper recovery, a deeper fellowship, and a deeper higher power. Why? Because in addition to whatever else our addiction is, it is *spiritual* death!

    Today I don't hesitate to tell religious newcomers of any persuasion who come into the program, "If you're a lustaholic like me, your relation with God is wrong, regardless of what your belief or religious experience is. How could it be right if you're thinking and doing the things you

*Preface*

tell me you're thinking and doing? To recover, your relation with God must change"

With the "impossible" addiction of lust, these four needs—a deeper sobriety, a deeper recovery, a deeper fellowship, and a deeper connection with God—are increasingly forced upon us. As one of the impossibly addicted, I must have these four deeper realities. I wonder how many in the addiction fellowships or church have the same need, feel the same longing. For my own recovery, I could not realize the first three without also experiencing the fourth—the real Connection. And just as I felt the burden of necessity moving me to express and share my sexual sobriety experience years ago—to carry the message—I now have the longing to express and share this present reality of the saving Son of man: a Christ for the impossible, the lust-possessed.

As I bear witness in this book, instead of merely accepting and believing the truth about someone called Jesus Christ, I am coming to know the saving Son of man. And this comes about in my continuing experience with my sinful human nature. The bridge connecting the Jesus of two thousand years ago with my lust addiction today was not made through Christian knowledge and belief. The bridge was made through the actual Connection itself—the repeated saving union in temptation after impossible temptation. Experiencing this "power of his resurrection" each time, and now looking back into Scripture, I am coming to see the "how" behind all of this—how it was made possible and why it is effective within me today. That's what I want to share so others can make this marvelous breakthrough.

A lifetime of trying to "have faith" without this real Connection proved deadly to me.

Thus, my aim is not only to lift up this Saving One but to move the reader into spiritual self-awareness and action. I want us to see our way out of the fog of certain religious illusions which I came to see within myself. I want to help shatter some false presuppositions floating about, concepts

*Preface*

keeping us in bondage, keeping us from the real Saving One. What I write about is what I am discovering for myself, what works for me, what has struck my deepest being and is my source of freedom and joy. This is how the Christ of Scripture is coming to be the Christ of my very own recovery experience. That my experience also resonates with others in recovery gives me courage now to come forward as I do.

But today I find that terms such as "Christ," "Christian," "Christianity," "Jesus," "church," etc., are so skewed in our pagan and media-driven culture as to be virtually *pseudo*-Christian. I see us having to go back to the beginning with John the Baptist at the river Jordan and hear the Gospel for the very first time: *"Repent, for the kingdom of heaven is at hand."* And then to look where he points and behold *"the Lamb of God who bears away the sin of the world,"* the One who takes our lust on himself—today.

It's taken me years of recovery even to begin to discover and enter this new way of life. Did it have to take me so long? I don't think so. That's another reason I'm writing this book. So others can experience this reality of the Savior within themselves sooner and more fully than I.

Another thing: This book is not a substitute for working the Steps. How can we behold the *saving* Lamb of God without repentance, which is what the Steps are designed to bring about? This book points toward the fulfillment of what working the Steps prepares the way for and offers promise of what our lust was really looking for.

I feel I am only touching the hem of his garment, but that's everything to me! So share it I must. Union with the real Son of man is my continuing prayer— "that I may know him and the power of his resurrection and may share his sufferings, becoming like him in his death." Because it works! Because he's real!

*Preface*

Although this book talks a lot about lust, this is really a metaphor for addiction, as addiction itself is a metaphor for sin (John 8:34; Heb. 2:15). The book is thus for sinners, that is, the powerless, those who have consciousness of deep personal need, knowing how far short they fall. It is for those who have no option but to come to know a personal, loving, saving, rescuing Friend—in their powerlessness. In the hope of helping such, I share this most personal aspect of my own recovery—getting to know the One who is keeping me sober and sane one day at a time.

> *Don't be afraid. I, I am the First and the Last and the Living One. I became dead and behold, I am living for ever more. And I have the keys of death and hell.*
> 
> Rev.1:17-18

Even so, come quickly in our midst.

# INTRODUCTIONS

# 1

## What It Was Like:

## The Boulevard Motel

My name is Ron; I'm a recovering lust and sex addict.

This particular scene in that last sex binge of mine proved more than I had bargained for. It took place not off the back alleyways of the red light district where my obsession had finally taken me, but in that rather nice motel room facing the boulevard. This was her place—the actress-dancer-prostitute—who was, as a sudden "gift," the embodiment of all the lust images, fantasies, and dreams I had ever known or wanted. Finally, I had everything—everything my lust had ever yearned for. I knew, sitting there, that I was willing to give away all to continue to have this wo—

I almost said "woman." But I didn't know her or really care—for her. I did care everything about the magical rapture of out-of-this-world ecstasy and intoxication that she mediated. Person, no; High Priestess and Goddess of Desire, yes!

It would mean giving away all—my second family (I had years before lost the first to lust), home, job, career. And God.

And, I would have to share her with other men. But I made that decision there on that couch, surrendering my will and my life absolutely to Lust. I gave up. I had no choice. Lust was my one and only wife, mistress, goddess, and slave master, and I was its thrall for life.

## What It Was Like

That motel room was where thirty-nine years of sex addiction had driven me. It was where I would come out of the closet to live the double life no longer. There was no strength left to keep up the pretense. The cumulative effects of repeated failures left me finally weakened to the point of simply giving up and giving in completely to lust, with no hope to change. I had fought it with everything: will power, church and Bible, prayer, psychiatry, and even exorcism—with a stint in the Christian ministry thrown in for good measure. The secret life of the sex drunk would finally burst out into the open; no more having to keep it under wraps. In its own tragic way, it was a relief, just like the time I'd been arrested, thanking God for that "final" blow, that I'd never have to do it again.

And it had all begun in total "innocence." First escapist masturbation as a child, then with girlie magazines. What at first had felt so good and promised such escape, turned into dark genital slavery, trying ever harder to recapture the original transport, release, and escape. Resorting to the ever-more-explicit images and ideas and becoming easy prey to the forces possessing the models I so longed to possess, I was forever blind to what was on the other side of idolatry.

And affairs. "Dancing in the Dark . . . ." What had held such glorious promise of new life and pleasure each time had left me morally, emotionally, and domestically bankrupt. I had, much as the compulsive gambler, spent all I had on my habit—my very life—and was left with nothing but emptiness and striving after wind. But again and again I would reach out and cry, the addict craving yet another fix, "Connect with me and make me whole!"

And prostitutes. The first one had also been a "gift" out of the blue. How eagerly I had crossed that line too. This was the real thing! The elixir of divine madness. Glorious delirium. (Lust has a poor memory for the bad stuff that usually goes along with it.) And "I'll never have to masturbate again!" Only to find that resorting to prostitutes, affairs, pornography, and masturbation all kept escalating. Never satisfied, always wanting more.

But now, here in this motel room, the Great Promise a reality, finally to have it all—

Then the moment of clarity. Sitting there, coming down off that lust high. Glimpsing, just for a moment, the truth, that having even this, I would nevertheless, within three days, be looking for another.

It was the end of the line, where alcohol had dumped the alcoholic—into "pitiful and incomprehensible demoralization." For me, the lust-aholic, the party was over.

# 2

### What It's Like Now:

### Bus Stop

I pull into the store down the street to make a phone call. Suddenly, in the corner of my eye I see the image of a woman at the bus stop. There's something about the figure and body language that wants to grab me, a powerful magnetic force pulling at the center of my soul. She looks like a prostitute I knew! I want to look and connect. The memory of that past encounter is the most overpowering trigger for my lust. I'm a goner! The compulsion to take that first look is irresistible. I know that I must look—and "drink." I'll die if I don't.

But I don't. Something intervenes within me. As I go on my way to the telephone, there's a deep lingering sadness for not taking that look. But then, in what has come to be my new pattern of reaction, I lift my spirit upward to my Lord and God and say, "You see that my heart really wants to lust; come be victorious over my lust." I thank Him for the trial and thank Him for the victory. And as I am making this surrender, I still have the craving and feel great loss. I don't want to die to my lust. But I do—upward to Him. And moments later there is complete freedom from that tyranny of the "drink" denied. I've been loosed from my lust. I can breathe again. And in place of that hunger which only wants more, I am satisfied. Filled with light and a feeling of goodness and Presence. Having overcome, I am now stronger. Victory over my sin—His victory—has given me an increment of life. Himself. I've made the real Connection.

*What It's Like Now*

He is my sin-bearer, my Resurrection, and my Life!

How can this be? How can I, for thirty-nine years a lust and sex addict, not take that first "drink"? Twenty three years ago I would have had to not only drink in that image for sustenance but act out sexually as a result. What's been happening with me that makes this continuing miracle possible?

# 3

**What Happened:**

**The Fellowship of Recovery**

What happened to make the difference inside me between where I was in the boulevard motel and where I was several years later at the bus stop and where I am today? Where all else had failed, what took me from that "seemingly hopeless state of mind and body" to sexual sobriety and freedom?

I encountered a fellowship of very defective people who were hopeless drunks of another sort but were living sober, joyous, and free. That's what happened.

It was April 20, 1974. I had just come home from work. Opening the door to our home, I saw the new issue of *Time* magazine with the mail. The cover story was on "The New Alcoholism." Standing there at the kitchen table, I quickly devoured the article, mesmerized. They were talking about me! But I wasn't thinking alcohol—I would uncover that problem only later—I was thinking sex. Every word the alcoholics and professionals were saying about the problem of alcoholism was describing me. Whatever it was that the alcoholic had was exactly what I had. The label didn't concern me. Whatever they were, I was. I picked up the phone, called AA, started going to meetings, and embarked on the incredible journey of sexual sobriety, progressive victory over lust, and now, what I had always been looking for but did not realize, personal union with the Friend of *sinners*.

I stopped drinking alcohol and using tranquilizers so I could stay in AA; there was something there I wanted and had never seen anywhere else, including church and group therapy. People led with their weakness! They actually were on the outside what they were on the inside. I had never experienced that, and it was immensely attractive. That honesty seemed to be the key to my conviction that the answer for me was with these people. What I was on the inside was as different from what I was on the outside as night and day.

The journey was rough. After staying sexually sober for a year and a half, I slipped and went on a sex drunk for three months that left me suicidal. Later I would see that sober was not well: I had not been masturbating, not been using pornography, not having affairs, not seeing prostitutes .... I had to learn the hard way that recovery is more than "putting the plug in the jug." That's not what the real Twelve Step program is all about. "Not" is not enough. The original recovery program of Alcoholics Anonymous is a threefold program of action: Find God, clean house, and work with other drunks. I had been going to meetings but not working the program.

Now—thousands of Twelve Step meetings later and sexually sober with progressive victory over lust—finding God, cleaning house, and working with other drunks, sex and otherwise, has not only kept me sober, but has set me on the road to discovering the real Connection with the One who is meek and lowly in heart and who offers Life and rest for the addicted soul.

Ostensibly heterosexual, I discovered that my sexual orientation had not really been to a particular gender at all, but to the spirit of Lust. Possessed of that spirit, I was an idolater, in rebellion against God. Now in recovery, surrendering my will, life, lust, and *mis*-orientation to God, I am being released from the slavery of Lust-worship one temptation at a time, time after time. And the sex-perverted love cripple is awakening to the love of the redeeming God and—wonder of wonders—to the love of woman. Really awesome!

## The Fellowship of Recovery

Sexual sobriety for me today is abstaining from any form of sex with myself (including resorting to erotic or pornographic materials or fantasy) or with partners other than my wife, and, positively, progressive victory over lust and the relational misconnection, my mis-orientation. I have discovered what I had never experienced before, in or out of marriage: marital sex in recovery without lust; totally optional; free of necessity, demand, and addiction; and coming from love. Recovery continues with progressive healing in myself, my marriage, and relations with others, one day at a time, by the grace and love of God, in fellowship.

I'd like to discover, with you, what's behind my impossible joy.

# Part I

# ENCOUNTERING THE REAL JESUS

# 4

## Jesus' Identification With My Sinful Human Nature—Introduction

*I speak after the poor fashion of a man lost in what is too great for him, yet is his very life.*
George MacDonald

The reality I am discovering and will be trying to share in this and some following chapters is Jesus' identification with our sinful human nature. This is the key to my victory in Christ. I'll begin by showing how I came to see him as I do.

After I was sober and into recovery for a while, I began working the Eleventh Step on a daily basis: "Sought through prayer and meditation to improve our conscious contact with God." I had never considered meditating; I automatically associated it with fads coming out of the 1960s. Prayer, yes; meditation, well, I didn't know what it was. Every morning, as soon as I arose, I'd do some devotional reading and pray, ending with surrendering my lust to God for that day and asking him to keep me sober.

Later on, seeing how meditation was suggested in the Twelve Steps, I became willing to be open to it and discovered to my surprise that it was kind of like prayer, only being still and quiet, with a unique value all its own. At first, it was only for a few minutes at a stretch. My mind would wander or fill with noise, and it would be useless to continue; it only invited the lust images back. But gradually, and without my having any agenda, the period slowly grew longer, until eventually I would lose consciousness of time.

## I—The Real Jesus

That quiet space, including reading, meditation, and prayer, has come to be the best part of each day. If I experience a dry spell, I don't push it; there are ebbs and flows in the spiritual life too. Now I add a quiet time in the evening before retiring. This began as a safeguard against sexualizing and romance in dreams, but is coming to be as precious in its own right as the morning time.

After a few years of my current sobriety, which included reading Twelve Step program literature, I began reading Scripture again. And for the first time in my life, instead of just giving me knowledge about God and His will and a certain amount of comfort, Scripture was validating and illuminating my own experience in recovery; it was ringing true. What a marvelous discovery that was! It was all real now, because it was first real in my own life! My experience with God was now preceding my knowledge about God, not the reverse, as it had been in church and seminary. I had unwittingly discovered a truth I later saw in so much of George MacDonald's writings: To know God is to obey him. No one could ever have told me that most of my religious experience had been having only "the form of godliness but denying the power thereof" (2 Tim. 3:5).

### "That I Might Know Him"

After a few years and well along in sobriety, I remember starting to pray specifically that I would discover what the death of Christ meant for me. I knew and believed what the Scriptures said—"Christ died for our sins"—but as far as my life was concerned, it was just a doctrine. I had a hunch I didn't really know what it meant for me. Coupled with this, I began praying Paul's prayer in Philippians 3:10, "That I may know him and the power of his resurrection, and the fellowship of his sufferings, being conformed to his death." Recovery was giving me a longing to know him better.

But something else was at work. I see now that it was my program activism which had to a large extent been

*Introduction*

keeping me sober. I had begun to sense that I was in jeopardy, that something was wrong, that Twelfth Step work was not enough. And sure enough, the moment came when I was "utterly defenseless against that first drink." That was my "Post Office" experience, which I will talk about in a later chapter. It was there that I first discovered the saving Presence that shielded me in that impossible temptation which I knew would put me over the edge.

I wanted to know that One whose presence came between me and the lust within and without, the One keeping me sober. So I just kept on praying and asking over months and months and months. And the hunger deepened. Years later, it's still deepening. (Perhaps it was this very hunger that had driven me all along trying to make the substitute connection in lust, sex, and misconnection. At times I have the strongest feeling that sex drunks have this God-hunger to an unusual degree.) Did I dare pray Paul's prayer? Knowing the power of His resurrection was one thing; deliberately asking to know his sufferings was quite another!

> *Lord, help me to know what your death means, not as a doctrine, or for the world out there, but for me. Does it mean you somehow died for and bear my lust? How? And can I connect with this today, now?*

Slowly, the more I read in the New Testament, the more I began to see how Jesus' life and work were indeed part of the recovery experience I was undergoing in the Twelve Step program. I began to see the lineaments of my own experience traced out in this grand Good News. And this is what brings me to connect my experience with the truth of the Gospel in this book—just how this condition and experience of mine are reflected in Scripture. I want to understand and share what's really going on in and behind my recovery, which is the great joy in my life today.

*I—The Real Jesus*

**The Sinless Humanity of Jesus**
If getting to know myself has been a startling discovery, getting to know the real Jesus is the wondrous surprise of recovery. Apparently, as I gradually came to face my real self, I became better able to grasp Jesus' true humanity as it bears on victory over my sin. Getting to know his victory in times of temptation to lust, resentment, fear, and other defects is slowly opening my heart to apprehending the truth about Jesus as revealed in Scripture and apprehending, connecting with the Person himself. Therefore, in this and later chapters, I'd like to examine what the Scriptures say about Jesus' humanity. We'll then be able to see how this bears directly on victory over the obsession. It will be necessary to go into this in considerable detail, so crucial is this to the whole argument and so profound our inability to comprehend and accept it.

Since the emphasis is going to be on Jesus' humanity, I'd like to start by making clear my position on his victory over sin, "any attitude or action that shuts out the presence of God." In 2 Cor. 5:21 we read, "For our sake he made him to be sin who knew no sin." The author of Hebrews writes, "who in every respect has been tempted as we are, yet without sin," (4:15) and Peter says, "He committed no sin; no guile was found on his lips" (1 Pet. 2:22). John tells us, "You know that he appeared to take away sins, and in him there is no sin" (1 John 3:5). The record is clear, including testimony from the two men who probably knew him best, Peter and John: Whatever his nature, Jesus never sinned. His own statement remains unchallenged: "Which of you convicts me of sin?" (John 8:46). No wonder that he stands unique in the history of the human race. He was and is Son of man, Son of God.

But in saying he is sinless, we must be very careful not to rob Jesus of his human relation to sin. Because it is his relation to sin that saves.

*Introduction*

Was his victory over sin due to some immunity from sin as the Son of God, or were his temptations, resources, and possibilities the very same as ours? If they were the same as ours, we too have sure hope of victory and joy. We can make the same saving Connection he did.

So I will try to show from Scripture that Jesus shared not some abstract, generic human nature or some special pre-Fall innocence, but our fallen human nature and was tempted by it just as we are and that he overcame all temptations to sin, not in his own strength but through his connection with the Father. Thus, in addition to being Son of God, he becomes the first son of man to overcome sin, thereby becoming the pioneer and perfecter of our faith—the one who leads the way. This is our key to true victory over lust.

**The Manifestation of Christ Must Deepen for Us**
It seems to me there is, on the part of believers, an evolving consciousness of God's self-disclosure in history. As our need grows throughout history, so does our longing and readiness to have that need filled. As human consciousness and culture develop over time, so must our understanding of ourselves and the Savior, so that the Good News, the Gospel, remains forever relevant and powerful to save. The needs of the church during the great Christological controversies of the early centuries were different than our needs are today. Our culture is different. The meaning of the person and work of Jesus should be ever more fully realized today. Jesus does not change; he is the same "yesterday and today—forever." But human consciousness, experience, and culture change, and our perception of him must deepen to suit our current condition. This is the story of church history from the beginning till now.

> Those of his disciples, that is, obedient hearers
> . . . would, in part, at once understand them
> [the Lord's words]; but as they obeyed and

## I—The Real Jesus

> pondered, the meaning of them would keep growing. This we see in the writings of the apostles. It will be so with us also, who need to understand everything he said neither more nor less than they to whom first he spoke; while our obligation to understand is far greater than theirs at the time, inasmuch as we have had nearly two thousand years' experience of the continued coming of the kingdom he then preached . . . .[1]

In our increasingly pagan culture we are approaching a condition where we may be ready for a deeper manifestation of the person and work of Christ. Our need is so incredibly great today! We, those of us especially who are the lust/sex/relationship addicts, must discover for ourselves, in our time, the real Jesus and our saving Connection with him.

**Christ in the Likeness of Sinful Flesh**
We'll begin with a very simple statement from Paul that will serve as my thesis and introduce the various other passages on this subject.

> For God has done what the law, weakened by the flesh, could not do: sending his own Son in the likeness of sinful flesh and for sin, he condemned sin in the flesh (Rom 8:3).

Jesus? In the likeness of sinful flesh? Wait a minute! What a powerful statement. And what does "likeness" mean? C.E.B. Cranfield, in his landmark commentary on the Greek text of Romans, says, regarding the word "likeness," that the Son of God was not, in being sent by His Father, changed into a man, but rather assumed human nature while still remaining Himself. He assumed the selfsame fallen human nature that is ours, but that in His case that fallen human nature was never the whole of Him—He never ceased to be Son of God.[2]

In other words, the innocent life of the garden of Eden was not reproduced in the life of the Son. (This is what I'm trying to show in Scripture and how it relates to my own recovery and lust breakthrough.) That could not and must not be, because His mission took place on account of sin. "Christ took precisely the same fallen nature that we ourselves have" and yet remained sinless because he constantly overcame any impulse to sin.[3] "Yes, the Word became flesh—sin-controlled flesh."[4] All because it was not unfallen but fallen human nature which needed redeeming. That fallen nature is me. What an incredible Gift!

(This may be hard to comprehend, but we'll get at it slowly.)

The first inkling I must have had of this truth appears in my personal journal entry of 9 May 1975, one year sexually sober: "We must find out the picture of the real Christ. If he really assumed the nature of sinful flesh, then almost every moment in his 33 years was 'contending against sin' [Heb. 12:4]." Back then I must have felt something was wrong with my concept of Christ even early in recovery, and sobriety was beginning to make it possible for me to yearn after the real Saving One. And for my condition, there simply had to be more.

It was while studying Romans and Hebrews in August of 1986 in an isolated cabin in the high Sierras which a program friend had let me use that I began to trust this identification of Jesus with my fallen humanity. The discovery dawned on me quietly, then with increasing clarity and force as I continued studying Jesus' life and the biblical witnesses. That was a very powerful awakening for me and a turning point in my own personal recovery. At the same time I was telling myself, This can't be so; it doesn't square with the image I've had of Jesus my entire life. But the more I experienced his saving grace in the new lust-transferral victory which such reality was making possible for me, the

## I—The Real Jesus

more convinced I became that here was something which had been lost to me (and perhaps lost to the church) but which was indispensable for my own continued recovery. And the more I delved into Scripture, the more clearly I saw how this had to be.

After I began connecting these thoughts and experiences together and writing about this view of Jesus' humanity, subsequent research uncovered the fact that some Bible scholars have held similar views. I was emboldened; I was not alone in this as I had thought. Passages from these nineteenth and twentieth century theologians of various persuasions, Protestant and Catholic alike, holding to essentially this same view of Jesus, are included in Appendix 1, together with an historical survey of the creeds of Christendom on this point.

I do accept the fact that some may have problems with this interpretation. Writing about the time of World War II, a famous theologian wrote that earlier theology, up to and including the Reformers and their successors, exercised on this point of Jesus' humanity a very understandable reserve. And that reluctance was calculated to dilute the offence of Jesus sharing our fallen humanity. Unfortunately, that reluctance also weakens the high positive meaning of passages like 2 Cor. 5:21, Gal. 3:13.[5] All I can say about this is that in this book I am simply bearing witness to the truth of my own experience as that experience is illuminated by the light I see in Scripture. (I'll leave it to others to come to their own conclusions and relate this to historical theology.)

An objection to this view about Jesus' humanity goes something like this: If Jesus had our sinful nature, as I propose, would he not himself have needed atonement? My response is, Who says that having such a nature in itself requires atonement? Jesus never obeyed the flesh; he never sinned. He is the righteous one. This is extremely important for me as a lustaholic sinner: It is not being temptable or tempted that brings spiritual death; it is surrendering to sin.

*Introduction*

The *wages* of sin is death. This is my glory today, that it's okay to be a sinner—to be temptable with lust, resentment, fear, etc.—because Jesus is saving me from my sins today.

**The Friend of Sinners**
The distinction between the principle or power of sin in a person and the acting-out of that in sinning is of primary importance. It is the difference between having the tree of death inside the Garden of Eden and partaking of its forbidden fruit. There's nothing wrong with having the tree of death in our nature; it seems to be our lot as humans and the avenue of God's glory. This is why Jesus could have the principle or power of sin in his being (our human nature) and be tempted through it, and yet be sinless. The Tree of that forbidden fruit dangled its delicacies in front of him constantly, as it does with us, but he never took and ate.

Yes, I believe this means Jesus could have been tempted to lust, including sexual lust. Apparently at times he avoided certain types of women. That may be why in the incident with the Samaritan woman at the well, his disciples were so surprised he was talking with her. Maybe she had her "switch" on—that mode where we have our radar scanning for the misconnection at every potential encounter. At other times Jesus associates freely with women without question and even lets them minister to him physically.[6] Who but one who had encountered lust and victory over it could have the authority to proclaim as Jesus did, "I say to you that every one who looks at a woman lustfully has already committed adultery with her in his heart" (Mat. 5:28)? It's Jesus' victory over lust and the false connection that will make him the merciful and faithful high priest, who will not only know and sympathize with my temptations but give me grace to help.

## I—The Real Jesus

**Jesus' Emotional Humanity**

There was apparently never any problem with anyone and everyone knowing this intensely human nature of Jesus. Once we "step outside the box," we see it everywhere: thirst (John 4:7; 19:28), fatigue (John 4:6), hunger (Mat. 4:2), joy (Luke 10:21), sorrow (Mark 3:5, Mat. 26:38), anger (Mark 3:5), weeping (John 11:35). Even his brothers did not believe in him! (John 7:5). At one point in his early ministry, his family and friends think he is beside himself, out of his head (Mark 3:21). I'm guessing that at that point they were afraid of his intense enthusiasm, exhibited in his words and works, in this case perhaps his casting out of demons.

In Matthew 22-23 we have one of the most, if not the most, remarkable and dramatic scene in all of world literature, if we can but visualize the scene and put ourselves into it as if we were witnessing it. Jesus goes through a range and intensity of emotions no one else could have gone through. No one is *human enough* to experience the full range and depth of human emotions he went through on just this one occasion. Knowing that the religionists are baiting him so they can kill him, Jesus challenges them with a conundrum: If the Messiah is son of David, how then does David call him Lord?

The religious politicos, feeling the charismatic power of Jesus' assertion, are silenced, and slink off to the fringes, while Jesus vehemently warns the people to flee their example. In a most penetrating discernment of human nature, Jesus exposes the utter sinfulness of the religious blindness in seven Woes of graphic denunciation, sparing nothing and no one. He *feels* the wrongs as intensely as though they were perpetrated on him—which they were. And the crescendo peaks as he explodes in fury at their hypocrisy, angrily exposing their murderous intent upon himself: "Go on then, finish off what your fathers began!" (New English Bible, NEB).

*Introduction*

Finally, as if reeling from the gut-wrenching intensity of the burden of his own emotions—his prophetic burden—Jesus cries out in anguished travail over the soul of the city in a devastatingly yearning plea reverberating across time: *"O Jerusalem, Jerusalem, the city that murders the prophets and stones the messengers sent to her! How often have I longed to gather your children, as a hen gathers her brood under her wings; but you would not let me...."* (NEB) Fury and compassion. Compassion within the wrath. Jesus is more human than anyone. I would say he was the most human of any the human race has ever known.

The problem people had with Jesus during the days of his flesh in Palestine was not with his being as human as we are, but with his claim to being Son of God. "It is not for a good work that we stone you but for blasphemy; because you, *being a man*, make yourself God" (John 10:33, emphasis mine). And we must remember that in those days and in that culture, there was constant intimacy of association, not the isolation we have today. Back then you lived in the close presence of others. Think about it. And Jesus lived in the humblest and closest of human relations. Had Jesus been some "special" human, unlike us at the core of his being by not having the same nature as ours, people would have sensed it; it would have set him apart as "weird." But as it is, they see fully that he was one of us in every respect. His worst critics testify to it. As a matter of fact, they accused him of being a drunkard and glutton and having a demon! (Mat. 11:18,19; John 10:20). They were sure he was a sinner (John 9:24). They chose not to believe in him because he was *not* "different."[7] The Pharisees felt Jesus was too much of the earth; they wanted a more "heavenly" manifestation of irresistible glory (Mat. 15:1-4). Maybe that's the kind of Jesus Christ Superstar we too would prefer.

This, I believe, is one reason why we do not want to accept Jesus' full humanity; we too want someone out-of-this-world "different." That appears to make faith so much easier,

## I—The Real Jesus

doesn't it? But making faith easier—trying to give it a tangible proof—is precisely what takes the kingdom of heaven out of the spiritual realm. And then we're back to only an earthly messiah whose kingdom is of this world, not a Savior from *sins*.

Jesus eats often with tax collectors and sinners. Prostitutes. He is called their friend. Jesus identifies not with "the righteous," but with sinners who hunger and thirst after righteousness (Mat. 9:10-13; Luke 7:34). He is comfortable with these people and they are comfortable with him. How could he be such a friend of such people unless they knew he was one of them, that he walked where they walked—on the inside, where it counts—and that he was tempted exactly as they were? That's what attracted people to him, the common people. They knew that he'd "been there." He had what they wanted—victory over sin. That's why Jesus is surely for the sex and lust-addicted.

• • •

Thus, the great fact of Jesus' work for me is set forth in Paul's statement in Romans 8:3: "Sin in my flesh stands condemned because Jesus the Messiah (Christ) has my humanity and my condition and has overcome." He could fulfill his task, his calling concerning sin, because he shared my sinful flesh.

Thus, Jesus' relation to sin is the key to my victory over sin, the key to my victory over lust. (This will be developed more fully in subsequent chapters.)

Let's now see how this is revealed in his life, beginning with his wilderness temptation experience.

# 5

## Jesus' Identification with Our Sinful Human Nature— The Wilderness Temptation

Jesus' wilderness temptation, occurring just before the commencement of his public ministry, is very crucial in helping us see the real person. These temptations set the stage for and reveal his all-important personal relation with sin.

### Moses and Christ

A brief comparison with Moses' forty days on mount Sinai will point up the great contrast between these two epoch-inaugurating events. Moses went without both food and water for forty days; yet it is not described as a fast at all (Exodus 34:28). It's almost as though he was getting divine sustenance, because when he comes down from the mount, instead of being famished as Jesus was, his face is shining with the effulgence of God's glory. On the other hand, Jesus deliberately fasts—Luke says he ate nothing, implying he may have drunk water—and winds up desperately needing sustenance. Moses goes up and meets God; Jesus goes down into a wilderness and meets the devil. Moses' encounter is to reveal the righteousness of God in the words of the Law; Jesus' encounter is being battered by temptation and evil so he can *fulfill* all righteousness.

Thus, we see that at the very outset, Jesus' mission is to deal with sin and evil. From the very beginning and throughout his ministry—not just at his death—the Son of God is dealing with sin in the most personal and intimate of contexts. The ministry of the Christ will be characterized not

*I—The Real Jesus*

by the brief moments of glory at the baptismal river bank or Transfiguration, or whatever, but by his ongoing personal encounter with sin.

**The Scene**

Let's try to imagine the picture here. (The three accounts of the Baptism and Temptation are found in Mark 1:9-13, Matt. 3:13 - 4:11, and Luke 3:21 - 4:13. In all probability, Jesus related these life-altering experiences to his disciples, probably more than once, and even to other persons, his mother, perhaps, accounting for the differences in order, detail, and emphasis between the three Synoptic gospels.) John the Baptizer has been publicly proclaiming the coming of the Messiah and preparing the way for "the Lamb of God, who takes away the sin of the world." Jesus has traveled from Nazareth down to Bethany to be baptized by John (Mt. 3:13). There at the Jordan river Jesus is baptized along with many others. Having been baptized, Jesus is praying. Note that there is nothing special distinguishing him from all the others there; he is one among many (Luke 3:21).

As he steps out of the water, Jesus sees the heavens torn asunder (Mark's phrase) and the Spirit, as a dove, descending upon him. Imagine the scene as he experienced it. This is the first overt supernatural manifestation attesting his person and unique calling. A voice coming out of the heavens says, "You are my beloved Son; in you I am well pleased." Imagine the impact. At about thirty years of age, this young man is suddenly divinely apprehended in a unique and glorious manner. His awareness will never be the same. What might come next? Another heavenly experience?

The next thing he knows, Jesus is led by the Spirit—Mark says he is driven—into the wilderness, where he stays forty days alone, with the wildlife, eating no food. Matthew tells us he was led to the wilderness to be tempted; but did Jesus know that at the time? We know he was led there, but he may not have known what would transpire. At least this is how I understand it. Of course, after it was all over, Jesus would know exactly why he had been led there and would so relate it to his disciples. Perhaps Jesus, on his side of it, was there to get away from everyone, fasting, trying to comprehend the impact of what had just happened at the river, praying for guidance, meditating, communing with the Father and nature.

At the end of the forty days, Jesus is famished and probably weak to the point of collapse. Most of us have no idea of the great weakening produced by such a fasting experience. Thus, we might imagine he is resting; the unprecedented spiritual ordeal—for that's what those forty days must have been—is over. Jesus is sitting or even lying down on the ground, using a stone for a pillow, perhaps. He is suddenly confronted—arrested—by an extraordinary experience.

No doubt thousands of books have been written and will yet be written on the Wilderness Temptation of Christ (as though it were his only temptation!). Writers are divided on whether the wilderness scene took place physically, with Satan taking Jesus in tow and actually leading, taking, and setting him on the parapet of the temple, etc., as the verbs in Matthew imply, or whether the dramatic encounter between the two persons suggested by these verbs was in the spiritual dimension. Of course, some reject the whole Temptation as fanciful fiction. I take every single word very seriously. And I have no problem whatsoever seeing Satan in some kind of physical form leading Jesus around, but I'm inclined to think Jesus may not have recognized the instrumentality of Satan until the third temptation, where Jesus commands him to be gone by actual name (Matt. 4:10). Why else would Jesus continue in the encounter and not break it off, as he will suddenly at the third temptation?

Until I began restudying this event, I simply assumed the scene was physical. Now I feel that the essence of this very real and personal encounter with Satan took place in the

## I—The Real Jesus

realm of the spirit, within Jesus' consciousness. And it carries more meaning not only for Jesus but for ourselves that way, especially if we are lustaholics. Because it is within our spiritual consciousness where we most often encounter lust and the enemy. However, one doesn't have to agree with this interpretation; the reality of that awesome encounter stands any way one looks at it.

Jesus may have been tempted during the entire forty days, with these three temptations either winding up the attack or representing the essential types of temptation—the lust of the flesh, the lust of the eyes, and the pride of life, what I sometimes call the lust of the ego (I John 2:16). And as we shall see later in this book, Jesus' temptations do not end here. The Luke account implies that temptation will be a continuing, not a one-time experience for Jesus (Luke 4:13). And Jesus seems to imply this in such passages as Luke 22:28, where he says, "You are those who have continued with me in my temptations." This is widely ignored but very significant. Jesus' life as the Pioneer of our faith (Hebrews 12:2) shows that continuing temptations are not only our lot in God's kingdom as it was for Jesus, but are the very will of God for us. Putting it the other way around, experiencing continuing temptations was God's will for Jesus because this is the lot of the children of Adam whom he came to save. *One of the great fallacies in recovery is the notion that somehow we should get to where we are not tempted any more.*

The subject of Jesus' temptations is inexhaustible, and I confess I haven't begun to comprehend the depths of this epochal temptation encounter. I offer this one aspect of the scene, described below as I am inclined to see it today, and words fail me. Our understanding usually deepens with time and recovery. Whatever the scene, whether physical or otherwise, I want to try to understand how the truth of Hebrews 4:15 was realized in the Temptation, that Jesus was "one who in every respect has been tempted as we are." This is one of the crucial points this book will try to make for our own victory over lust.

So, let's suppose that Jesus is not yet aware that this is Satan, appearing as he most often does, we are told, as "an angle of light" (2 Cor. 11:14). (If it was an overt physical happening however, this was apparently Jesus' first personal encounter with any person from the other world.) Weak and literally starving, Jesus is confronted by this glorious personage, this powerful, aggressive, and articulate personality from another realm. Yes, Satan is a heavenly being, the prince of this age, the commander of the spiritual powers of the air (Eph. 2:2). But let's try to look at the *inside* of these temptations. If it was a physical encounter, the temptations still had to resonate within Jesus himself. The occasion of the temptation may be physical, but the temptation itself is always internal to the one being tempted; that's where our choices are always determined. Ask any lustaholic.

Without being dogmatic on the subject, I feel that I have been tempted by the adversary on some occasions, perhaps more often than I would care to think. Maybe the lust we sexaholics know so well is more a personal encounter with forces of evil than we might imagine. And those temptations are always in the realm of the spirit, regardless of what the physical circumstances may be. Often lust temptations are in the form of fantasy. Sometimes an image will pop into my head, even today, and I wonder, Where on earth did *that* come from? Who is to say that that erotic image you or I may have just had flit into our mind was *not* presented to us by the adversary-seducer? We know so very little about the spirit realm. But if we can see the full congruence between Jesus' temptations and ours, it can give us courage to bring him into ours *while we are being tempted.* Let me emphasize: *while we are being tempted*—the crying need of the lustaholic. Because that's when we're powerless and need salvation.

*I—The Real Jesus*

**The First Temptation**

Jesus is in an extremely debilitated physical state here, a very unusual state, as would be the case with even the strongest of humans. He has been fasting, meditating, and praying for forty days. Only those who have done so will know the change in consciousness that comes with even one full day's fasting. Perhaps we should all do it more often.

Jesus is perhaps lying down on the ground, faint, resting. He turns on his side, using his hand as a cushion between his cheek and the stone pillow, feeling its smooth rounded surface and seeing its loaf-like coloring. And at that moment, a thought is distilled into his consciousness: **Turn it into a loaf of bread!** He actually visualizes it; the stone turned bread so he can eat and live. The image is so very real and the impulse so strong he knows that all he has to do is reach out and take it and it will be so! He knows from his experience at the river Jordan that such power is now his. What a temptation to use it!

Jesus will later, knowing what really transpired, describe the temptation in terms of the Satanic seduction that it really was: "If you are the Son of God, command that stone to become bread!"

The word "if" in the tempter's challenge "If you are the Son of God" may be translated "since" here. Satan knows and affirms in a diabolical way, what had just transpired at the baptism. In effect, he is building on the divine power that was revealed there saying, **"Since you are the Son of God—now that it's been declared from heaven and you've been anointed with that Power—use the power! Turn that stone there into bread!"**

The idea seems to come with its own validation, yet tension mounts within Jesus: Yes, I have been anointed by God himself and empowered by his Spirit for a unique calling. I've gone through these forty days as Moses did, readying myself. I am Son of God—with power. Why not? As he entertains the thought, the temptation is distilled in his heart: **You stone there—! Be bread and life for me!**

But just as quickly, Jesus recoils from it. NO!! In an instant he senses the wrong in it for him and sends away his temptation to sin. Sitting up as if to confront the temptation directly, he affirms the Word of his Father: **"It is written, 'Man shall not live by bread alone but by every word from God.' And I shall so live!"**

Whatever the source, Jesus is tempted from within, and it is so very real, so powerful. Sin is knocking on the door of his heart, mediated by an angel of light. (Isn't this our very own story?) But Jesus sees that to obey this impulse would be *relying on his own power instead of his connection with the Father!* That is the action-point of the sin to be. He'd be thinking, "I can hack this thing on my own!" And this is precisely where we have the most trouble in overcoming lust temptations, isn't it? We want to rely on our own power instead of bringing him into it. Apparently we think we have the divine power—which Jesus gave up the right to use for himself (Phil. 2: 6,7)—so we can make lust disappear or deny its very existence! But if we brought him into our temptation, into the very evil itself, we would neither have to deny its existence within us nor try to suppress it, both of which are deadly and shut God out! This is one of the changes in our thinking that this book is trying to bring about.

The act of surrender brings peace. The impulse and its beguiling power pass, and Jesus breathes a sigh of relief. He lies down relieved, feeling the joy of divine victory. But the tempter will try again.

## The Second Temptation
As Jesus ponders what has just happened, affected by the unusual power of the experience, his mind drifts ahead to Jerusalem and the temple, the center and symbol of God's historic self-disclosure to the human race. And the power-field comes over him again. As he will later relate it to his disciples, we might hear him saying, "I was there! Standing

## I—The Real Jesus

on that lofty parapet of the Temple, high above the throng. **Jump off!** Is it the Father's voice? It's his Word I'm hearing!— **'He will put his angels in charge of you,' and 'On their hands they will bear you up, lest you strike your foot against a stone.'"** The potent feeling overwhelms Jesus: What a demonstration of power that will be! Caught up by angels, before that thronging crowd of worshipers, looking, waiting, hoping, praying—wailing for their Messiah. They'll believe!!

Some commentators make the point that such public display was not the issue here, since spectators are nowhere mentioned. In this view, Satan's suggestion is the demand for Jesus to commit an act of supreme, unconditional, blind, absolute, total confidence in God, what might *appear* as the highest form of devotion. But by experimenting with God, making use of God in his own favor, he would betray the cause of God by making it his own cause, by using it to fulfill his own self-justification before God. He would then have committed the supreme sin of tempting God himself, under the appearance of this most robust faith in God. Is not this the supreme sin of the religious man?[8] "See how much I believe?" (That could be a cogent insight into what is more and more being referred to as religious addiction, which we'll discuss later.)

This is exactly what I was doing in the ritual of the lust chase, thinking, God would protect me. This proved that my behavior was really saying, "*I* am in the right against God!" Can we see the pernicious sin of religious addiction here, using what appears as faith in God to support self-justification?

But again Jesus recoils, sending the sin away: **"It is written: 'Thou shalt not tempt the Lord thy God.' And I shall not tempt the Lord my God."** The power subsides. And he's free again. Thank God he chose to act for all of us and obey the Father, as he would continue to do, up to and including Golgotha.

## The Third Temptation

The first might be called the most "innocent" of the three temptations. And in each of the first two, the seducer is not directly in the picture. The thrust of those temptations is not directly connected with Jesus' personal relation to Satan. But in the third, this changes. The final temptation starts out like the other two: Jesus envisions the scene; from that limitless vantage point of the spirit, he actually *sees* the glory of all the world's kingdoms set out before him. And the tremendous power field is back, only imbued with confusion. (That's one of the tipoffs as to whether something is not right for us, too—a spirit of confusion accompanying the decision.) For him, it's a blinding vision that beckons gloriously. He feels the awesome power of total world-control. And it must ring especially true with him, since having just been anointed by God, he *is* the destined ruler of the kings of the earth (Rev. 1:5). Why should he have to suffer in relation to sin when he can have the adulation due him now?

But there's a new element in this third encounter, and the direct connection with Satan is finally out in the open. The devil comes right out with it. No longer disguising his identity and real intent behind injected images, he says, **"All these kingdoms and their glory, which are in my power to dispense, I give to you, if you will fall down and worship me."**

As the thought coalesces in his mind, Jesus recoils again, and the recognition hits him like a ton of bricks: Satan! No wonder! All along—! Thank you Father... Jesus now knows what's been happening in the other temptations, and immediately takes the required action to be done with the devil: **"BEGONE SATAN!! It is written, 'Thou shalt worship the Lord thy God and him only shalt thou serve!' And I will serve only the Father!"**

And the power-field collapses. The air is cleared of confusion. There is peace in Jesus' heart and the joy of the real Connection. *Jesus, truly tempted with sin as we are, was saved from sinning!*

This is our hope and very faith. *We* can thus be tempted with sin, yet saved from sinning.

**Conclusions**

Jesus was really tempted from within, just as we are. He saw into his own nature better than anyone to perceive, in each of these three instances, the real sin that would be involved, if acted upon. When Jesus said, "You shall not tempt the Lord your God," he was referring to himself as well as Satan. And when I tell Satan to be gone, I'm not only rejecting his temptation but my own; I'm affirming that it is written that *I* shall not tempt the Lord my God by surrendering to that sin.

Jesus called not on his own resources but on the Word in each case to overcome sin. It was surrender. It was the obedience of faith. How could Satan tempt him unless there was something within him that could be tempted; where was the point of contact? James tells us that God is not tempted with evil (Jas. 1:13). Thus, Christ, without a human nature such as ours, could not have been truly tempted with evil. The only validity to his temptation is that he shares our flesh and nature too.

The alternative to this interpretation isn't very attractive. To put it in question form, we'd have to ask something like this: You mean Jesus did not feel the power of those temptations, that they did not really threaten him? That would have been a sham. And would not Satan have known that? He knew Jesus was truly temptable; he treats him the same as he treats me, knowing where I'm most vulnerable. This wilderness scene was not playacting! Otherwise, Jesus' temptation, "for human need, struggle, and hope . . . bears no meaning; and we must reject the whole as a fantastic folly of crude invention; a mere stage-show; a lie for the poor sake of the fancied truth; a doing of evil that good might come; and . . . not in any way to be received as a divine message."[9]

Here is the point: If Satan has access to Jesus' consciousness, then he has access to mine and yours. If Jesus can be tempted to sin, then so can I and so can you. If it was part of God's plan for Jesus to be tempted with sin, then it is also part of God's plan for us to be tempted with sin. ***It's not a sin to be tempted with sin!***

And if Jesus deals with sin by sending it away, trusting the Word of the Father, then so can we! And if dealing with sin in this way brings the ministering of angels to Jesus, then dealing with our sin in this way brings the divine life to us. This very fact is what I am bearing witness to: Each temptation to lust can become sacramental, an occasion of grace, a Life-giving experience.

• • •

*Temptation! The great fear of the sexual compulsive, the no-man's land where both Lust and Faith do battle until one wins and the other is vanquished. Lord, you've been through that bleak wasted zone of terror and death, and more intensely than we'll ever know. You've met the Enemy under the worst possible conditions, your only defense the Word of the Father. And you have always come through obedient to that Word. Help us to follow you in temptation so we can be with you in your victory.*

# 6

## Jesus' Identification with Our Sinful Human Nature—His Life

We find that the same human nature Jesus exhibited in the wilderness temptation is manifest throughout his life.

### Jesus' Baptism

> *But Jesus answered him, "Let it be so for now; for thus it is fitting for us to fulfill all righteousness"* (Mt 3:15).

John the Baptist balks at baptizing Jesus. I can certainly identify with that. We shouldn't be too hard on ourselves or others for reluctance to see Jesus in such an intimate relation with sin in his flesh as I am proposing. John the Baptist had the same problem. He balks, saying it is he who should be baptized by Jesus. Maybe we don't want to see it either. But what better backdrop for a fuller realization of Jesus' person and work than the darkness of lust in our own time and lives? We, the impossible sinners, are the fortunate ones, as were the "publicans and sinners" in Jesus' day.

Perhaps we shy away from the true humanity of Jesus because we do sense something of our sinfulness and sins and powerlessness. Facing Jesus' nature, we are forced to see our own. "No!" we cry out at the very thought. "You can't have what I have, Lord; if you did, you'd be like me!" But his being like we are in his flesh is his point of contact with us.

## I—The Real Jesus

That's why the Word became flesh! Not understanding this may be why we are so reluctant to bring him into our lust temptations. *We think we have to be good first.* But our trying to be good is what keeps him out! If you can see this, you understand the whole point of this book.

Jesus insists that John baptize him. But lest we fall into a trap and try to explain that in his baptism Jesus was just going through the motions to "identify with Man" in some vague way (or some such evasion), we read: "But Jesus answered him, 'Let it be so now; for thus it is fitting for us to fulfill all righteousness.'" These are the very first words recorded of Jesus as he begins his ministry as an adult. The least I see here is Jesus' complete identification with us, not only in the baptism itself but in the way he says it: "it is fitting for *us*." Whatever else his life was, it was to be one with us in every respect. That gives me some hope. What about you?

More than this, I see that Jesus had to actively participate in fulfilling righteousness as we must. It was not automatic, just because he was Son of God. That would not be *fulfilling* righteousness. It's as though Jesus were saying, "John, don't treat me any differently; I have to fulfill all righteousness, and for me to do so, I have to encounter sin and go through the same surrender that baptism represents as others do. So, John, you see that you must baptize me, because I do now in this public confession testify to sending away sin and surrendering my will and life to the Father." (See Appendix 3 for another treatment of this aspect of his baptism.) Jesus thus worked the first three Steps of our program here (Appendix 4). This makes him the Pioneer of our own faith (Heb. 12:2). Jesus said, "Thus it is fitting for *us* to fulfill all righteousness." That one word "us" says it all; he is with us in every respect, from the inside out. If this is true, we can lift our hearts and say,

*Thank you, Lord, for fulfilling all righteousness. I want to fulfill righteousness too, but I know I can't; I've spent a lifetime trying. "Don't worry," Jesus replies, "I'm going to make it possible for you to overcome sin, but first I'm going to have to do it myself; you'll not be able to otherwise.*

## Jesus Came to Fulfill the Law

*"Think not that I have come to abolish the law and the prophets; I have come not to abolish them but to fulfill them."* (Mt. 5:17)

Is not Jesus saying the same thing here to the multitudes in the Sermon on the Mount as he said to John the Baptist? He tells us that his very mission was to fulfill the requirements of the law. How could he fulfill the law, if not in his own personal experience with sin and victory over sin? And how could he *fulfill* the law if it were different for him than for us? He might proclaim the law or teach it, but that's not fulfilling it. He's the only one who ever did fulfill the law of God!

And it is this fulfillment which becomes the place he is pulling us toward, the raising of our consciousness to the will of the Father. But he never pushes. He leads us by his having been there himself and calling us to follow him. It's as though he were saying, Follow me; you *can* do what I did in the same way I did, by relying not on your own power but on the Father's.

## The Sermon on the Mount (Matthew Chapters 5, 6, and 7)

It seems to me we have a couple of possible ways we can look at this Sermon: Either the Sermon was merely the recitation of truth Jesus "read off" to men, as an angel might merely be a messenger of God, or it sprang from the truth of Jesus' own

## I—The Real Jesus

experience, being learned through temptation and trial. Everything in me revolts against the idea of Jesus as mere heavenly messenger. I feel he learned this righteousness which he preaches from the inside out, being tempted within the same sinful nature I am but, overcoming temptation by the power of the Father. In Hebrews 5:8 we are told that he *learned* obedience through what he suffered. He knew these truths because he had first learned them in his experience. He could proclaim them because they were his life. He was thus bearing witness to the truth of his own experience, sharing his "experience, strength, and hope," as we say in the program.

> *And when Jesus finished these sayings, the crowds were astonished at his teaching, for he taught them as one who had authority, and not as their scribes* (Mt 7:28,29).

I believe this stamp of authority Jesus radiated issued from his living the truth of this Sermon on the Mount in his own experience. The scribes of Jesus' day spoke from the authority of Scripture and tradition, but there's a total difference between that and the authority coming from a person's *life*. Nothing rings true like the voice of experience, and the crowds intuitively sensed this.

Thus, Jesus was blessed because *he* was poor in spirit, because *he* mourned and was meek. He was filled because *he* hungered and thirsted for righteousness, etc. Do you see the color and force that imbue his life now as we look at this sermon in this way? Jesus, the Son of God, was at the same time fully temptable flesh and blood, like you and me. He called himself the Son of *man*.

On another occasion, Jesus explained to his disciples what he meant by his assertion that it was not that which goes into a man that defiles him: "For from within, out of the heart of man, come evil thoughts, fornication, theft, murder, adultery, coveting, wickedness, deceit, licentiousness, envy, slander, pride, foolishness. All these evil things come from within, and they defile a man" (Mark 7:21-23). How did he know this? Again, I think Jesus is speaking from the authority of his own being; he knows this because he felt the power of these sins within him and overcame through his connection with the Father. He's been there! "Jesus had to fathom every sin and every sorrow man could experience."[10]

And I say that except Jesus be fully man, he cannot stand in for me, the sinful man. If we can but see this, our hearts would lift in prayer:

> *Lord, now I see you were sharing, not preaching or telling. This was no Sermon at all; it was a speaker meeting and you were sharing your experience, strength, and hope. This draws me to you and gives me life. "Blessed are the pure in heart, for they shall see God." I can be pure in heart too! I who want to lust and resent and who am so obsessed with myself.*

### Peter's Remonstrance an Inner Threat to Jesus

> *But he turned and said to Peter, "Get behind me, Satan! You are a cause of stumbling to me; for you are not on the side of God, but of men"* (Mt 16:23).

Many incidents in the life of Jesus give us a penetrating insight into his humanity. We'll touch on only a few. On this occasion Peter takes Jesus aside and soundly rebukes him for predicting his own rejection, suffering, and death. Note the great familiarity with which Peter treats Jesus as he takes him to task. There was certainly no halo about Jesus' head in the days of his flesh. Peter acted as though Jesus was one of us in our common human nature. But Peter would hinder Jesus' work by trying to protect him from suffering. (Are *we* unwittingly trying to protect Jesus from suffering—suffering our lust in the next temptation by *not* bringing him into it?) So Jesus rejects Peter's misconception of him and let's him have it. (Isn't it nice to know some of us aren't the only ones hanging on to a false Christ?).

The vehemence with which Jesus resists this particular temptation speaks of how deeply he felt its power within himself. The occasion for Jesus to sin here was Peter's remark from without, but Jesus' temptation to sin came from within himself, as is true, always, with us. Again we ask, What was within Jesus that made such a temptation so threatening? Where was the point of contact, the threat, if not in the same fallen nature he shared with us? Jesus says Peter was a stumblingblock, "a cause of stumbling, to *me*". This means Jesus was actually being tempted to turn aside from the will of God, tempted to turn aside and stumble.

It is encouraging for me to see that Jesus placed the priority on his own program; his "sobriety" came first. He's not a people-pleaser; he tells it like it is: "Hey, Peter, knock it off! I have to surrender my ego to the Father's will, and your refusal to see it isn't going to stop me. Furthermore, if you want to follow the real me and not a false Christ, you're going to have to do the same thing. The kind of kingdom you want isn't it. I'm not here to usher in New Age consciousness and make a hit. I came to identify with man's sinful dilemma so I could be with him in that very dilemma. If any one wants to come after me, he's going to have to do what I do—deny himself and take up *his* cross" (v. 24).

> *Lord, thank you for denying your self; that gives me courage and great hope.*

## Jesus and the Greeks

Here's another incident giving us a deeper perspective on Jesus' humanity and our own temptations. In John 12:20-28 we see what must have been a very powerful temptation indeed. A contingent of people from Greece makes formal request to see Jesus, going through Philip and Andrew. Jesus doesn't pay them any mind and instead says, "The hour has come for the Son of man to be glorified," referring to his imminent death. Giving audience to the Greeks would have been a publicists's dream come true. Here we have men from a foreign country, a country representing the pinnacle of learning, philosophy, and civilization; and they want an audience with The Man. My reaction would have been, "Why are you dummies making them wait? Don't you know who they are? You can't buy this kind of promotion. That means validation, fame, success, glory. Bring 'em over!"

But no. What does he say? "The hour has come for the Son of man to be glorified. But it's not going to be gaining earthly glory through the Greek connection; it's going to be by my *losing* any chance of glory, by losing myself. Listen; listen to me now: I say to you that unless a grain of wheat falls into the ground and *dies*, it remains alone; but if it dies, it bears much fruit." Jesus is tempted by earthly glory, just as you or I. But he sees through it and surrenders. "I'll take the contrary action," he says, "take the action against the feeling, believe the Father, deny myself, and give up my life"(12:24f).

But that's not the end of the temptation; it was just the beginning. Having overcome this self-glorification temptation, rather readily it would seem, he then goes on to drive the lesson home to the disciples, preaching one of the most profound paradoxes of the kingdom of God: "He who loves his self is lost; but he who despises it will keep it unto life eternal." Then he adds, "And if anyone—these Greeks or you or anyone else—would serve me, they'll have to do the same as I. And if anyone serves me, that person will the

## I—The Real Jesus

Father honor."

Immediately Jesus is hit with an emotional temblor deep inside himself (verse 27). As soon as he's preached this truth about people who serve him being honored by God, he's struck forcibly and says, *"Now my soul is troubled. . . ."* He's caught in deep inner turmoil, as at Lazarus' tomb and again in Gethsemane. He's been delivering an intensely personal message and plea, asking people to follow *him* in losing their lives, and that if they do this they will be honored by the Father. Jesus was centering attention on himself as the Pioneer and One to be followed. And then— Out of the blue, he's in turmoil and overcome with temptation and pleads: *"Father save me out of this hour!"* Why? He's been absolutely in charge, on top of things in a powerful way. Why is he now pleading with God? What's the temptation here?

I have often been most vulnerable to temptation after preaching or bearing witness to the truth of my own experience. I feel exposed and alone, doubting my own motivations for calling attention to myself in such a way. Could it be that he was tempted here as he was in the Wilderness and Gethsemane temptations? That "the flesh indeed is willing, but the spirit is weak." Whatever the temptation is, he is so troubled he reaches out immediately and unselfconsciously in audible prayer: *"Father, save me out of this hour!"*

(Some versions place a question mark at the end of this sentence, making the prayer merely a question instead of a request, reading, "Now my soul is troubled, and what shall I say? "Father save me from this hour?" Evidence from the Greek manuscripts for the presence or absence of the question mark is apparently inconclusive, which explains why the versions differ. Thus, it's up to us to see which interpretation better fits the context. This is one of some 600 passages in the Greek New Testament where the differences in punctuation in the many manuscripts are particularly significant in interpreting the text[11].)

*His Life*

I feel his prayer was an actual plea and not a question. Jesus isn't wondering which way to pray; he just comes out with his plea to be saved from that hour. The same way I see his prayer in Gethsemane, when he asks the Father, "Remove this cup from me!" (Mark 14). There's certainly no possibility of misinterpreting his prayer in that temptation, and that's the way I take it here. He is being tempted, but how? Since the text doesn't describe his inner feelings, we can try to infer these from the larger context and from what we've already learned about him in this study. He knows very soon he's going to die, that he will lose *his* life. Not the death of his physical body; he never gave that a thought. Losing his whole aim in life, not fulfilling his very destiny of seeking and saving the lost, healing the sick and stricken, saving, drawing followers, teaching, ministering, dealing the bread of life to the hungry. . . . MY LIFE'S WORK WILL BE NO MORE; IT'S OVER! His humanity is real, just like ours, and his prayer instinctively voices his feeling: **"Save me out of this hour!"** He's real! He rings true as having our humanity.

Is he tempted with doubt? Doubt that following him really is the way to go for everyone else and that it is sure to bring honor from God? He's calling people to follow him in giving up *their* lives. Might that not lead to doubt about giving up his own life? Such doubt is not rational, but who says temptations are ever rational, especially, as we shall see, when they come from the Deceiver? The point here is that regardless of how we label the temptation, Jesus is tempted from within himself and cries out to be saved.

Then, he hears himself and corrects it immediately: **"No, it was for this that I came to this hour. Father, glorify thy name"** (12:27 NEB). Tempted in a most real and personal way, he "turns it over," and surrenders in the obedience of faith. In response, he hears the voice of the Father from heaven, "I have glorified it, and will glorify it," as though to say, "Yes, I've glorified my name in your earthly ministry, but I will glorify it again—in your death." This word of the Father brings forth the exultant proclamation from Jesus, the answer to his fear: *"Now is the judgement of this world. Now the ruler of this world shall be cast out."*

What does this mean? Satan is to be cast out of what? That his influence will be cast out of the *world*? That simply did not happen. When Jesus was arrested, he said, "Now it's your hour and the power of darkness." Satan was apparently still active then. Satan has not only been active in the world ever since Jesus made the statement that the ruler of this world would be cast out, but Satan's influence waxes greater and greater. I read only yesterday that there are 50,000 pornographic web sites registered to one credit card verification service alone (*L.A.Times* 2-16-99). So in what sense has Satan been cast out, and why did this revelation come to Jesus as it did?

In his surrender prayer, Jesus had just experienced dramatic victory over his own fear temptation. And that came about, not through his own strength, but through the word of the Father, just as it had in the Wilderness temptations, by the voice from heaven, revealing that God would be glorified in Jesus' coming death. So it is possible to infer that Jesus is connecting his own victory in temptation with the casting out of Satan's influence, first within himself, and then, because of the Father's promise that he will be glorified in his death, to the resulting casting out of Satan's power in *our* lives. That's how I see it today. How powerful! My victory over the power of evil in temptation issues from the same certitude Jesus felt here—the word of the Father. And if Jesus could be victorious, having our sinful flesh, so can I, so can we, the same way, by trusting not in ourselves but in the word of the Father!

Then Jesus adds, *"And I, if I be lifted up from the earth, will draw all men unto myself."* His troubled plea to the Father has brought the assurance from heaven that by surrendering to losing his work and dying, God's will and work will be accomplished and Jesus will draw *all* men to

*His Life*

himself. Because Satan's authority will be nullified in that death. Satan shall be driven out of his power in men's lives, just as he was driven out just now in Jesus' own temptation. The death-resurrection event will make it all possible. Can you begin to see the awesome power of Jesus having our humanity and how that applies so directly to us today? It's okay if it hasn't dawned on you yet; we'll keep at it from different angles.

**The Event Horizon—The Either/Or**. As I understand it, the event horizon in astrophysics is that point on the "rim" of a black hole beyond which nothing can escape, not even light. The gravitational pull is too strong to overcome. There is an event horizon in every temptation. It is a decision point, an action point, where one can go either way. Choice. One can either stop and pull back or—an invisible instant later—be lost in the pull. This is where Jesus was, as soon as he heard himself ask the Father to be saved.—on the edge of the black hole of temptation. The unforseen circumstances of life brought him to that event horizon.

It's the same action point you and I have in every lust, resentment, fear, or other temptation today. So, Jesus' impulse to sin comes from the same humanity he shares with us, his sin-controlled flesh. His flesh is weak too, just like ours. Maybe even weaker. (Remember he comes from a dysfunctional lineage going back to Solomon and David.) He is actually tempted from within. But he doesn't go with it. It hits him, perhaps even overwhelms him, but he doesn't drink. He doesn't obey it. He surrenders it. The event horizon, the action point, the Choice, the Either/Or comes between these two statements, between the "Save me" and the "No." What determines which way he'll go lies in the prior attitude and disposition of his heart. As it always does with us. *That's what the Twelve Steps are designed to change—the attitude and disposition of our heart.*

*I—The Real Jesus*

It wasn't a sin for Jesus to be *tempted* to self-glorification or fear, or whatever. It's not a sin to be tempted with sin. It's not a sin for me to feel the pull of the black hole of temptation to lust, to feel the power of lust impelling me to drink. But I have a choice today. So do you. The same choice Jesus had. The same choice Adam and Eve had between plucking the fruit or leaving it on the tree. It's the choice to drink or die to the drink. To look or not look. This is the action-point for us. It's the point were time touches eternity, the point between saying Yes or saying No, of "saving" your life or losing it.

• • •

We've come to a place where I'd like to say again that this view of Jesus' humanity is what I have come to see in the record of his life. It may be difficult for others, as it was initially for me, to accept him as being Son of God *and* Son of man in our very own human flesh and nature. This is not for everybody. All I ask is that as you pray and read his Word, you ask the Lord to reveal himself to you as he will.

But let's pause for a moment and ask, What would a man be like if he did not have the same nature shared by the rest of humanity? How would he act? How would he respond in everyday situations? It's hard to realize how very different such a person would appear, how much he would stand apart if he did not share our true humanity. I think he would appear non-human, "other," out of this world. He would be different at the core of his being, and that would show through. I wonder if such a one could attract people to himself the way Jesus did. Could he have real compassion? How could there be any *feeling* for another human being without the ability to sympathize, suffer with us, which is what *sym-pathos* literally means? Did Jesus really *suffer* in temptation as we do? I believe he did; that's why he had to pray. That means I have a chance—if I do what he did.

*His Life*

Thank God.

When you think about it, it's our sinful nature that bonds us to others. At least that's the way it is in the recovery programs. We lead with our weakness, and that's how others identify with us and are attracted to us. (I admit that's not how we typically relate in the rest of our lives, including church, perhaps, but I don't call that intimacy.) If someone did not fully have our nature, his reactions to us and relations with us would stand out like a sore thumb. Our first impression would probably be, "He's a hypocrite! He's pretending to be something he isn't. He doesn't ring true." Mothers would sense the difference right away and keep their children away from him. And children would intuitively sense the difference and avoid such a cosmic stranger. The only one in the universe different, he'd stand out. But he drew children to himself. We underestimate the vast difference in kind between us and such a hypothetical person, for with all the weirdos who have inhabited the planet, there has never been such a person as one not having our very own human nature. "One who went to the truth by mere impulse would be a holy animal, not a true man."[12]

Unfortunately, we seem to prefer some such haloed humanoid for our Christ because we create that person in the image of what our religious addiction wants to see. People have been making Jesus other-worldly throughout church history, and we have inherited that legacy without realizing it. But as a lust addict, I have no choice; I must discover and connect with the real Jesus. Thank God! So let's turn and dare look at that momentous event intersecting time and eternity which makes his Connection with us possible.

# 7

## Jesus' Identification with our Sinful Human Nature—His Death

We have now come to the holy of holies. Nowhere do we feel the force of Jesus' full identification with us as we do at Gethsemane and Golgotha.

**Gethsemane**
Jesus began to feel the force of Golgotha and its inner conflict even before Gethsemane. We can trace the movement within Jesus of the progressive revelation of his passion. As Jesus embarks with his face set toward Jerusalem for the last time, knowing what will befall him, his disciples are first astonished and then afraid (Mark 10:32). They must have picked up something of what Jesus was sensing of the impending struggle, that the course toward the ultimate temptation and trial was now irrevocably set. Later, in Jerusalem, when he is describing how the grain of wheat must fall into the ground and die, referring to his own death and resurrection (and ours by identification), the foreboding breaks in upon him: "Now is my soul troubled. And what shall I say? 'Father save me from this hour?' No, for this purpose I have come to this hour" (John 12:27).

Here we have a premonition of the darker side of Jesus' agony, preparing him, as it were, for the ordeal to follow soon in Gethsemane. The verb translated "troubled" implies he was shaken, distraught, agitated, even perhaps with a sense of terror—an intuition that this was something that had not yet fully dawned upon him. He recoils from it.

## I—The Real Jesus

Again, in John 13:21, speaking of his coming betrayal, he is "troubled in spirit," the same verb. (This verb is first used in Jesus' reaction to the death of Lazarus in John 11:33, which may have been the first foreboding of the true nature of his own impending agony.)

Finally, in the olive garden of Gethsemane, the full force of the impending ordeal is upon him (Mat. 26:38-41):

> *Then he said to them, "My soul is deeply distressed, even to death; remain here, and watch with me." And going a little farther he fell on his face and prayed, "My Father, if it be possible, let this cup pass from me; nevertheless, not as I will, but as thou wilt." And he came to the disciples and found them sleeping; and he said to Peter, "So, could you not watch with me one hour? Watch and pray that you may not enter into temptation; the spirit indeed is willing, but the flesh is weak"*

Falling on his face and crying out? "My Father, *if it be possible...*"? Jesus? Asking if there's any way around it? I know of no greater demonstration of Jesus' fully human nature than this, his own words and this awesome experience.

Several questions come to mind. Why did Jesus have to agonize in prayer if he was not in real conflict? Why pray at all? If he was in conflict, it had to be between choosing between the will of God and his own human temptation to disobey. If he was only Son of God without our fallen nature, why all this tremendous inner disturbance and dread? Does this not imply that his own watching and praying were because *his* spirit indeed was willing but his flesh weak? In his flesh, Jesus does not want to take that cup of spiritual death—to become the sin offering; why else would he ask that it pass? The conflict within him was so great it was manifest in extreme emotional symptoms, "even unto death."

## His Death

It's hard for us to even begin to comprehend this. Jesus craves the support of his disciples when he pleads with them, "Watch *with* me"—apparently the only time where he so pleaded with them. Note also Jesus' sad devastation at the discovery that his three closest companions did *not* watch with him, that he had to bear the trial all alone. Only one who is truly human can be so attuned to such human intimacy and companionship as to be so needy in such an hour. And how could he feel all these emotions if he does not suffer in temptation as we do? Mark 14:33 has the startling phrase that he was greatly amazed and sore troubled . . . a "feeling of terrified surprise."[13]

First, he is astonished, then he is distressed, and finally, he is hurting in his soul to the point of death (Mark 14:34).[14] In terrified surprise, Jesus confronts not simply the prospect of physical death, but for the first time apparently sees he will have to actually *become sin*. This is the Great Dread. The only way I can even begin to imagine such horror is to think of having to bear all my own lust all at once. Today, progressively removed from it, I can tolerate less and less without terrible consequences; one visual drink is devastating; to act out would be—! And the thought of having all the lust I've ever known come into me at one time? Too terrible, even for a moment. And all my other sins and those of the whole human race—? This is the scandal—and the utter paradox—facing Jesus ahead on the Cross.

Jesus foretold his physical death from the very beginning, without any hint of backing away from it (John 2:19; Mk. 8:31; 10:33,38, etc.). He moved toward it knowingly and willingly. And his reaction to his arrest and crucifixion was fearless and courageous, with not the slightest hint of aversion. Note, for example, the first three Words of the Cross (recorded statements): He is concerned not with the physical pain of crucifixion but about first the soldiers, then the penitent thief, and then his mother. Also, he declined the offer of the tranquilizing drink. So his terrified astonishment

## I—The Real Jesus

in Gethsemane must refer not to physical death at all; he had foretold that in every detail, and not only never shirked it, he drove relentlessly toward it. His terror must refer to the fact that the full impact of the awful price he would have to pay for obedience to the Father finally dawns on him. *He will become sin!* He who overcame every sin in his surrender to the Father, must now be overcome and be vitiated by sin, which will destroy that union with the Father and bring spiritual death!

Can you sense the unspeakable horror? In my bus stop experience, I felt I would die if I did not "drink." Everything in my being screamed out for that drink denied, but it was all a lie. Not to drink was to live; to drink was to die. But here Jesus knew he would die—*spiritual death!*—by obeying the will of the Father! I had to die to my sin; He had to die to his own righteousness and connection with the Father. He gave up all for me, his connection with God, which is eternal life! And on Golgotha, when the sin-death actually took place, he was gone, done for, abandoned by God! That's the death the Son of man was recoiling from.

There's one other aspect of Jesus' temptation in the Garden that lurks behind the scenes here. He knew that in obeying the will of the Father and taking on our rebellion and disobedience he would then be subject to evil—and to the Evil One himself. There would be no defense possible, since he would be cut off from the Father. That seductive evil, which he overcame in the Wilderness temptation at the beginning of his ministry, would now overcome him. Note that at the Baptism and Transfiguration, the cloud accompanying the glorious Presence was bright. Does the darkness during the final hours of the crucifixion suggest that the Power of Darkness was now in control, that Jesus was finally under its power?

John Calvin, in some remarkable passages, says, "Why was it that he dreaded death except that he saw in it the curse of God, and that he had to wrestle with the guilt of all

*His Death*

iniquities, and also with hell itself?" and "engage, as it were, at close quarters with the powers of hell and the horrors of eternal death."[15] Perhaps Ephesians 1:21, where it says he was raised *above* all principalities and powers, implies that he became, in his surrender to sin, *subject* to those very powers. And when the chief priests and captains came out against him, led by Judas, Jesus, not resisting, says, "This is your hour, and the power of darkness" (Luke 22:53). That is, "This is your hour, and Darkness is in charge."

I believe Jesus willingly gave himself up to sin—our sin. How else could Jesus bear sin? It could not be forced upon him mechanically. Sin is spiritual, and for Jesus to bear it, he'd have to take it, not unknowingly as scapegoat, but knowingly surrender to Sin. And surrendering to sin opens us to the power of Darkness! Can we ever even begin to see the real agony of Gethsemane and Golgotha?

He knew he would be given over to the lost state and be subject to the Power of darkness! The stupendous terror of it, knowing that cut off from God, he will be totally given over to sinful nature, without remedy, without God, to suffer the lostness of being sinful and whatever consequences being subject to the powers of evil would imply. He must submit to the power of darkness! He would be subject to Satan without defense, and he would know the death-pain of eternal lostness.

It seems clear to me that the reason Jesus knew "the flesh is weak," so pleading with the three disciples, was because he experienced the weakness of his own flesh—just like we do! The whole scene demands it. As in the Temptation, how could his agony in Gethsemane have been real if he did not have the inner conflict wanting to keep him from the will of God? And where else do we find Jesus on his face, wanting support from others? Something within Jesus tempted him to shrink from the will of God. What could that have been if it was not the very same nature that is within me and you and entices us to shrink from obedience in every temptation? The fact that the conflict was there tells me that Jesus himself knew that conflict between flesh and Spirit, just as I do.

So it's okay to be tempted and feel powerless; He was! It's okay to have the Tree of Death inside our Paradise! It must be so! **It's not a sin to be tempted with sin!**

Gethsemane is where Jesus' dealing with my sin begins to come to its sharpest focus; it tells me Jesus had my sinful flesh! Thank God! That means it's not only okay, but necessary for me to have it too and that there's victory over it one temptation at a time, because he was victorious over the same body of sin I have.

> *Thank you, Lord, for suffering in temptation. Now I know I can too, and it's all right; I don't have to be afraid of sin within me. Victory over it is your glory—and mine.*

## Golgotha

Jesus' experience on the cross seems sharply divided into two phases: the first three hours, and then the three hours of darkness following those. In the first phase we see the same Jesus we saw after the victory in Gethsemane—resigned to the will of God, serene, his remarks full of concern for others, even though his body is wracked with terminal torture.

The second phase has a drastically different mood to it. We have no record of what was happening during those three final hours. The darkness, (which apparently could not have been an eclipse[16]) and the final Words of the Cross call attention to this dramatic shift in Jesus' subjective experience, what was going on inside of him. That's the real essence of Calvary: what was going on inside the mind and soul of Jesus during those three hours of darkness. The continuing darkness obscures the externals of the physical execution taking place on the cross, overshadowing the awesome cosmic conflict within him. Finally, piercing that darkness,

*His Death*

we hear the agonized cry of the Son of God abandoned by God—"My God, my God, why hast thou forsaken me!"

There is some question as to the exact order of the last Words of the Cross; one can best see the problem by looking at the various accounts in a harmony of the four Gospels. I come up with the following sequence at the conclusion of the three hours of darkness:

Word 4 — The loud cry, "My God, my God, why hast thou forsaken me?"

Word 5 — "I thirst." (He is offered sour wine, and he drinks it.)

Word 6 — Another loud cry. (I do not connect this cry with any recorded words. The Greek text of Luke 23:46 actually separates the cry from the Word, the RSV notwithstanding.)

Word 7 — "It is finished."

Word 8 — "Father, into thy hands I commit my spirit."

I list the second cry as the sixth Word because it is recorded by Matthew, Mark, and Luke and may tell us as much or more than if it contained words. (In this reckoning, there would thus be eight Words of the Cross instead of what is conceived traditionally as seven. This is the way I see it.)

There's something different about Jesus here after the darkness descends—different from the spirit of the first three Words. Whatever happened during the darkness has produced a great change. Could it be that now the sin-transaction has actually taken place, that the mystery of those three hours is the mystery of the Atonement itself? Now he appears as the one "stricken, smitten by God, and afflicted." "It was the will of the Lord to bruise him; he has put him to grief" (as prophesied in Isa. 53).

## I—The Real Jesus

When Jesus became the Great Sinner on Golgotha by submitting to being overcome by sin, the same thing happened to him that happens to us when we sin. Sin separates. And it separated him from the Father, as inconceivable as that must be, which we cannot fully understand. Why else would he cry "abandoned!"? Sin creates disunion within myself and between myself and God. Must it not have had the same effect in Jesus? What an incredible thought. Christ (and thus God in Christ?) suffering the same effects of sin we do? The same disunion in his person, the same dissolution? The same spiritual death? How inconceivable! No wonder someone has said such a thought is morally and metaphysically impossible.[17] But who said anything about Golgotha is logical?

If this interpretation be correct, then Jesus' death for our sins—his sin-death—took place *before* his actual physical death, though necessarily a part of it. Jesus' spiritual death occurred at the Abandonment, which elicited his cry of being actually forsaken by the Father, the Source of life. At that point, Jesus is *dis*connected, spiritually dead! Sin has wrought its penalty, and Jesus is lost. He has been made sin.

Listen to John Calvin again: "Nothing had been done if Christ had only endured corporeal death. . . . not only was the body of Christ given up as the price of redemption, but
 . . . there was a greater and more excellent price—that he bore in his soul the tortures of condemned and ruined man."[18] Thus, Jesus knows what it means to be cut off from God as we are. This draws me to him. *He identifies with me*—in the very sense we speak of identification with one another in the program! He's actually "been there." Yes! And I identify with him.

Seen in this light, the resurrection and ascension take on new force. God is the Overcomer of Sin and Death! That's who God is! In himself. So it's been done. Sin is over and done with! Finished! That's why it's a supreme exaltation of ego to even think we have to be righteous first

## His Death

to be accepted by God or to think that we should somehow prevail over lust ourselves. God meets us in our sin. And he himself is its Remedy. (We need to dwell on this and ponder it until it breaks in upon us.)

The very next Word is "I thirst;" and Jesus takes the offered drink of sour wine, the ordinary drink of the Roman soldiers.[19]

Jesus then cries out again with a loud voice (Word Six by my reckoning). We aren't told why or what he cried, so let's recap what happened: He has been enduring the abandonment of the unspeakable sin-death during the three hours of darkness. At its end he cries out the loud anguished "WHY ... ABANDONED. . . ?!" He then asks for a drink. He must be weak to the very point of death. He takes the drink. Now we hear this second loud cry, the one without words. This whole final sequence may have only taken a few moments.

Has the darkness ended here? If so, it leads me to believe that this second cry, instead of being another cry of hopeless anguish, is a cry of hope and faith. Having drunk, he has a moment of renewed strength and sees that things had to be this way. He accepts it, as he finally accepted the will of God in Gethsemane. Not automatically as some divine android, but through suffering and pain and temptation to doubt. *This* was the last temptation of Christ, and had he put words to the feelings of this cry, we might hear him say, "Yes! it had to be this way. I've fulfilled my mission; it's *not* a failure. This was the Father's will. I accept it. It was supposed to be. It's over. I'm cut off, abandoned, and lost, but I put my trust in you, Father!" That cry of exultation and praise, echos across time to us even now. The original "Joy Response."

That's why we hear, finally, **"IT IS FINISHED!"** (John 19:30). He is at peace again, as before the darkness, and we hear the last Word, "Father, into thy hands I commit my spirit" (Luke 23:46). Even in that state of being cut off,

*I—The Real Jesus*

he believes—*as you and I must believe.* He is now one of us in every respect. He is truly the Pioneer of our faith.

In that sin-cursed alienated state, he has no guarantee that any kind of salvation will take place. Can you believe that? All he can do now is trust God in the same way we must, putting his fate into the Father's hands. (We actually have it easier because we see him now raised from that death.) So Jesus works the first three Steps of our program and turns his will and his life over to the care of God. He is now in the same place we are. His identification with us is now complete. This is "the obedience of faith" (Rom. 1:5). He stands exactly where we must stand—as sinner, abandoning himself to God absolutely.

I connect with Christ because he died. The Son of God died—spiritually. Nothing but sin could have separated him from the Father. Therefore, it was the sin he bore—*our* sin—that caused God to forsake him. "He himself bore our sins in his body on the tree" (1 Peter 2:24).[20] He was made a curse for us (Gal 3:13). Thus, the proof that he actually took my sins upon him was his spiritual death—the Abandonment. This cannot be overemphasized. His lostness has to be our lostness! So his resurrection can be ours! Do you see it? I, for one, need such proof and assurance.

**When we focus merely on the physical agony of the crucifixion, we trivialize the death of Jesus the Christ.**

• • •

The Abandonment is thus the circumstance, above all others, where Jesus is united most fully with me, the sinner. He who had never sinned was made sin on my behalf (2 Cor 5:21). My sin made him bear the unthinkable death and hell of separation from the Father. More than that, my sin bore its death in him since he opened himself up to my sins, and that destroyed him.

## His Death

Let me then ask, How could Jesus bear my sin *without* having my same sinful flesh? How could he experience my sin without a point of contact with it in his own human nature? How could he bear my sin—*in my stead*? How could the effect of my sin destroy him—sever his union with the Father and cast him into lostness and outer darkness? How could he taste the death of my sins, how could he feel the consequences of my sins in himself, if there was nothing within him with which sin could connect? Otherwise, he would have been *immune* to all that sin; it would not have phased him at all. Otherwise, bearing my sin could not have had any ill effect on him because he had no nature sin could harm. But in obedience to the Father, he felt sin, knew it, bore it, and it destroyed him.

He who had overcome every temptation to sin let himself be overcome by every sin of mankind. All so *he* could identify with, have union with *me*. So he could relate to my sinful being. So he could loose me from my sins. When we thus stand at a distance and survey that wondrous cross, we can only conclude, with the Roman centurion who witnessed it all, "Truly, this man was the Son of God."

*Our true connection with the one called Jesus is with his humanity.* How can it be otherwise, since we are human? And that connection makes us fall down, as did doubting Thomas, and cry, "My Lord and my God!" Can you begin to see now why I say I believed in an unreal Jesus and that that is why I was never saved from sinning?

What love of God! I always had it the other way around, that Jesus came so I could become one with him. The truth of the matter is that God so loved the world that he gave his only begotten Son *so that he could become one with me the sinner.* Do you see the incredible? The Father wanting to be reconciled with the rebellious child, reaching out first, through Jesus, and denying himself, to be one with *me.* He takes the sinner to himself![21] And at what incredible cost!

## I—The Real Jesus

> *When I survey the wondrous cross,*
> *On which the Prince of glory died,*
> *My richest gain I count but loss,*
> *And pour contempt on all my pride.*

Do you see now how the terror of today's unmentionable word—SIN—is gone? That most-shunned word few dare utter any more? Sin. That we can open ourselves up to a concept we have been shutting ourselves off from most of our lives—yes, even in the church? Had I only understood this while raising my children, I could have been a real father to them and husband to their mother, accepting them for what they were because I could accept myself for what I was. Accepting their sinfulness and sins, as I would have mine, instead of trying to force it out of them as I tried to force it out of myself.

> *Lord! in my next temptation to lust, resentment, fear, or self, help me to see and know and be one with your death and thus be one with your love. That I may know you and the power of your resurrection and the fellowship of your suffering, being conformed to your death, that I may attain the resurrection out of my sin and death*
> (Phil. 3:9-11).

# 8

## The Gallery of God

How can we ever f~~...~~e what really happene~~...~~ss? Words fail us. But ~~...~~ven "from afar." Let us take a holy look ~~...~~. How did it happen that Jesus became sin (~~...~~)? (I make no claim to certainty in this interpretat~~ion. H~~owever, this is the only one that strikes me as being consonant with the scriptural data I consider in this book, and it offers a new challenge to our relation to Jesus.)

*[Overlay: Chapter 8 has been significantly revised as an insert. Its message can best be understood in the light of previous chapters 1 through 7.]*

Just recently my wife and I were touring another part of the state and stopped by to visit an artist friend I hadn't seen since my early days of initial sobriety. His new home was designed as a gallery for his work, and his paintings lined the walls in almost every room. The man's thoroughly professional work was populated by a number of female nudes, beautifully rendered. I had forgotten this predilection of his, and it caught me off guard. Nevertheless, appreciating the fine art, I found myself captivated by his work again. There was nothing salacious or of prurient interest, but the mere fact of so many nude female figures hanging about and the character revealed in the face of his self-portraits created an atmosphere I never came to terms with until after we left the place.

The ability of this artist to see his own soul as clearly as he does in his self-portraits is amazing, putting some of us to shame. His own term in describing one such portrait, was

## I—The Real Jesus

"debauchery;" the visage is marred from inner dissolution. The searching self-appraisal was communicating something powerfully in all these paintings, and I was feeling the power of that revelation hung around me on those walls.

It was not until my quiet time the next morning when I finally faced my reaction to the art. There in the stillness of mind and heart, I again felt the power the images in that gallery had held over me. The paintings had communicated a spiritual force trying to gain access to my soul. And all the while I was in that house and for some time afterwards, I was under the influence of that power. I had unwittingly been invited to drink whatever it was that had possessed the artist's subconscious and which he had expressed so artfully. As I think on it, this is very similar to the common plight of sexaholics tempted to look at any image which is a trigger for lust. In the case of such images accompanying masturbation, the "drink" analogy is very apropos. As we start drinking in the image, we open our soul to a spiritual force lying both behind the image and within our very souls—Lust. We open our souls to connect with the negative force.

On my knees that morning after, it came to me that each of our lives hangs as a portrait in the Gallery of God. The very heart of what we are in the utter reality of our secret self is displayed there. We are known. From the inside out. This Gallery exists in the spiritual realm; it holds every soul-portrait of the human race. It is the spiritual atmosphere of the human race. It is God's Gallery of Man.

Jesus had a cup to drink, one he did not want to drink. In Gethsemane, we see Jesus beseeching the Father not once, but three times that somehow he would not have to drink it. At one point he comes out flatly and pleads, "Take this cup away from me!" (Mark 14:36). Intuitively he recoils from it as though to say, "I don't want to drink this. I *can't* take it into me, into my being. It's death to me!"

Sharing our sinful human nature, Jesus was already hung with the Gallery of Man, for one man's sinful human

## The Gallery of God

nature is the nature of Everyman, and that of the whole human race. The portrait of anyone's soul as it appears in this divine gallery, is the portrait of all. Each of us is a reflection of that Gallery of the human race, and the whole Gallery is portrayed within each of us.

> When therefore, we see our sin and guilt in the light of the Word of God's grace, we do not merely see it as our own, but in our own we see the sin and guilt of man, of every man and all men. In our own person we see all mankind sinful and guilty before God.[22]

There is no one's sin I am incapable of committing. I have what everybody else has; we share a fallen human nature in common! *That's* why the love of God can move me concerning other sinners and I must never sit in judgement. Under God, our sinfulness is all the same! So the gallery of Jesus' soul was hung with the portrait of Sin, as each of ours is, but he never drank of it as we do. He lived and walked daily in the halls of that gallery, feeling its power, yet overcame every temptation to take a drink. Incredible, but true. But now, on the cross, the Righteous One must taste death for every man. Now he must *drink* to the dregs that awful cup of Sin.

So, the moment of truth has come, the last temptation of Christ. The first Adam eats and dies; the last Adam is to drink and die, the first Adam in disobedience, the last in obedience to the Father. Both die spiritually. During the first three hours Jesus is slowly dying physically there on that cruel cross, but everything is right within him. Then, the darkness descends, and we know something terrible is happening—inside him. It's as though at this point in his dying, the Father's will must now be accomplished. And for the first time ever, in blind obedience to that will, Jesus opens himself to the Gallery within. Sin. Not something in the

## I—The Real Jesus

abstract. My sin, your sin. The spirit of sin, and hence all mankind's sinfulness. He *drinks*!

Take the most shameful thing you've ever done and imagine it hanging in the Gallery of God. (It's already there, whether we acknowledge it or not.) Now imagine everyone else's sin-portrait in the same gallery, each representing his or her most diabolical sin-event. What a gallery of horrors! Who could stand to view it, much less drink it in and be possessed by it? The very force of it would change you.

Looking at it another way, imagine—if you are fortunate enough to have some sexual and lust sobriety under your belt—imagine what happens when you take a single visual drink of lust. You know the effect—immediate loss and disturbance. Just that one drink. It cuts us off from God, from love, and from life and sets up the craving for more. The farther we are removed from lust, the more we can detect the death-wages, the death-effects, of a single lust incident inside our being. Now imagine acting out sexually on your lust as you used to do. For the sober recovering member, that's destruction! Then imagine letting into your being all the lust you've ever known and experienced, then add in the rest of all your sinfulness—let it all in, all at once. What would it do to you?

Jesus opens himself up like that. The hour has come for that final obedience of faith, the moment on which all eternity pivots. He drinks the cup of Lust, Hate, Self-obsession, Fear. . . . and all the rest. He opens his soul to the entire Gallery of Sin and Death. He lets it all in. He becomes Sin! That's the meaning of 2 Cor 5:21.

In the Transfiguration, Jesus let the divine Glory out; we saw it burst forth for a moment. But here on Golgotha he must let the demonic Darkness *in*. So the darkness descends on the crucifixion scene, for what is happening is too awful to conceive. Merciful darkness that the spectators cannot see his shame! We must not look upon his face now, for to look would be to see the debauchery, the lewd and debased defilement of our own spiritual countenance creeping over that holy tortured visage. Our defilement! As in Isaiah,

> *"As one from whom men hide their faces...."*

But we must look! Every sinner. You and I in our lust-sin. *We* must not hide our faces from him. We must look deeply upon the very face of the serpent! To live!

> *"As Moses lifted up the serpent in the wilderness, so must the Son of man be lifted up"* (John 3:14). [Yes, that's what the man said. He was to be as the serpent!]

> *"Many were astonished at him— His appearance was so marred, beyond human semblance, and his form beyond that of the sons of men....*
> *"We regarded him as one stricken, smitten by God and afflicted."*
> *"It was the will of the Lord to bruise him, to afflict him with disease....*
> *"You make his soul an offering for sin....*
> *"He has poured out his soul into death."*
> (Isaiah 52 and 53)

The sinful nature we all share was let loose within him, not because he wanted to sin, but because it was the Father's will that he bear sin, *become* sin. What did it do to the Son of man, taking that cosmic Drink of Sin? What happened? The wrath-connection is what happened. Wrath was revealed from heaven against that unrighteousness! (Appendix 5 deals with this at length.) Every effect that sin has on the human organism took place inside Jesus as it does in us. Every kind of death that issues from sin became his. Christ *died* for our sins.

## I—The Real Jesus

Oswald Chambers comes close to this:

> The Cross of Jesus is the revelation of God's judgment on sin. Never tolerate the idea of martyrdom about the Cross of Jesus Christ. The Cross was a superb triumph in which the foundations of hell were shaken. . . . The Cross did not *happen* to Jesus: He came on purpose for it. . . . Beware of separating *God manifest in the flesh* from *the Son becoming sin*. . . . God became incarnate for the purpose of putting away sin; not for the purpose of Self-realization. . . . The Cross is not the cross of a man but the Cross of God, and the Cross of God can never be realized in human experience. The Cross is the exhibition of the nature of God, the gateway whereby any individual of the human race can enter into union with God. . . . The Cross is the point where God and sinful man merge with a crash and the way to life is opened—but the crash is on the heart of God.[23]

• • •

So, what did Jesus' sin-death accomplish? First, we are *known*. You and I. In all our sinfulness! He's been there; and is now the revealer of sin. But Jesus is now with us as co-sinner. Unthinkable! If we could only grasp it. Now he will call us his brothers and say, as he told Mary at the empty tomb, "I go to my Father and your father, to my God and your God." The curtain of the temple is torn, ripped open from top to bottom—that which keeps us all from the Real Connection. The way for sinners is now open, and he leads the way out of the tomb!

> *The self-surrender of God to our human condition was so that God could know our sin and be one with us.* And those of us in the thralldom of defiling lust now have a Savior who can come inside our every lust craving—inside the lust itself—and bear its death so we can be free and clean.

> *"Get you up to a high mountain, O Zion, herald of good tidings; lift up your voice with strength, O Jerusalem, herald of good tidings, lift it up, fear not; say to the cities of Judah, Behold your God!"*
>
> Isaiah 40:9

### An Afterthought

All of this points up why lust addiction is so ultimate; because lust is drinking spiritually. And this is why Jesus' sin-death had to be spiritual and why he had to *drink*. The spiritual drink is the real essence of sin; behaviors are simply physical manifestations of what is going on in the heart. Sin is really spiritual. The essence and origin of sin is attitude, not action. Jesus can't move a muscle on that cross; he can't *do* anything. He can't *do* a sin. This is one of our great religious delusions today: "I'm not *doing* anything wrong, so I didn't commit a sin." But it's the being behind the doing where all the mischief lies, and we cannot, we will not see that! That's why we are so very sinful today and in such denial.

Thus Jesus was not "committing" any particular sin, as we tend to narrowly think of sin. He opened himself to Sin and let himself be overcome by it. All this forces us—*forces us*—to a deeper view of sin, which we've lost. As we have lost the real Jesus, so have we lost the real meaning of sin. Recovery from lust forces us to discover within ourselves the real nature of sin and thereby become able to see and know the real Jesus. Thank God!

# The Lustaholic's Gethsemane

Let's pause for a moment and go back to the garden of Gethsemane and witness again the Son of man encountering his final temptation. We see him greatly amazed, overcome by a feeling of terrified surprise, and we hear his anguished plea, *"My soul is overwhelmed, unto death."*

Unless you have let yourself feel the power of your own "unto death" encounters with lust, you can never know the joy of being "raised with Christ" in that next lust temptation. Sadly, many of us just go ahead and take the "drink" to escape the feeling of deprivation and desolation. But lustaholics who are willing to cross the lust-death barrier live through such feelings into freedom. As we turn away instead of looking, we have the feeling of being hit with a ton of bricks. We're knocked out, helpless and powerless, knowing nothing in us can resist this. We are utterly overwhelmed. It's nothing less than the threat of soul death!

It seems presumptuous to think we might have experiences analogous to what Jesus had, but we do. Our Gethsemanes can be just as overwhelming to us when we encounter the impossible as his were to him. Turning to him *in* the lust temptation is dying to the sin, and dying means not knowing whether we'll make it or not. But thanks be to God, Jesus was obedient—obedient unto death—and was raised victorious out of that death. So we too can be raised with Christ out of our soul death in any temptation, as he was in his. The resurrection of Jesus the Christ is God's guarantee that we will be raised, if we too trust and obey. And we are so raised, praise God! (Eph. 2:5; Col. 2:13, 3:1; 2Cor. 4:10)

This book won't do you any good unless you are willing to go through the fear of being overwhelmed, start dying to the looks, and take that first leap of faith onto him, not knowing whether you'll make it or not. Those who do so are discovering Life on the other side—his loving, saving Presence—what our lust was really looking for all along.

So stop trying. Go to *him* when that next "impossible" hits, and put him to the test.

# Part II

# ENCOUNTERING THE REAL ME

# 9

## A Startling Discovery

In Part I, Encountering the Real Jesus, we encountered the reality of Jesus' full identification with our sinful human nature in his Wilderness experience, in his life, and in his death. This reveals the Jesus I have slowly been discovering in my own recovery experience. So I ask, What had to take place in my life before I could begin to know him so? Something "violent" had to happen inside me that would tear away the blinders which self-will had put over my eyes to prevent me from seeing what I really am. I would have to enter violently into the kingdom (Luke 16:16); that is, I would have to forcefully face the unfaceable—my sinful self. So let's encounter together, in the light of God's word, the reality of our own human natures.

Lust for me, the so-called Christian, separated me from the real Jesus and blinded me so I could not see the delusion of my idolatry. Thus, my misapprehension of Jesus and of the Gospel—as a believer trying to kick my habit for 39 years—had a twofold basis: not knowing the real condition of my own sinfulness and not knowing Jesus' real identification with that sinfulness. For me, it turned out that I could not know the real Jesus without first knowing my own sinfulness. I'll venture further and say that the measure of knowing our own sinfulness and need is the measure of knowing the saving Son of man.

So how did I come to know my own sinfulness, and what is it? That realization did not begin in church, where sin was talked about occasionally. I would have vague feelings that would get me out of my seat and take me on that long lonely walk down the aisle-to-nowhere with every altar call. Neither did the realization of sinfulness begin at home, where I was so often reminded of how far short I fell. And it didn't begin in Sunday School or in the theological educational system either. Realization of my true condition began when I put down my overt drugs which were blinding me from my true condition—sex, lust, alcohol, and tranquilizers—and began the process of recovery. I cannot emphasize too strongly that I was blind to my true spiritual condition—as a believer—until I put down all those behaviors that were helping conceal it. The realization of my true condition is still continuing. Thank God; I hope it never ends.

At the most obvious level, one might think that sexual sobriety in itself would immediately have brought recognition of the true nature of the effects of what I'd been doing sexually. But awareness of the profound nature of the evils sex addiction was working on myself and others would be a long time coming and is still in process. (That's the awakening the first Eleven Steps promise to bring about.)

The first realization of intrinsic wrongness came to me when I discovered the power of lust. The initial experience of sexual sobriety exposed raw nerve endings, which picked up the slightest lust signals, which were then amplified a thousand-fold. My eyes were alive with lust, "full of adultery." Abstinent from sex, I was struck with the awesome, supernatural force of the lust power, caged within as a wild, ravenous beast. Had I always been like that? Had sex merely sedated, covered over this monstrous appetite of lust to snatch, ingest, and possess through eyes, body, and being? Yes, apparently the sex drug had quieted this "imperious urge"—for the moment. No wonder sex had to continue as an addiction; it was too frightening to look at what lay beneath it, inside of *me*!

## A Startling Discovery

What an awakening! Had I not put down my habits, I would never have guessed that what lay hidden in the secret recesses of my own soul was such a dark force for evil, over which I was absolutely powerless. This is one reason why I suggest long open-ended periods of sexual abstinence in marriage—by mutual consent and for the purpose of healing—especially when first entering sex addiction recovery. We have to break through the drug-connection with which sex has become associated. The addiction to lust and sex does not stop just because we are having sex only with our spouse. In such abstinence periods, the member should strive for increased non-sexual contact, care, and communication, lest the spouse read abstinence as rejection. (See the pertinent articles in *Recovery Continues*.)

The next phase of this progressive revelation of the defective self for me was characterized by my discovery of resentment—the big number two. How well I remember. And so do my wife and younger son, as well as the back door or our house, which was slammed a lot in early sobriety! Sexual sobriety—eliminating the sedating effect of the sex and lust drugs and thus threatening the free play of lust—forced the real me to the surface. And the volcano of resentment erupted, first in my mind, and then out upon those closest to me in the safety of my home, where I could "be myself." What was *this* force? Where did it come from? I was such a gentle creature, I thought. Pseudo-gentleness covers such a multitude of sins, doesn't it? How could I have such intense animosities that lingered, fuming, for not just hours but weeks and years? My sister told me that in my teens and twenties I had a perpetual smile on my face. (I sometimes wonder whether that was the smile of the pacified masturbator or the man still in the womb or the people pleaser, or all of the above?) Resentment was a power as demonic in force and effect as lust was, and maybe more so. I had an overpowering need to resent. It was as though I *had* to find someone to have bad feelings about. Resentment was

## II—The Real Me

a drug I had to have! A *spiritual* addiction. And I was as powerless over it as I ever was over lust. There was no way I could prevent resentment from knocking on the door and entering. Of course, in the beginning, I was the one opening the door and ushering it in! But I could not see that then. The practice of sin produces blindness.

The third discovery of the exposed self—the third in that commonly experienced threesome recovering sex drunks seem to know so well—was fear. Not physical fear; I seemed to be pretty fearless when it came to most physical dangers. Spiritual fear. Those nameless, formless specters that rise out of some abyss deep inside. Trying to label them would only weaken any attempt at description. One has to experience it to know what I'm talking about. *Fearfulness*. Again, here was a vast subterranean realm of the secret self I was powerless over, where all manner of dark forces clamored for possession.

This list of the discovery of what I am in the "thoughts and intents of the heart" continued and is still going on: an unforgiving spirit, judgmentalism, self-obsession, self-glorification.... It never ends! Thank God! Yes, I'm grateful to have a continuing compelling need for a loving, saving Presence within this very sinful nature of mine.

One day, as I pondered this continuing litany of my defective self, getting to know slow but progressive victory over some of its various manifestations by the grace of God, it dawned on me: All these defects, these "sins" of mine—what are they? At first, we discover that the addiction is merely a symptom of underlying spiritual pathology. This was discovered early in AA. But there's got to be something underneath *all* of this stuff. When taken all together, what does this whole picture tell me but that I am a sinner; that is, whatever else I am, issuing from a good Creation in the image of God, I also have a sinful nature that wants to express itself in any or all these many ways. It also tells me that I cannot change that nature of mine by myself. Progressive victory over its manifestations, yes! But that does not eliminate what it is in itself inside of me. All the evidence points to the presence of some lowest-common-denominator force within—what some of us call our negative force or "*lower power.*"

So let me now try to show how my experience coincides with and illustrates what Scripture reveals about my sinful nature. I will later try to show how Jesus' identification with that selfsame sinful nature is the basis of my progressive victory over lust. That's the key, the theme of this whole book. Jesus' identification with that selfsame sinful nature is the key to my victory over lust. But first, a brief illustration from life, an eye-opening run-in with this alter ego of mine.

# 10

### The Woman in Line

*One day you will be compelled to see, nay, to feel your heart as God sees it; and to know that the cankered thing which you have within you, a prey to the vilest of diseases, is indeed the centre of your being, your very heart.*
George MacDonald

Several years ago I had an experience that tells me what I really am; it opens a window into my soul. I include it here because many people, when they first read this, will think, whether they say it or not, "Ron, you're making a big deal out of something that seems so minor. Aren't you getting a little pathological here? Lighten up!" But it is for this very reason that I include here what some would say is such a minimal offense. I might have included a more lurid story; I have plenty of the "scarlet" variety from which to draw. Instead, I choose what would probably not even be considered a "little" sin.

I was at the government offices where several people were waiting at the counter for service. While traveling there, I had had the premonition that I might have to do some line surrendering when I arrived (after all, I'm a "line loser"), but dismissed it. I had that "charmed" feeling of invulnerability. There are times when I have had that same feeling I used to have in the lust chase, where I did insane and dangerous things, yet felt I was somehow immune from harm, even divinely protected.

When I got to the counter, there were too few clerks waiting on too many people. Soon, a woman came up behind

## II—The Real Me

me, and I engaged her in conversation about how the Planning Department should have a system of taking numbers for more equitable service. She agreed wholeheartedly, obviously in some kind of hurry herself. After considerable waiting, a clerk was available and I was next; but who rushed in in front of me but the very woman behind me with whom I had been talking! I couldn't believe the audacity of it all, and after a few moments resolved to express my feelings. I walked up to the offender and in a quiet voice calmly said, "Lady, you are really something!" I was proud of being able to express myself and without guile, resentment, or malice. Pure Responsible Adult! or so I thought, feeling pretty smug.

Instead of defending herself, the woman immediately accepted blame, sincerely apologizing to the effect, "I *knew* you were ahead of me. I don't know why I did that; I'm terribly sorry." And how did I respond? "Oh that's okay; I've done the same thing; I understand. Why don't you go ahead. Thanks for the making it right." No, I said no such thing. Without saying a word, I turned on my heel and walked away. Stalked is more like it. Twelve years sober! There was never a better example of a "little murder." My reaction gave the lie to my "pure" response to her. That response was sinful, and I knew it. I knew that my calm quiet voice was deceiving even me. But I willfully covered it over with rationalization—all in an instant.

I take this as pure evil in its most essential form: I refused forgiveness. I willed her into non-existence, lostness. Total rejection. As I inventory the act now, I see first of all that my basic mind-set expected her to defend herself with either rationalization or denial. That's probably because I would have wanted to defend myself that way. Intrinsically, in the flesh, regardless of how I may moderate it at the time by "practicing the program," my first impulse is that I am right. Sinful instinct first; Program second, if at all. I was willing her to be damned to unforgiveness. I played Judge, Jury, and Executioner. I was playing god.

## The Psychology of Sin

That's the essence of my sinfulness, isn't it? Being god of my life. The mechanism of that transaction was identical to that of lust or resentment. Let's take it apart in slow motion:
1) In a conscious decision of my will 2) I turn from God in rebellion, 3) choose to pervert the reality of that situation, 4) in an ego-demand, so I can lust after someone or judge someone by what I want to believe, 5) and abuse that relation, 6) all to keep from seeing the truth about myself. This is the sin-process, the "psychology" of sin.

No wonder my wife and children were discounted and suffered.

Talk about playing God, this is the kind of god only humans can devise, the kind some of us could never accept and fled! This is the negative god—just like the ruler of darkness. Thus the essence of my sinfulness is no less than his whose pride

> Had cast him out from Heaven,
> with all his host
> Of rebel Angels, by whose aid, aspiring
> To set himself in glory above his peers,
> He trusted to have equaled the Most High,
> If he opposed; and, with ambitious aim
> Against the throne and monarchy of God,
> Raised impious war in Heaven and battle proud.
> (John Milton, *Paradise Lost*)

This book may not speak to any who do not feel the power and despair of their sinfulness. I accept that, and I accept all who do not feel the weight that I feel in the above encounter with the woman at Planning. I ask only that you believe that I believe this is symptomatic of sinfulness in essence. Remember, however, that it was—and is—the despair *over* my sinfulness that leads me to union with the Lover of my soul, and that without progressive recovery, I

*II—The Real Me*

could never see, much less despair over my real condition.

This is what I am as a believer, sober—in my flesh. Impious war against the rule of God. This is what lies underneath everything else in the many-layered depths of my inner psyche, heart, and soul. It's what I've been all along. There's just too much evidence like the above incident for me to deny it or say it should be otherwise. This is my nature—my sinful nature. Today! And this is what I really am today, in my flesh. As a recovering addict. As a believer! This is the essence of my First Step powerlessness.

***I cannot retain a low view of sin and survive.*** I, the lustaholic, do not have the luxury of retaining a low view of my sinfulness and continue to survive and recover.

Sometimes, in a meeting, I feel like jumping up and saying, "My name is Ron; I'm a sinner!" There's great freedom in that today, because being a person with a nature wanting to sin, no longer means the impossible tyranny of having to obey sin. That subtle, misunderstood, but all-important difference is the very reason for my impossible joy. Take time to dwell on this. If we can grasp and experience this, we can begin to see sin, the Savior, and salvation for what they really are.

# 11

## The Sinfulness of the Believer—Romans 7

Now that we have begun to see this Jesus, this sin-bearer, sin-conqueror, let's turn for a deeper look into the sin question itself. How we view ourselves must change if we see the Son of man aright. And how we view ourselves must change if we want recovery from lust. (The Twelve Steps are designed to produce such a change.)

I have shown that I have a sinful nature. Today. Right now. And when I imbibe, take the drink, inevitable consequences ensue within me. I have used lust and resentment as obvious indicators, but these are only a couple of the more obvious sins of the spirit underlying and fueling the sins of the flesh. So the question now is, Does this old nature of mine, this sinful nature, does it remain when I become a believer? The answer must be Yes. Let's see what the Scriptures say.

Sin as a force in the child of God comes most clearly into focus where Paul is bearing witness to his own personal experience in Romans 7.

> Sin, finding opportunity in the commandment, wrought in me all kinds of covetousness. . . . For sin, finding opportunity in the commandment, deceived me and by it killed me. . . . It was sin, working death in me . . . in order that sin might be shown to be sin, and . . . might become sinful beyond measure. We know that the law is spiritual; but I am carnal, sold under sin. I do not understand my own actions. For I do not do what I

## II—The Real Me

> want, but I do the very thing I hate ... so then it is no longer I that do it, but sin which dwells within me, that is, in my flesh. I can will what is right, but I cannot do it. For I do not do the good I want, but the evil I do not want is what I do.... When I want to do right, evil lies close at hand. For I delight in the law of God, in my inmost self, but I see in my members another law at war with the law of my mind and making me captive to the law of sin which dwells in my members. Wretched man that I am! Who will deliver me from this body of death?" (Romans 7:8-24)

This is an absolutely perfect description of my inner self. Today! As a believer! In joyous recovery! Not all Bible scholars would agree. But then, how many Bible scholars are lustaholics in recovery? The New Testament scholar C.E.B. Cranfield, of the University of Edinburgh, Scotland, has put to rest any thought that this passage of Paul cannot refer to the Christian experience. Cranfield's careful argument against commentators holding the contrary view, which is too lengthy to include here, is utterly convincing for me. (His is a landmark commentary on the Greek text.) "In fact, a struggle as serious as that which is here described can only take place where the Spirit of God is present and active."[24] And one look at Romans 8:10 (and such passages as Galatians 6:8) should quickly confirm this. "But if Christ is in you, although *your bodies are dead because of sin,* your spirits are alive because of righteousness." Our bodies being "dead because of sin," even though Christ is in us, is the very imagery of the passage we just read in Romans chapter 7!

The point here is that our bodies—our "flesh," our "members"—are still dead because of sin, but God can give us life. There is victory *over* the sinful nature and sin! There is Life in death! This is our very hope and joy as Christians. It's the continuing token of our final resurrection, and God's glory, because we can't take any credit for the victory. We can continue to be tempted from within, but we can have continuing victory over temptation through him who loves us.

Also, Paul carefully qualifies this indwelling sin in our natures by saying it is "in my flesh" (v.18). He's recognizing that there is another side to his nature that is alive to God. Thus, in this whole passage in chapter 7, Paul, because he is living in victory over sin, knows the true state of his heart—and mine. The farther men advance in the Christian life, and the more mature their discipleship, the clearer becomes their perception of the heights to which God calls them, and the more painfully sharp their consciousness of the distance between what they ought, and want to be, and what they are. [25]

"Evidently conversion for Paul meant becoming aware as never before of the power of sin in his own life . . . a power still in play insofar as he was still a man of flesh."[26] Amen! I find that not only in my own recovery experience, but in the recovery of those I sponsor, see, and hear in the fellowship, recovery means becoming aware as never before, of the presence and power of our sinfulness, whether we use that term or not. This is an indicator of true recovery. I'll go further to say that no one can be in true recovery without such a progressive awareness of the sinful self.

Thus Paul says to *believers*, "Walk by the Spirit, and do not gratify the lusts of the flesh" (Gal. 5:16-17). Paul, do you a mean that a Christian's flesh wants to lust? Yes! Walking each temptation in the Spirit is how we overcome the flesh, one temptation at a time. Because, that's how Jesus did it.

**A Glimpse of the Utter Reality**
I'd like to share a very personal experience here. Talking about my sins is one thing and is easy to see; trying to comprehend the underlying sinfulness behind all this is quite another. And I do see now that something lies beneath any and all my sins, fueling it all.

Many years ago in my current sobriety, I had a glimpse into my real self—a glimpse that went all the way

## II—The Real Me

through. I believe it took place in the morning quiet time. For one time-suspending moment—it was timeless eternity—I was suspended within myself, as in a dark cosmic abyss, cut off from everything. Everything! Totally alone inside myself. Time space and matter did not exist in that inner dimension of being. The intensity of that separation makes all talk of aloneness or isolation pale into nothingness. The veil before my inner self was gone. Any insulation, any covering of my deepest self was simply not there. I was totally naked spiritually in the innermost core of my being. It was instant recognition of what I really was at the core of my being, yet without reference to anything specific. It was a glimpse of absolute and perfect clarity into what I was. No argument, no discussion, no doubt whatsoever. There was no light there and not a vestige of righteousness or hope.

There's simply no way of describing the pain because it was absolute; the whole experience was spiritual, not physical at all. The pain was so intense and unbearable it was beyond the limits of what consciousness could bear, yet unconsciousness never came. There was the awful certainty that what I was *was* destruction. It was eternal death. And I knew it was perfectly just. It was The Hopeless Unending. Suspended in that annihilation without end, in that absolute lostness and aloneness of the naked self.

And then, in that very annihilation, in that eternal lostness, I was enfolded in God's love, an assurance sweeping through and possessing me of the love of God: *"Underneath are the everlasting arms."* As I rested in that love for the first time in my life, I wept.

What was this experience? I'm in the strange position of not wanting to tell for fear of being thought a fool or madman. Yet I know exactly. I experienced myself as I really was, apart from grace, apart from God. Separated from the Source of my Life. It was my totally naked human condition, as I was, shut up to myself. Just like Paul says, "In me, that is, in my flesh, dwells no good thing." That's what

I sensed. I *knew* it. Without words to describe it, I just knew it.

I know too much about myself now to continue living in any denial about this natural core of my being, as I am apart from God's presence. The hell of aloneness—and that *was* hell—is so absolute, how utterly desperate we all must be for our true Connection! And no wonder that the lust-drive holds such great promise of fulfillment in all its *mis*-connections. Maybe the intensity fueling my lust-drive was the necessity of fleeing from that very hell. If we can only see it. But today we have too many means of distracting the unease at the center of our being.

So this passage in Romans 7 is the very cry of my own heart today. The passage describes the anatomy of my own sinfulness, what I am in the flesh. So let's look at it again, putting it in more personal terms:

I am carnal; that is, in me there exists that which is radically opposed to God.

I am sold under sin; that is, my flesh is under its power and authority. I venture to say that most lustaholics would readily admit that they are sold under the power and authority of lust. Isn't that what we admit to in our First Step? Understood in isolation from the larger context of Romans 7, these words would give a wrong impression of the Christian life. But within that context of the whole epistle they bring out forcefully an aspect of the Christian life which I gloss over to my undoing:

> **When I fail to take account of the fact that I (and my fellow Christian members) are still subject to the power of sin, I am dangerous both to others and to myself because I am self-deceived.**

All of this puts I John 1:7-9 into proper perspective: "If we are walking in the light as he is in the light we have

## II—The Real Me

fellowship with one another, and the blood of Jesus, his Son, is cleansing us from all sin." Present tense. Being cleansed from all sin is being cleansed from my sinful temptations today. That's the righteousness of God at work in me the sinner. Sure, the Bible speaks of sinful acts: "Thou shalt not this, thou shalt not that. . . ." And certainly we commit known sins. But instead of focusing on such acts, as though if we could only steer clear of these "biggies" we'd be okay, we should focus on the cleansing.

Focusing on the "thou-shalt-nots" is a great misconception many of us have in the Christian community and lust-sex recovery program. It's part of our legalism, part of our salvation-by-works error. But instead of focusing on such discreet acts as to whether they're a sin or not—"Did you commit any sin today?—we should focus on Jesus *cleansing* us in that next sinful temptation. That's the key, if we can grasp and hold on to it.

I tend more and more to interpret this remarkable passage in I John in a very practical way, especially since it resonates with my current victory experiences in being loosed from sin *in* my temptations. The continuous present tense is used throughout this passage in every verb. That makes it a "Today" experience. Being cleansed from sin is being cleansed from my sinfulness today, overcoming temptations today. It is the continual cleansing of Jesus, the sin-bearer; his Presence taking on our sin, guarding us from sinning.

Our perception of whether we are about to commit such-and-such a sin or not in that incident sidetracks us. We turn into Pharisaical lawyers, and it distracts us from making the instant transfer onto Jesus the sin-bearer. Note that Jesus' blood is active now—present tense—in our cleansing. That's a key verse for the concept that Jesus' death for sin is also a present, not just a past, reality (ref. Part III). Thus, perhaps we should understand this aspect of "cleansing" from sin to be what John describes as being "loosed" from our sins in Rev. 1:5, (where "freed" is better translated "loosed").

## The Sinfulness of the Believer

The more seriously a Christian strives to live from grace and submit to the discipline of the gospel, the more sensitive he or she becomes to the fact of their continuing sinfulness, sensitive to the fact that even their very best acts and activities are disfigured by egotism, which is still powerful within them—and no less evil because it is often more subtly disguised than formerly.[27]

This is the glory of my life today, that is, the glory of God—being tempted from within my sinful nature, but being cleansed or loosed from it through the Presence of my sin-bearer. Praise God! I don't have to pretend I'm a saint any more. *He* is my righteousness because *he* delivers me out of that temptation by taking the sin into himself.[28]

• • •

At this point I'd like to relate a very personal experience which illustrates the meaning of Paul's self-appraisal in Romans 7, which is my self-appraisal. Let me relate it to you as though it were happening right now, though it happened quite some time ago:

### The Ice Cream Connection

I do not understand what's going on here . . . I'm sightseeing downtown L.A., leaning against a wrought-iron railing, looking down at the flux of people coming and going. I notice this woman on the opposite side of the courtyard licking an ice cream cone. My very first thought is that she's trying to attract a man. Me! And I am attracted. And immediately I am tempted to connect.

I delight in the law of God in my inmost self, I really do. But here and now, I see in my members another law at war with this. I'm in recovery, but there's a war going on—within the very core of my

## II—The Real Me

being. And the battle begins. I see myself in conflict on how to react to what I see. Shall I keep reading into her actions what lust wants to see, or shall I obey the purifying presence of God within me? I delight in the law of God! How can I have this impulse to lust or mis-connect? Where does it come from? It must come from a principle dwelling *within my very members!*

I've felt this polarity tension thousands of times before; it's no stranger. Matter of fact, I'm learning to expect it without fear. Something's always going to be "couching at the door," as God tells Cain (Gen. 4:7), waiting for the next trigger opportunity. It must be sin which dwells within me, in my flesh. My *human* being is dead because of sin; but my spirit is alive because of righteousness, the righteousness of God's presence at work within. That's how I can even be having this conflict.

I proceed around the courtyard in her general direction, wondering if the situation will turn more overt. (Translation: Will something overwhelming happen so I'll not be responsible for giving in?) But then, I just keep walking. A quiet help supervenes within that would shield me from giving in to the sin force. Part of me doesn't want to, but I leave the area. The sadness of loss persists for a while, but then I'm free again! I've just witnessed another sample of sin-in-my-members—that sin "might be shown to be sin." And the Spirit of life in Christ Jesus doing his work in delivering me *from* that sin.

Therefore (now we go to Romans 8:1) there is no condemnation. There's no condemnation in having a sinful nature, in being tempted with sin from inside me. This is the way things are with me, the sex drunk: I in my flesh want to lust; I in the Spirit want to obey God. These forces/desires are opposed to one another. The great Either/Or. I have no remedy within myself.

## The Sinfulness of the Believer

No strength, no power. But the Principle of Life is active within me as I choose not to shut him out. Thus, I don't have to have guilt or shame for feeling this inner conflict—unless I choose to yield to sin. There is no condemnation in being tempted! Praise God, I'm free to be what I am—a sexual misconnect. Having sin in me, I'm free not to sin!

> *Thank you for your Presence, Lord. Thank you for knowing my sin and loving me in it, taking it on yourself, and leading me out of it. You are my Savior, my Shepherd.*

(Note: I was under great stress and in escape mode, which always makes me more vulnerable to temptation, even though the avenue chosen for escape may be benign. I hadn't reacted like this for a long, long time. It was sobering and reminded me, as I've heard from AAs, "The farther away you feel you are from your last drink, the closer you are to your next.")

• • •

For two thousand years Christians have wrestled with the question of the origin of sin in Romans chapter 5—the concept of man's sinful nature and why we all sin. I don't think the issue will ever be logically resolved, since man can never fully know himself, much less know the mind of God. However, to put all of this in another perspective, consider the growing evidence for the neurological aspects of addiction, described so well in Gerald May's *Addiction and Grace* (HarperSanFrancisco). Addicts, and all humans, are victims of the neurological programming of their own choices, which take place in the context of cultural predispositions. (See my *Lust Virus*, which goes into the cultural predispositions of our particular malady.)

# 12

### The Great Delusion

*"Gone, gone, gone, gone,
Yes my sins are gone...."*
From a Christian chorus

We're still talking about encountering the real me. Understanding our real selves is a key to understanding the real Jesus. True, I cannot understand the real Savior without seeing him in his Word. But regardless of what is revealed of him in the Word, I cannot *know* the real Savior if I'm in denial about the reality of myself.

### 2 Corinthians 5:17

If in my flesh, as we saw in Romans 7 and elsewhere, I am "sold under sin," meaning I have a sinful nature as a believer—what about 2 Cor. 5:17? As the King James Version has it, "Therefore if any man be in Christ, he is a new creature: old things are passed away; behold, all things are become new." The words of the King James version were the ones I memorized and heard preached, again and again. They're still in the pulpiteering air. Misinterpretation of this passage has helped energize the notion that once a person "accepts Christ," the sinful nature is no more, that Romans 7 must refer to Paul before his conversion and to unbelievers. This verse in Corinthians was a tremendous stumbling block in my own experience. I somehow was faced with the fact that I had to be good now, yet all my inner life and much of my behavior was testifying otherwise. So the

## II—The Real Me

misinterpretation of this verse helped fuel my denial and created great confusion for me personally. And yet I quoted it often to others in trying to describe the benefits of Christian faith while I was still living the lie.

I had to put this false concept to rest before I could proceed in recovery. Of course, I speak only for myself. It was one of the "old ideas" that simply did not work for me. Something in me must have wanted to buy into such a deception, or delusion, as I call it here. We are no more new creatures in Christ in the sense of no longer having our sinful nature than the man in the moon!

Here's how I interpret the passage: When we finally come to the end of ourselves in admitting our powerlessness and surrendering our lust and resentment to God, when we stay sober and start making the principles of the Steps a new way of life, there is a new principle of life at work in us instead of the principle of death; light instead of our darkness, freedom instead of slavery. But this new creation is the beginning of victory *over* sin, not the elimination of our sinful nature and temptations to sin. There is a very importance difference between saying our sinful nature is no more and saying we can have victory over sin. How can we even be tempted as believers if we have nothing in our nature that is temptable? This is the very argument we used when looking at Jesus human nature in Part I.

**Making Peace with What We Are**
I, as a Christian, in my own nature (in the flesh) am sinful. My human nature is sin-controlled. This is the key to getting victory over sin through the Son of man. We'll see this again and again. It connects me with his work, for as we shall see, it is his identification with my *sinful* nature that is his point of contact with me, the basis of his being able to deliver me, to loose me from my sins each time I am tempted. Thus, I make peace with this nature of mine, just as it is, and I don't have to be afraid of temptation any more. Thank God! Sin

becomes only a *three*-letter word.

The end of this whole matter of my sinfulness is not despair, but joy. Impossible joy. And this is the glory of Romans 8:1 and the great significance of the "Therefore" with which it begins, in reference to our true condition revealed in Romans 7: "There is therefore now no condemnation" for having a nature inclined to sin, because the Spirit of life in Christ Jesus sets me free *in* the temptation to sin.

**Awareness of Sinfulness a Sign of Progress in Recovery**
The revelation of the righteousness of God (Romans 1:17) becomes apparent against the backdrop of my unrighteousness. Thus, I believe, a true mark of recovery is the progressive awareness of one's personal defects and shortcomings—one's sinfulness. "Growth in grace is measured not by the fact that you have not gone back, but that you have an insight into where you are spiritually."[29] I question whether those who have not begun to see their sinfulness are in true recovery, whether they use that shunned S-word or not. I was not in true recovery when I was in denial about what and who I really was. Dwell on it; this is not easy medicine. And suddenly, Romans becomes not a theology textbook but the Word of God making a claim on me—the claim of repentance, a change of attitude in first seeing, then sending away my sins, one temptation at a time. Being done with them, as in our Steps 6 and 7.

But who can see or acknowledge this? I was often led to believe, perhaps true of some of you also, that we actually are or must become "new creatures" in the sense that our sinful nature is gone. That this never squares with reality doesn't matter; we seem to hang on to this fallacy at any cost. (Maybe that's our ego in there, saying, "I believe now, and that belief is gonna do it!)

Thus, the legacy within myself of the perversion I've created as the result of my choices since childhood is the defective nature that I carry about today. I make no apology

## II—The Real Me

for what I am. I must see it and I do see it, thank God. I have no choice; it comes with the territory. That's the incredible beauty of our First Step. I make peace with it. I acknowledge it and I know that this is me. This is not something I used to be "before I was a Christian." It's what I am now! You'd better believe it, because you're talking to an expert in sin. I know too much about myself now to think for a moment that my sinful nature has been removed. And this truth about myself forms the basis for my victory over lust and sin of any kind to which I choose to apply it. The Man said, "I came not to call the righteous, but sinners to repentance," and "The whole have no need of a physician, but those who are sick."

My sinfulness is the window of opportunity for my temptations, regardless of the occasion "out there." But to be tempted is our lot in life, the same as it was Jesus' lot in life. More than that, it is *necessary* that we be tempted. Each temptation can become, through connection with our Friend, a life-giving experience, I might even venture to say, a *sacramental* experience.

If and when we see what the Son of man really went through in Gethsemane and Golgotha, we will fall down, as Peter did on his first encounter with Jesus, and say, "Depart from me, for I am a sinful man, O Lord!" It is *then* that he tells us, as he did Peter, "Don't be afraid" (Luke 5:8-11).

I am not afraid to call myself a sinner today because I'm free not to sin, one temptation at a time, if I so choose. Thank God—through Jesus Christ our Lord.

# 13

## Religious Addiction— "Believism" as Unbelief

*You care not for the arms of your Father; you value only the shelter of his roof.*
                                        George MacDonald

These words of MacDonald sum up the essence of what I call "believism," putting the focus on formula-belief instead of *knowing* the Savior. Two things had kept me from knowing and connecting with this real saving Son of man/Son of God: lust and "believism." We've talked a lot about lust; so it's time to take a hard look at one of the greatest stumbling blocks to recovery among believers today—believism.

One of the glaring realities I see in my past Christian experience and in today's Christians trying to recover from sex and lust addiction is that our belief in Christ is not working. Too many Christians believing in Christ as I did are not experiencing sobriety and progressive victory over lust and the defective self. Since I have to believe there is nothing wrong with Jesus, the fault must lie on our side, in our "belief." And this is precisely what I discovered in my own experience. My "belief" in Christ was somehow keeping me from knowing the One who is now saving me from my lusts.

**Source of the Belief Formula**
The source of our modern belief-formula error lies in the scriptural vocabulary itself. Various forms of the word "believe," referring to the necessity of believing in Christ, appear hundreds of times in the New Testament, most often

## II—The Real Me

in John and Acts. John's very purpose in writing his gospel was "that you might believe that Jesus is the Christ, and that believing, you might have life in his name." But the error which I identify in our modern use of the belief formula lies not in scripture but in our lack of understanding and abuse of it. What we fail to see is the historical context in which "believe" words are used.

Believing that Jesus was the promised Messiah was the decision people were faced with initially. This man had suddenly appeared on the scene one day at the river Jordan, and was announced to be the promised One. The ensuing call to believe, was accepting this man as the Messiah, the Christ, not as political savior but Savior from sin. This took more than intellectual persuasion, since the man was and appeared to be one of them in every respect, even with his miraculous powers. The great hurdle people had to jump over and tripped on was the fact that this man's kingdom lay not in delivering the Jews from Rome, but in setting their hearts free to know the Father. But back then they had to begin by believing Jesus was the Promised One of God. They could not commit their hearts and lives to him without accepting that fact. Thus, the Gospels and Acts are full of "believe" terminology. But this is not the situation we have today.

By the time we get to James, the first New Testament book to be written (about the year 47 or 48), and to Romans (written in the year 57), some 17-27 years have elapsed after Jesus' death in the year 30. By then the Christ event had become established in a vast and growing multitude of believers spreading throughout the known civilized world. The issue was moving from focus on believing Jesus was the Messiah to personal *actions* (James) issuing from *"the obedience of faith"* (Romans, developed in a subsequent chapter). And this emphasis takes us back to the very beginning with John the Baptist, who started everything off by calling for personal "repentance unto the sending away of sins." So we need to interpret the "belief" terminology in the light of the whole historical context.

Based on my own experience and observations, I'm saying that we've turned belief into believism. Let's delve into this a bit further.

**Believism as Works of the Law**
The Good News proclaimed by Paul says, "No human being will be made righteous in his sight by works of the law" (Romans 3:20). Paul was living and writing in the context of Judaism and the law of Moses. But there were probably as many Gentiles as Jewish believers in the imperial capitol of Rome, the destination of Paul's letter.[30] Why then all this talk about the Jewish law to the Roman believers? Is it possible that there is in every Christian age and people something that corresponds to the "works of the law" and which is the supreme stumblingblock to the righteousness which comes through the obedience of faith? Again, since I want to stay within my own experience, let me say what I believe this is for me.

I was not raised under the Jewish law and traditions current with first-century Judaism; I was raised in the church of the Twentieth Century. But since I want to apply the truth of Romans to my own life today, I must ask, What is it that corresponds to works of the law in my "Christian" experience? What in my life would take the place of being made righteous by faith? What keeps me from a faith that works, a faith bringing about victory over sin?

My mind goes back many many years before recovery to one of the religious formulas of that time, a small tract entitled The Four Spiritual Laws. We used it in evangelism, going door-to-door, pointing out the four questions to the prospect. They went something like this: 1) Do you believe Jesus was the Son of God? 2) Do you believe he died for your sins and rose again? 3) Do you believe the Bible is the word of God? 4) . . . . We would then say something to the effect, "Well, if you believe these things, you're saved! All you have to do is believe; isn't it great! Why not come on over to our church Sunday?"

I believed those truths, but there was always this nagging doubt that there was something fishy going on in the disparity between those truths and my own life and attitudes. There was never any *change*. I was never freed (saved) from my *sins*. Just the opposite happened; my defective thoughts and acts kept getting worse and worse and buried deeper and deeper inside of me.

I wonder if such believism is today's counterpart to Paul's "works of the law," what the Jews felt they had to obey to be saved. In my case I believe it was. I was using my belief in Christ, the Bible, and church as "works" to make me right with God, to give me "salvation," whatever that was. That belief, however, never made me right with either God, myself, or others. Paul says "he who through faith is righteous shall live" (Rom. 1:17 RSV). My belief was not faith-making-me-righteous, so my belief wasn't saving faith. For me, believing was thus a form of works. I was in exactly the same situation as the Jews of Jesus' day, to whom he said, "You search the scriptures, because you think that in them you have eternal life; but those very scriptures that you idolize bear witness of me; yet you refuse to come to *me* that you may have life" (John 5:39f, paraphrase and emphasis mine).

Today we glory in the Bible and "justification by faith." But what are we really doing? Sometimes I wonder. Judging from my own experience, we presume to take this matter of believing into our own hands, to carry it through as the work of our own robust faith. In that way we have a part in our salvation and can be certain of it. I am believing; I am somehow exerting faith; and that exertion, that believing is a force going out of me that is making it happen. Since I must believe to be saved, I make sure I have my "believing switch" turned on at all costs, against all odds. Note however, that without realizing it, we have put the emphasis here on what *I* am doing and must continue to do! Do you see it? This is not justification by faith; it is works of the intellect and will. Believism.

In the early spread of the Gospel recorded in the book of Acts, Christians from Cyprus and Cyrene traveled to Antioch and preached the Lord Jesus to non-Jews. We are told that "the hand of the Lord was with them, and a great number that believed turned to the Lord" (Acts 11:21). Note the wording. Why didn't the historian simply say that there were a great number who believed on the Lord? Why does he add that many who believed *turned*? He makes a distinction between believing on Jesus and turning to him, *a change in course of action*. (And as we know from the Gospels, many did believe in Jesus, but did not follow him.) If this still isn't clear enough, we read that when this news reaches Jerusalem, the leaders send Barnabas to Antioch, who "exhorted them all to remain faithful to the Lord with steadfast purpose" (verse 23). Remain faithful? Steadfast purpose? I thought all I had to do was "believe." The demons believe—and shudder! (James 2:19).

**The Hypocrisy of My Believism**
In Romans chapter 2, I see that the very fact that I judge others indicates I am a sinner, "doing the very same things (v.1)." Paul drives closer to home here when he says, "Therefore you have no excuse, O man, whoever you are..." Again, he's speaking to me; there's no partiality, whether Jew or Greek (v. 11). Putting this in present-day terms, God shows no favoritism to "believer" or unbeliever. Let's read Romans 2:17-24 in such a generic light. This is my own paraphrase of the passage:

> But if you call yourself a worshiper of God and rely upon the Bible, your church, or your religious practice and boast of your relation to God and know his will and approve what is excellent, because you are instructed in the truth, and if you are sure that you are a guide to the blind, a light to those who are in darkness, a corrector of the foolish, a teacher of children, having in the Bible

## II—The Real Me

or your church the embodiment of knowledge and truth—you then who teach others, will you not teach yourself? While you preach against stealing, do you steal? You who say that one must not commit adultery, do you commit adultery in every look? You who abhor idols, do you create your own within you very heart? You who boast in the Word of God, do you dishonor God by breaking it? For, as it is written, "The name of Christ is blasphemed in today's world because of you."

That's my own biography, in black and white. What a perfect description of me the seminarian, the church-going, Bible-believing, Sunday-School-teaching, gospel-preaching "Christian." I called myself a believer, boasting of my relation to God. I did that from the pulpit and with Sunday School students. I knew his will and approved what was excellent, being instructed in Scripture, sure that I was a guide to the blind, a light to those in darkness, a corrector of the foolish and teacher of children. I thought and acted like I was the embodiment of knowledge and truth. But while I taught others, I would not teach myself. Preaching against stealing, I stole what was not mine and possessed it through my eyes and hands and body and soul. Preaching against adultery, I was an adulterer. Abhorring idols, I was an idolater. Boasting in Scripture, I dishonored God by breaking the law. Surely, if in Paul's time the name of God was blasphemed among the Gentiles because of the religious God-worshipers (v.24), is not the name of God and his Christ blasphemed today in the world because of us "Christians"? He is a Christian who is one inwardly, and real believing is a matter of the heart, spiritual and not merely a matter of going by words (v.29).

Let's listen to the Son of man again, if we dare: "Not everyone who says to me, 'Lord, Lord,' shall enter the kingdom of heaven, but he who is doing the will of my Father who is in heaven. On that day many will say to me, 'Lord, Lord, did we not prophesy in your name, and cast out demons in your name, and do many mighty works in your name?'

And then will I declare to them, 'I never knew you; depart from me, you evildoers'" (Mt 7:21f). What a devastating indictment! There is no blindness such as the blindness of religious addiction. Take it from an expert witness. Are you willing to examine yourself in this light?

**Believism Means Failure for the Lust Addict**
This is where we get down to where it really hits us and where it counts. For the Christian lust/sex addict who wants to recover, this Christian *mis*-belief system translates directly into his or her misguided formula for trying to stay sober and get victory over lust temptations. This is one of the key reasons so many Christians cannot proceed in sobriety and real victory over lust. Most of us have no other model but the believism model we've picked up from the religious environment. It's all we have. So we try attaining sexual and lust sobriety in the same way we practiced our religion. Thus, we wrongly believe that salvation from lust will come about if we take the situation into our own hands to carry it through as the work of our own robust faith to stay sober. Does that ring true with anybody here? A force going out of me that will make it happen. This implies that because I have a part in it I can thus be certain of it. A killer delusion!

What is all this but another form of willpower? It certainly doesn't ring true with our First Step powerlessness, does it? The Twelve Step program is supposed to show that we cannot get victory over our powerlessness through willpower, even religiously exercised. And this is precisely why willpower and believism do not work, why so many Christian lust/sex addicts in the sex addiction recovery movement are not experiencing being loosed from lust.

Many Christians seem to believe as I did, unwittingly, of course, that the church or the Bible is the Way, the Truth, and the Life. Some even call this "bibliolatry," worship of the Bible. Its corollary is religious addiction, *a system of religious practice that shuts God out.* (See Matthew 23 for a

## II—The Real Me

quintessential expression of it, my story in the ministry.) This is the essence of the works of the law—a system of belief and practice that shuts Life out. And this is precisely what I was doing in my Christian belief. My belief system, Bible-based and "centered on Christ," shut the living Jesus out. That's why there was no salvation from sin and lust for me. Reliance on my Christian belief system kept me from seeing the truth about myself; it kept me from seeing and knowing my sinfulness. Hence, it kept me from seeing the Savior. *He* is the Way, the Truth, and the Life, the *living* Word.

Believism is works of the law. It doesn't save. Believism is unbelief!

Thus, for me to have salvation from lust, I must undergo a radical change of attitude toward myself and the Son of man that results in my actually doing the will of the Father.

### The Way of Salvation As Originally Preached

The way of salvation, salvation from sin *today*, is the same as that which was proclaimed by the disciples of our Lord. This is most clearly seen in the book of Acts, the marvelous history of what Jesus continues to do. See such passages as 11:18, 20:21, and 26:18-20. It is the same as the original two-fold message of the Baptist and as announced in Paul's own commission from Jesus himself: repentance toward God and faith in our Lord Jesus Christ, *"to open their eyes, that they may turn from darkness to light and from the power of Satan to God, that they may receive forgiveness of sins and a place among those who are sanctified by faith in me."* This is happening. This is real. Today! Will you receive it and enter in?

> *Lord, search me and know my heart; try me and know my heart; and see if there be any wicked way in me and lead me in the way everlasting.*     Psalm 139:23-24

# 14

## Idols out of the Id

A wrong view of Jesus, ourselves, and salvation-by-believism leads to blindness to the effects of sin and lust upon ourselves. Let's look for a moment into what's going on in a typical lust episode to see if we can discern one aspect of what is really happening—idolatry.

There are some 35 million legal over-the-counter "men's interest" magazines sold every month in the United States (according to *The 1993 Janus Report*), and millions of hits a day on Internet porn. It takes little imagination to visualize the physical scene going on with the person so engaged. However, what's going on internally within a person's mind and soul tells the real story. One of the great follies of our time is making judgments on externals, ignoring the spiritual components of any given behavior. Take for example the following statement: "Masturbation, a means of self-pleasuring, is generally appropriate and healthy." (Lutheran "Report on Sexuality," *L.A. Times* October 23, 1993.)

The following anatomy of a look is what I came up with when I tried to describe the psychology of a typical lust event as I saw it within myself when a real person is involved as the object of the "drink." However, the same process is in effect when images or fantasy are used as the input trigger, with or without masturbation. And note that the whole scenario can take place before masturbation actually begins, indicating how lust is really asexual.

## II—The Real Me

(I doubt whether any but lust drunks can fully identify with or understand what this blank verse is trying to depict. And if the reader has been victimized sexually, he or she may find the following tough going, since the abusive nature of lust is dramatized.)

### Anatomy of a Look

There it is—
Over there.
That image in the corner of my eye.
Light rays impinging on the retina of my peripheral vision.
Rays coming in. Neutral. Passive.
Innocent.
Brain processing the data as a computer.
Man the benign machine.

Then, the image moves closer and more data is processed.
The computer sets a flag: "Trigger material."
Recognition.
Now I, the practicing luster, face a moral predicament:
*Decision*!
To drink or not to drink?
Suddenly I'm a spiritual creature with a higher will *using* the computer. Man the autonomous Being!

I choose to drink.
Not just look. *Drink*.
Only the lustaholic knows the difference.

What is the drink?
Instead of light rays coming in passively and
registering a neutral image,
Something is now going *out* of me.
Taking. Plundering.
Against the knowledge and will of the other person.

*Idols Out of the Id*

And lightning-fast.
Doesn't have to be the hard "drool."
Can even be oh, so "gentle."

Lust is always an act of violence.

Rebellion. Demand. I want. I must have.
I must have or I'll die!
So I take. And get. . . .
It's free! And secret. No one knows!
Or will ever know.
I don't even acknowledge it to myself.
The perfect steal.
Man knowing Good and Evil,
on the same order of being as *God*.

But it's an act *against*.
Against the man or woman, yes.
But what about a mere picture or fantasy?
There's something in *me* I have to transgress.
Something in *me* I must turn against.
The light inside. God.
Lust proves there's a conscience,
and knowledge-of-good-and-evil, and God.
The tree of death is *within* me!
I *choose* to eat of "that forbidden tree
whose mortal taste brings death into the world
and all our woe."

An act of defiant will.
Against the light I take. And shut God out.
Isolation. Separation. Escaping inward, getting lost
inside myself.
Losing my *self*.
But *seeming* to gain a shot of life.

*II—The Real Me*

And instead of the image serving oneness with that person,
I choose to use it *against* the natural.
Perversion.
Greedily I ingest and possess,
And am possessed.

The one glance is enough.
I now process the image any way I choose.
It's no longer a person or picture out there;
It's something *in here*, from a part of *me*.

The image is invested with a super-natural
Power and Presence.
Larger-than-life.
Infused with *spirit* to fill the god-emptiness within.
*Spiritual intercourse.*
With myself! —
(Or is it?)

This creative power I get is from being in the image of God.
*That's* what I use to imbue this thing with it's super-force.
Thus—
*I pervert the very image of God!!*

And this is what I want.  Must have!
It's taking me out of myself!
Mood-altering.  Mind-altering.
Self-transcending!  Spiritual!  Ecstasy!
What power!  I'm in total control!
I!
Create!
And possess!
I'm GOD!!!

*Idols Out of the Id*

The saliva of the false god juices a voracious appetite.
I gulp and devour this inner entity.
And am devoured!
Lust is self-consuming; I'm doing all this to *myself!*
No wonder it unleashes the negative force:
Rage,
And the litany of all my sins.

And what was once neutral, innocent reality,
 a person, a mere picture in the brain,
Is now a perversion—
Twisted distortions of reality out of the inner darkness.

I, the Destroyer at work.
I, now the god of my own life,
Creating my own God(dess) of Desire,
*In my own lust-image!*
False worship.
Idols out of the Id!

And I have what I truly want:
my own god—*Me!*
The giver of "life" to me.

To what end?
Death!
Shutting out the light and love of God and man—
And woman—
Blinding me to the truth about myself.
For to see *that* truth would be to fall down and cry:
"God be merciful to me the sinner!"


[My *Lust Virus* has an extended analysis of this lust episode.]

*II—The Real Me*

Of course, women are not exempt from such a scenario. Listen to the female editor of *The Boomer Report*, a publication on consumer trends. She's writing in November 1992: "Every woman I know is having sex dreams about Bill Clinton. We're finally getting a President our own age who we can imagine having sex with."[31] This statement reportedly "captures a new dimension in the national psyche," but we in the recovery movement know the epidemic of sexual lust had spread to women long ago.

**"Christian" God-Hating Idolaters**
Now let's sum this up by looking at Exodus 20:4-5:

> *You shall not make for yourself a graven image, or any likeness of anything that is in heaven above, or that is in the earth beneath, or that is in the water under the earth; you shall not bow down to them or serve them; for I the Lord your God am a jealous God, visiting the iniquity of the fathers upon the children to the third and the fourth generation of those who hate me, but showing steadfast love to thousands of those who love me and keep my commandments.*

When I would engage in such a lust scenario such as we've just seen in "Anatomy of a Look"—with or without masturbation—I was actually changing, perverting, the image of a woman into *an image of spiritual worship*. Of course, the same perversion takes place in same-sex lust. The transmutation energized by lust changes that neutral image in our visual field into an image to be ingested, worshiped and served. In essence, I would bow down before those images (or bodies) and become possessed by the lust mediated through them and the negative force I let into myself. Although I never saw this as a religious connection or exercise, that's exactly what it is. Note how often the Bible uses sexual imagery to speak of idolatry. Without my realizing it, masturbating to the image of a person, mental or otherwise was a religious exercise, an act of worship. "Believing" in Christ, I was actually serving the false god of Lust. So much for believism.

Notice the results of such behavior revealed in this Exodus passage. Bowing down to and serving images is directly connected with the punishing effects upon one's offspring, mediated through the sinning parent. How painfully aware we are of this in our own family histories! Also, such behavior is hating God, regardless of one's religious beliefs and practices. No wonder we have so much so-called heterosexual sexual perversion today, and no wonder it spreads into all forms. (Ref. *Lust Virus*. Also, Appendix 5 shows how all of this leads to the revelation of wrath.)

# Part III

# REAL VICTORY IN CHRIST

# 15

## Jesus' Identification with Our Sinful Human Nature—His Present Saving Work

*To the one loving us and who loosed us out of our sins by his blood.*
Rev. 1:5-6

*The glory of that Father is not in knowing himself God, but in giving himself away....*
George MacDonald, 1892

Now that we've taken a new look at encountering the real Jesus and our real selves in Parts I and II, let's see how all this bears on the "how to" of real victory over lust.

If anything should be clear by now, it is that I, the believer, am powerless over a sin-controlled nature, and that I need a continuing deliverance from this force. Incredibly, it turns out that I am not only being loosed from my sins, but much more. Let's turn to Scripture for an unusually lucid picture of Jesus' present saving work—the best hope for those of us hopelessly given over to the sin-process. Given over especially to lust, resentment, fear, and Self.

The view of the person and work of Christ which is given in the Epistle to the Hebrews is in many respects more comprehensive and far-reaching than that which is given in any other book of the New Testament. It is interesting that of the various names by which our Lord is spoken of in the letter, that which is distinctive is the human name, Jesus. This occurs nine times, and in every case it furnishes the key to the argument of the passage where it is found.[32]

## III—Real Victory in Christ

Remember that we're focusing on Jesus' humanity, as it touches our sinful humanity.

I was overwhelmed when I discovered Jesus in Hebrews in 1986. And I had read and studied that letter many times. But this was new for me. Not having even scratched the surface of this marvelous and somewhat difficult epistle, I'm still overwhelmed. I come across glorious shafts of sunlight illuminating the spiritual landscape every time I pause in reflection and study. Nowhere do we get deeper insight into the meaning of the human nature of Jesus as in Hebrews, so much so that I wonder if this may not be one of the reasons this letter seems so neglected in preaching and teaching today. Maybe in our one-sided defense of the Son of God or blindness to our sinfulness we've lost sight of the truly human aspect of Jesus' life. Maybe we simply don't want to know *this* Jesus. Had this One been presented to me before recovery, I too might have rejected him. But now I have to know this One who is revealed here. The more I see of my own sinful nature, the more I need such a Savior. So let's look at the major passages in Hebrews that tell us about saving help made effective through the humanity of our Lord. First, a brief reminder of Jesus' uniqueness.

**The Son of God**
In this book of Hebrews, where we shall view the deepest revelations of Jesus' humanity, we have one of the most profound revelations of his Sonship.

> *In many and various ways God spoke of old to our fathers by the prophets; but in these last days he has spoken to us by a Son, whom he appointed heir of all things, through whom indeed he made the ages. Being the expression of God's glory and representing His being, bearing all things by the word of His power, when he had made cleansing of*

*His Present Saving Work*

*sins, he sat down at the right of the Majesty on high.* (Heb. 1:1-3)

The one appointed heir of all things, the one reflecting the very image of God's being in our own sinful likeness, the risen Lord who now has all authority in heaven and on earth, upholding all by his word of power—*this* is the one who has made a cleansing of sins, himself becoming sin for us, for you and for me. This is the wonder and paradox of Bethlehem. This is the love and power of God to sinners like me.

**Jesus Has My Sinful Nature So He Can Deliver Me from Temptation**
Hebrews 2:8-18 is one of the crucial New Testament passages on Jesus' humanity. As often elsewhere in this book, the following is a more literal translation so we can connect with its importance to us.

> As it is, we do not yet see everything in subjection to him. But we see Jesus, who for a little while was made lower than the angels, crowned with glory and honor because of the suffering of death, so that by the grace of God he might taste death for every one.
> For it was fitting that he, for whom and by whom all things exist, in bringing many sons to glory, should make the pioneer of their salvation perfect (or complete) through suffering. For he who sanctifies and those who are sanctified have all one origin. That is why he is not ashamed to call them brothers, saying, "I will proclaim your name to my brothers, in the midst of the congregation I will praise you." And again, "I will put my trust in him." And again, "Here am I, and the children God has given me."
> Since therefore the children share in flesh and blood, he himself likewise partook of the same nature, that through death he might destroy him who has the power of death, that is, the devil, and deliver all those who through fear of death were subject to lifelong bondage . . . . Therefore he had to be made like his brothers in every respect, so that he might become a merciful and faithful high priest in the service of God, to make expiation for the sins of the people. For because he himself has suffered and been tempted, he is able to help those who are tempted.

## III—Real Victory in Christ

Obscure at first reading, this is a startling revelation. Would that we might come to the full realization of the power of this truth. Again and again in this important passage, as we will see below, the writer calls attention to and progressively describes the nature of Jesus' humanity and how it relates to us now. Let's take it apart, statement by statement:

**Jesus As Pioneer of Our Salvation (verse 10).** The word translated "pioneer" refers to founder, leader, or captain.[33] Jesus is the one forging the way first. Jesus pioneers our salvation, but he does so by actually taking part in what he establishes. The term signifies his full identification with us in his humanity, which is then developed further in this passage.

Furthermore, Jesus the Pioneer is "made perfect"—that is, made complete or fulfilled—through suffering. The word translated "made perfect" conveys the idea of bringing to fulfillment developed by the author of Hebrews, both in the experience of Jesus and believers.[34] The word conveys the idea of fulfillment of destiny or fully realized selfhood and mission. The point here is that Jesus' life was characterized by a dynamic process of progressive realization, and that it took place through suffering.

I confess to having had too static an idea of who this person Jesus is. Hebrews gives us a vivid and natural filling-out of our concept of our Lord's life on earth, if we can only see it. (And I wonder if as our need, so our sight. Maybe we can only see when we come to that place of desperate need. And I believe that with our enormous need in the lust/sex/relationship illness we are really crying out for a progressively deeper experience with the Son of man.)

From his birth on, Jesus was moving toward a fuller realization and expression of his being. Isn't that what happens with us? Everything is there in the babe, yet there is a progressive unfolding and realization of it as we mature. Jesus' life was a process too, just as mine is! He was human;

## His Present Saving Work

he went through the same process. This gives me great joy and hope; there is a Savior I can identify with! And he with me! That's how he can *know* me. Better yet, that's how I can know myself—as he knows me. And as though this were not enough, the fulfillment of Jesus' humanity was realized through *suffering*. Read the passage again; there it is!

What is this suffering of Jesus? It's the suffering of death (verses 9 and 14) and suffering in temptation (18). Jesus tasted death for every one. But what about this death, this experience that was the crowning realization of Jesus' humanity? I have trouble with all the preachifying on the merely physical aspects of Jesus' crucifixion, as we saw earlier. The essence of his death was that in it he bore my *sin*. The wages of sin is death; Jesus bore my sin; so he bore the wages of my sin, which brought the ultimate desolation, lostness, and destruction that anyone can experience—the death of separation, death of his union with the Source of his life, the Father—spiritual death.

Think for a moment about this concept of Jesus' suffering as it relates to his human nature. How can anyone *suffer* temptation and death as Jesus did, in the realm of the spirit, unless his spirit can suffer? How can his spirit suffer as man's does without man's nature? Either Jesus must be fully man or no man at all; we can't have him some special kind of divine humanoid. And being fully man in no way diminishes his being fully the Son of God, as reflected in such passages as Hebrews 1:3, etc.

"The two natures were inseparably combined in the unity of His Person. In all things He acts Personally; and, as far as it is revealed to us, His greatest works during His earthly life are wrought by the help of the Father through the energy of a humanity enabled to do all things in fellowship with God (comp. John 11:41f)."[35] This is precisely how *I* am enabled in victory over my lust and sin—fellowship, connection with God. The Pioneer has shown us the way. His way worked for him. We follow him. It works for us.

## III—Real Victory in Christ

He is the Way.

Thus, the crowning realization of my humanity is also suffering on account of sin. We follow him. It is the suffering of surrender in every temptation to sin, as I did at the bus stop and ice cream connection incidents. It is the sending away of that sin. So he can bear its consequences in himself so I can be released from that temptation—be released *in* that temptation—and be free and clean. Free from having to act on the sin, and thus clean, with nothing between my soul and the Savior.

This is the prayer of Philippians 3:10-11, that I may know him and the fellowship of his sufferings. This is Paul's great affirmation, when he says, "I am crucified with Christ." This is the fellowship of suffering together with Christ, our fellowship of light, the only true fellowship of the children of God. And this is the fellowship I crave, and my hope and prayer for our own recovery fellowships today—the fellowship of following Jesus in suffering on account of sin. We sex/lust/relationship addicts are the lucky ones; we have within us a continuing source of "suffering"—temptations coming out of our sexaholism. And each temptation becomes the opportunity to know him.

**Jesus' Identification with Us As Family (verses 11-13).** Jesus calls his people "brothers" because he and we are all of One, that is, of the Father. He says, *"I will proclaim your name to my brothers."* That means me; he's reaching out to me as his brother; what an inconceivable gift. And what perfect identification with our human nature. How could we be in the same family if his human nature were different than ours? John 20:17 comes to mind here. After the resurrection, Jesus tells Mary Magdalene at the empty tomb, "Go to my brothers [referring to his disciples] and say to them, I am ascending to my Father and your Father, to my God and your God." Think of it! He's putting himself with us. His identification with us has become complete because of his

## His Present Saving Work

suffering our sin-death on Golgotha. If I ever really connect with what he was trying to tell Mary here, I think I'll break out weeping.

"*I will put my trust in him*" (verse 13). Jesus must put his trust in God as we must—an extremely significant point. Because Jesus' humanity is just like ours, he must trust the Father as we must. That's how he did it; that's how we do it. He pioneered the way.

"*In the midst of the congregation I will praise thee*" (verse 12). That is, he will be one with us in the fellowship of praise, standing with us praising God. He's putting himself side by side with us, with me, in the congregation of those praising God for victory. He's one with us—*part of!* (We begin to experience what it means to be "part of" in true recovery fellowship.) This draws me to Jesus today, far more than any one-sided, religious devotion that would ignore his true humanity. I suddenly know who I'm dealing with here—an elder brother who's "been there!" He calls us his brothers and children; and he's "not ashamed" in doing so (2:11). Are *we* ashamed to call him brother, friend? Children in a family share the same flesh and blood and same family nature. He is proud of this. It's the very purpose and end of his calling—his destiny. *He* has made himself one with *us*!

My Lord, and my God!

### Having Our Nature Makes It Possible for Jesus to Nullify the Devil and Set Us Free (verses 14 and 15).

> *Therefore, since the children share in blood and flesh, he himself also in just the same way partook of the same [nature] so that by means of his death he might render powerless [incapacitate, nullify, render ineffective] the one having the power of death, that is the devil, and might set free all those who through fear of death were all their lifetime subject to*

## III—Real Victory in Christ

> *bondage.* [For our purposes we could substitute the word "addiction" for bondage. See "The Luster's Fear of Dying" in a later chapter.]

In this passage we approach most closely, as in the Gethsemane/Golgotha experience, the inner sanctum of Jesus' humanity.

The word translated "in just the same way" is used in situations where no difference is intended.[36] Thus, a special point is made of the fact that Jesus had the very same nature as we, that in his humanity, there is no difference between us. The whole argument here is that he had to become like the children.

Think of it: In every temptation of mine to lust, resentment, fear, etc., Jesus can render Satan powerless and set me free from it because he's been there. And he unites with me in my sin *now*! That's the key to our impossible deliverance from lust.

**Having Our Nature Makes It Possible for Jesus to Be our High Priest (verses 17 and 18).**

> *Therefore he had to be made like his brethren in every respect, so that he might become a merciful and faithful high priest in the service of God, to make expiation for the sins of the people. For because he himself has suffered and been tempted, he is able to help those who are tempted.*

That says it all. But can I really believe it? Do you mean to say that the Logos, the Christ, had to be made like me in *every* respect? I am temptable and tempted. Do you mean that he knows the conflict between flesh and spirit as I do? Yes, thank God! Otherwise, where is my hope; where's the

*His Present Saving Work*

Pioneer of my faith?

The "therefore" introducing both verse 14 and verse 17 refers to Jesus' work in making the devil ineffective, powerless, and delivering those of us subject to the lifelong bondage of lust addiction. In other words, because Jesus' destiny is to render the devil powerless and deliver man from the bondage of sin and death, he must of necessity be made like us in every respect so *he* can be subject to our sinful condition in temptation and death. It's as though once God set about to render the devil powerless and save man from sin—saving you and me from the power of that next lust—it became necessary for him to enter into that sinful condition and redeem it from the inside out. In order to make expiation for the sins of the people, the Christ must subject himself to the process of sin in us. He must experience it fully—its power in temptation, subjection to evil, and spiritual death.

The word translated "expiation" (or "propitiation") seems to pose problems for the modern mind; the term seems strangely alien to us today. The same Greek word is used in I John 2:2. Westcott notes that such phrases as "propitiating God" or God being "reconciled" are foreign to the language of the New Testament. *Man* is reconciled (2 Cor. 5:18ff; Rom. 5:10f). Propitiation as appeasing the one who is angry is not the idea. Propitiation is dealing with what there is in me that *causes* the anger, the alienation—my sin. So propitiation is what Jesus does; he's dealing with my sin, my lust, and taking it out of the way so it doesn't alienate me. Propitiation, when applied to the sinner, neutralizes the sin.[37]

So my victory over sin, Satan, and spiritual death is Jesus' victory because he tasted it and went through it all for me. He's the Pioneer and Perfecter of my faith; I don't have to make it happen. He's my Savior from lust in this next temptation *toda*y so I don't have to make it happen. But the action-point of my faith is my sin and his relation to sin.

Jesus does not simply guide or teach; he himself is the Way, the Truth, and the Life (John 14:6). He pioneered the

## III—Real Victory in Christ

way man has to go; I follow him the same way. There's no way for me to go other than the way he went—suffering temptation to sin and death to sin in the obedience of faith toward the Father. In the program, we call it Surrender. Since Jesus' work for me meant that he had to identify with me in my sinful flesh, my receiving that work means that I must identify with him. Thus, whenever I am tempted, as we'll see later in this section, I can die to my sin, cast myself onto him, and be raised by the power of God, just as he was raised. The great joy here is that I can go the same way he did. You can too! He leads the way. He calls us to follow him. We follow his way.

This is not religion; it's following the One who pioneered the way through suffering, sin, and death. He had my nature and went that way; so I can go that way! He calls me to it. It's that simple. Do you see how, from this perspective, this saving work of Christ for us today in the next lust trigger is based on the truth of his real humanity? This passage in Hebrews is not easy; it takes work to get at the ideas being presented. But what a payoff!

The words, *"For because he himself has suffered and been tempted"* (Heb. 2:18) are better understood when literally translated, "For in that he has suffered *being tempted*." Every temptation Jesus went through was a suffering. Sound familiar? Don't you and I suffer in that crisis of surrender? Yes. We have to. Suffering death to the self. "Ego deflation at depth." Go back to my "Bus Stop" and "Ice Cream Connection" stories, and you'll see it. I'd like to make this a headline in every newspaper in the world and shout it from the street corners:

JESUS SUFFERED IN TEMPTATION TOO!
BECAUSE HE WAS VICTORIOUS, I CAN BE TOO!

And he felt it more than we do. He sympathizes with me—suffers with me—because he suffered temptation more than I. He knows what I'm going through when I'm tempted to lust resent and fear. In the language of the program, he *identifies* with us. Can you believe that? He identifies with *us*! This is why I can bring him *into* my lust, into my resentment, into my fear, into my ego-lust as soon as the temptation hits!

Communicating the importance of these Hebrews passages and making them relevant for us today is not easy, and my ability is very limited. But it's worth staying with it. We should stop and take time out to meditate and pray as we read, so that we may experience the truth of who the Savior is and his relation to us in a new a powerful way.

*"He is able to help those who are tempted."* The King James has "able to succor." The idea behind the word here is to run to help one in trouble, often used of physicians.[38] How appropriate for me. He is able to run to my help when I'm in trouble in that next temptation. Isn't that the kind of Higher Power you need as a lustaholic? Does any other kind really work? I'm sorry, but unless you have this kind of Higher Power, the only recourse you have is still within yourself. If you're a lustaholic like me, that won't cut it. I'm asking for help all the time—lust, resentment, a judgmental and unforgiving spirit, self-glorification, ego, fear, bad feelings about people.... (And at times I *cry* out for help.) I feel the death in these sins more and more. So in these, I gladly call for my Physician. On my heavenly cell phone. He makes house calls! Instantly. He comes to me whenever I call him. Inside myself. He becomes the ultimate phone contact, because he's there within, always—if we make the call. And the more I call for help, the more confidence I have, the more help I get, and the more I want to bring him into my sin-process earlier the next time. I don't have to be afraid of sin any more.

What a marvelous freedom! Compared with living in my own guilt and weakness and "trying." Or playing around with lust in so-called sexual sobriety, with all the subtle

*III—Real Victory in Christ*

compromises, the garbage we still carry, trying to "control and enjoy." "If the Son makes you free, you will be free indeed" (John 8:36). This is the essence of the entire Gospel, the Good News of salvation. That's our goal. We don't have to lust at all! It's the Promised Land! Enter in!

We thus see that the author of Hebrews makes a special point of progressively developing the humanity of Jesus, all so we can flee to this One for refuge. And, as if this marvelous passage were not enough, the author comes back to the subject again and again.

### Jesus Experienced Temptations the Same Way We Do (Heb. 4:14-16)

Notice how each of these passages we're dealing with in Hebrews is telling us something very, very significant about Jesus' relation to sin and temptation.

> *Since then we have a great high priest who has passed through the heavens, Jesus the Son of God, let us hold fast our confession. For we have not a high priest who is unable to sympathize with our weaknesses, but one who in every respect has been tempted as we are, yet without [committing] sin. Let us then with confidence draw near to the throne of grace, that we may receive mercy and find grace to help in time of need.*

The word translated "weaknesses" here can be translated powerlessnesses, our beautiful First Step word.[39] We have One who can sympathize with our powerlessness. And "sympathize" doesn't mean mere understanding that would condone something, or simply the compassion of one who regards suffering from the outside, but the feeling of one who enters into the suffering and makes it his own.[40] *Sympathos*—suffering with. He's been there, so he knows the full

*His Present Saving Work*

extremity of our powerlessness. That's why he wants us to invite him into our weakness and sin.

He's able to suffer *with* me in my powerlessness over sin because he's been tempted *as I am tempted*. See how the writer of Hebrews keeps bringing the truth of Jesus down to where we live? Not only did Jesus suffer in temptation (2:18), but his temptations were experienced just as we experience ours. This is very crucial for someone who's powerless over lust. Because if he is able to suffer with my powerlessnesses, then I can bring him into my sin and weakness. Yes, bring him right into my next lust temptation! At the very time I least want to! Try it. You'll discover what I did, the impossible joy of having him bear it away.

**Because He Learned Obedience Through Suffering in Temptation, He Is Salvation to All Who Obey Him (5:7-9)**

> *In the days of his flesh, Jesus offered up prayers and supplications, with loud cries and tears, to him who was able to save him from death, and he was heard for his godly fear. Although he was Son, he learned obedience through what he suffered; and coming to full realization of his selfhood, he became the source of eternal salvation to all who obey him.* (Paraphrase mine.)

This incredible passage brings me to embrace this One and fall before him in gratitude and worship. And obedience. His complete and utter humanity draws me to him. This is the One my soul longs to know and see and follow, the Lover of my soul.

I don't think the author is talking only of Gethsemane and Golgotha here; Jesus' prayers, loud cries, and tears were *in the days of his flesh. That's* what went on in those solitary mountain vigils during his ministry. Jesus knew better than

## III—Real Victory in Christ

we that acting on his temptations would bring spiritual death to him. But it was the godly fear of learned obedience that saved him—the obedience of faith. That's the very same obedience you and I can have, the obedience which saves us in our moment of lust or resentment. If he in his weakness could do it, so can we.

No one who can feel the force of Jesus' loud cries and tears can say that he did not feel the power of sin from within his own being. He *knows* what I'm going through—and more. He suffered more than I against sin, felt its power more keenly, knew its consequences more fully. And he in his sin-controlled flesh overcame, not through his own power or goodness or merit or Sonship. He overcame through an attitude of learned obedience to the Father, the source of his deliverance and victory. Do we dare see this? Do we dare believe it? Do you see what hope this gives the sinner? I'm talking about me—*the lustaholic believer!*

I have translated the words "being made perfect" (RSV) with the words "coming to full realization of his selfhood." His life was a process of completion, fulfillment, as we saw in 2:10, above. He learned obedience; he wasn't automatically immune from disobedience just because he also happened to be Son of God. Remember, he gave up the independent exercise of the divine prerogatives when he was born into our nature and flesh (Phil. 2:6-7). He learned obedience through suffering and thus fulfilled the destiny of his selfhood. This is what makes him so attractive to me. This is what gives me hope that following him, I can fulfill *my* destiny, my selfhood, as a child of God. Coming to fulfillment through his suffering, Jesus is now the Source of salvation in my temptations to lust, resentment, fear, etc.

Yes I, the unclean sexual sinner, can have the righteousness of God fulfilled in my life; and this Jesus is my only and precious hope. I need neither deny nor despair over my temptations to sin. They become the avenue of the great Connection.

## Jesus Struggled Against Sin (Heb. 12:3f)

*Consider him who endured from sinners such hostility against himself, so that you may not grow weary or fainthearted. In your struggle against sin you have not yet resisted to the point of shedding your blood.*

Westcott's translation of this last sentence seems to reveal the original better: "Ye have not yet resisted unto blood, contending against sin." The implication here is that Jesus struggled or contended against sin too, not just against sinners; that's why he knows our fallen human nature. That's why I can bring him *in* to every temptation. And our conflict is really not against sinners "out there," but against sin in here. Yes, this is what lust addicts contend against—sin! Inside! This is the very name of the game, and our victory is in and through that of the Victorious one.

*Thus, to freely and joyously acknowledge our sinfulness in our temptations becomes the key to our union with Christ and victory over the sin, so we can be free and clean in that temptation.*

The Lord is telling us, "Don't despair when you find your sinfulness knocking on the door! Don't grow weary or fainthearted. It's all right to be tempted. It's the way things are. I accepted it; you can too. Trust the Father and believe me."

The difference between having the power of sin within us (our sinful nature) yet not sinning, is something like having a virus present in the blood stream, but not breaking out into the illness because our immune system is intact. It's okay to experience the power of sin in temptation; it's our lot in life as it was in Jesus'! How can we otherwise ever get to know him better? Experiencing, feeling the power of sin is okay because we can have victory *over* it so we don't have to

## III—Real Victory in Christ

sin. Because Jesus is our spiritual immune system. *He* is my immunity, my shield, my defense, even while feeling the very pull of that sin bowling me over. "Experiencing the power of sin in temptation is really the opportunity to exercise the choice of obedience, the opportunity to realize the grace of God. If we did not really feel the pull of sin, how could we ever know the wonder of grace and victory?"[41]

"You shall call his name Jesus, for he will save his people *from* their sins" (Mat. 1:21 AV emphasis mine). That refers primarily to his saving me in my temptations to sin now, today. I'm afraid the prevailing religious mind-set in so many of us sees this only as "forgiving my sins so I can go to heaven." It's much deeper than that; it's referring to the sin-process today. He can, will, and does save me today *in* my temptation. As the old A.B. Simpson hymn has it, *"I'm living in heaven today, for heaven is Jesus and Jesus is mine."*

I'm free to be a sinner today because I'm free not to sin! Praise God, through Jesus Christ our Lord! This is what makes me want to jump up and shout for joy, "MY NAME IS RON; I'M A SINNER!!" Can you begin to see the freedom this brings? It's revolutionary, isn't it?

**The Joy of Jesus**
One final thought on this revelation of the humanity of Jesus in Hebrews:

> *"Who for the joy that was set before him endured the cross, despising the shame. . . ."*
> (Heb. 12:2)

What was that joy set before him? Set before him even at the sin-death on the cross. I think it was the joy of identifying with our sinful needs, bearing their death for us, coming into our temptations, and saving us from our sins—this was the motivating joy-force of Jesus' obedience. His joy is in supping with us as we surrender sin and invite him in (Rev. 3:20; John 14:20). This is the love of God! If we can only receive it, take it, and appropriate it, work it! That's where the work of the Twelve principles must prepare the way before we can realize this. There's no way you and I can ever enter into this sin-relationship with Jesus without having worked those Twelve Steps and getting the junk, the wreckage out of the way.

This passage again proves that Jesus' struggle was real and of the same kind as ours, only more so. It was not mere duty that forced him to fulfill his destiny of suffering for me; it was the prospect of joy. In a similar way, is not this our own motivation in the recovery program? Think about it. Is not our joy made full when we hear our friends, the impossibly addicted, overcoming in faith and discovering the life of God that sets them free when they start overcoming lust? There is no greater joy than seeing life spring up in others in a fellowship of which we are a part. They are part of the process of our own recovery, and we theirs. We are Jesus' brothers and sisters—children of the Father. And Jesus is seeing us through as the Author and Fulfiller of our faith. In the process we become brothers and sisters to others on this pilgrim path.

# 16

## My Point of Contact with Jesus Now

*"Jesus Christ—yesterday and today, the same forever."*

Hebrews 13:8

Jesus is the Way to real victory; hence I have to join myself to him. But how do I do this? Is not the work of Christ "out there" somewhere—in history two thousand years ago, in heaven, whatever? Is there a "bridge" between what happened back then and my need here and now? How do I connect with that? What's my point of contact, here and now with what happened then?

**The Advent of Jesus Into Our World**
The question is, Is he here in my world today? We have seen in previous chapters how Jesus' life and death laid the foundation for our victory over sin. But his death in itself—however powerful the event—has no power to save. When Jesus died, he was done for, abandoned by God, the helpless victim of sin and death. Had Jesus stayed in the tomb, all our faith would be futile, and we would still be in our sins (I Cor. 15:17). But he was raised by the glory of the Father so that "we too might walk in newness of life." He was raised so that we might be "united with him in a resurrection like his . . . so the body of sin might be rendered powerless and we might no longer be slaves to sin" (Rom. 6:4-6). When seen as part of the one divine Event of God's identification with us, the incarnation, Jesus' life, death,

## III—Real Victory in Christ

resurrection, and ascension, together with the subsequent outpouring of his Holy Spirit, become the historic reality with which we can now connect in our time, today.

The advent of the Holy Spirit becomes the final historical event—the bridge—that connects us here and now with what happened two thousand years ago. Fifty days after the Passover meal, on the day of Pentecost (the Jewish festival of weeks), an event took place that would mark the change from Jesus' earthly ministry, restricted to the few then and there, to the advent of his spiritual presence and rule in the larger world of all who follow him throughout time. This Advent is what makes Jesus' redemptive work available to us and to all who follow in our needs today. This is how all of us can personally experience the saving presence of Christ. This is how thousands of people, scattered around the world or gathered together in the same place at the same instant of time, can individually experience the full real personal presence of Jesus within them.

This is why Paul can say, "If Christ be in you, although your bodies are dead because of sin, your spirits are alive because of righteousness. If the Spirit of him who raised Jesus from the dead dwells in you, he who raised Christ Jesus from the dead will give life to your mortal bodies also through his Spirit which dwells in you" (Rom. 8:9-11). Jesus dwells in his people through his Spirit, and where the Spirit is present, the manifestation of Jesus' life is present. Conversely, the person whose life bears no evidence of the Spirit's sanctifying work does not have the Spirit and is not Christ's. "Any one who does not have the Spirit of Christ does not belong to him" (Rom. 8:9).[42]

What I'd like to have you do is imagine in your mind a bridge. This bridge spans not only space, but time. It's a bridge between Jesus and me, between you and the Savior. We'll look at this bridge from two points of view, first from Jesus' side, then from ours.

## Jesus' End of the Bridge

> *"Consequently he is able to save to the uttermost those who draw near to God through him, since he ever lives to make intercession for them."* (Heb. 7:25)

This is a very very important passage, if we can ever grasp it. Here's my attempt: The words translated "to the uttermost" mean that Jesus is not only able to save forever, but whenever he does save, he saves fully.[43] Think of it: The living Jesus—the *living* Jesus—having borne our sin and death, then being raised victorious over it, is now, today, in the business of making intercession for you and me. And he's the one who can deliver us *fully* in and from that next temptation. Do you know what it means to be delivered fully from a temptation? Where there's no situation whatever where he won't save you? This is the amazing grace of our program, when we can experience his presence *in* that temptation. We can encounter a fear, a lust, a resentment, make the real Connection inside ourselves with the Saving One, and have him bear that and take it on himself so we can be free and clean.

Have you ever experienced the freedom of being fully loosed from a lust or other temptation so you're absolutely freed from its power, even though a moment before you were powerless and helpless, with no defense? *That* is what we need. And that is what is promised here—he is able to save fully now. That's just what I need and want—I the lustaholic, the resentaholic, the fearaholic. I've got to have that kind of salvation in the instant of temptation. That's why salvation must always be considered in the present reality as salvation from sin. Yet many, like myself, were trained to believe that the salvation being referred to was merely salvation from hell. What I need and want is not only one who can help me not act out on my temptations, but one who saves me fully in that encounter, in that desperation. In this right union with Jesus, every temptation surrendered thus works toward fulfillment of my personhood. I actually feel fulfilled after it's over. I have more Life in me after it's over than before the temptation ever hit. Because I've connected with his Life.

Listen to how a newly recovering sex addict describes the aftermath of an impossible temptation: "My feeling of inadequacy was invaded by a peaceful presence of Him who is most willing to cover me from the ultimate defeat of shame, bewilderment, and guilt." His inadequate self—he couldn't do it—was invaded by the peaceful Presence of the One who ever lives to make intercession for us. Yes, for *us*, the polluted lust junkies of this world. Jesus, when he delivers us, does not leave us empty; he imparts his very life, his peace and joy. "Peace I leave with you; my peace I give unto you." And we lust addicts must get something better than what lust had to offer. It's called "The expulsive power of a new affection." That's what we're after in this book, a new affection with the Savior.

This objective aspect of this bridge from Jesus' work then and there to the saving acts in my experience here and now is beautifully described by a twentieth century Swiss theologian. He puts it into the form of the question, How does the atonement made then and there come to us and become our atonement? [44] Excerpts from his work which follow form an eloquent commentary on our Hebrews passage. (Emphases are all mine.)

> "... He did not continue to be enclosed in the limits of the time between His birth and death, but as the One who was in this time He became and is the Lord of all time...."
>
> "His being on the way from Jordan to Golgotha, His being as the One who suffered and died, became and is as such His ... present-day being every day of our time."

"He not only did bear the sin of the world, *He does bear it.* He is the same here and now as He was there and then: the Mediator between God and us men."

"Therefore He not only did but does stand before God for us—not in a different form but as He stood before Him for us 'in the days of His flesh,' as the Judge judged and the priest sacrificed."

"The eternal action of Jesus Christ grounded in His resurrection is itself the true and direct bridge from once to always, from Himself in His time to us in our time."

"He receives for us to-day as on Easter Day the grace of God which we have not deserved."

"[The intercession of Christ] is not simply the origin and the lasting basis of our righteousness and hope, but its continual turning point, the way which is always open to God. . . . the eternal act of the crucified and risen One for us, the one truly contemporaneous divine act to us, the Today, Today! of atonement against which we must not harden our hearts." [See Hebrews 3 and 4.]

[The ascension was a sign] "of His *transition to a presence which . . . embraces all times.* . . . With the end of the time of this particular event there began the time of another form of His parousia [coming or presence], His living present. . . ."

God "will not allow life to be split into a 'here' and 'beyond.' *He will not leave to death the task of freeing us from sin and sorrow.*"[45]

*Yes! That is our impossible joy. Thanks be to God.*

• • •

## III—Real Victory in Christ

Let's look at another view of this same bridge we're talking about. Aaron, the high priest under Moses, prefigures the work of Christ. He was a type of our Savior today because Aaron dealt with sin. And in the Exodus experience, through Aaron, we get a precious portrait of Jesus our priest as the one who "ever lives to make intercession for us":

> So Aaron shall bear the names of the sons of Israel in the breast piece of judgment upon his heart . . . to bring them to continual remembrance before the Lord [he actually wore a garment with a breast piece in which the names of the people were represented in it, worn always over his heart]. . . . Aaron shall bear the judgment of the people of Israel upon his heart before the Lord continually. . . .and Aaron shall take upon himself any guilt . . . that they may be accepted before the Lord (Exodus 28:29-38).

How can Jesus' work for us be put any better than this? Our Lord bears our names, our judgment upon his heart continually, and we are accepted! He bears *me* on his heart continually. He bears my judgement, the effects of my sins, continually that I may be accepted. Can you see that he bears yours on his heart too? Have you ever opened your heart to let him in—into your sin? If we can ever connect with this, we'll be changed people, and our suffering world will know that something from above has once again broken into human history.

In the parable of the Last Judgement recorded in Matthew 25, the righteous ask, "Lord, when did we see thee hungry and feed thee, or thirsty and give thee drink? And when did we see thee a stranger and welcome thee, or naked and clothe thee? And when did we see thee sick or in prison and visit thee?" And the King replies, "Truly, I say to you, as you did it to one of the least of these, my brethren, you did it to me." You mean Jesus actually *feels* our pain and suffering? The risen Lord tells Saul on the road to Damascus, "I am Jesus, whom you are persecuting" (note the present

## Contact with Jesus Now

tense, Acts 9:5). This implies Jesus was suffering what the Christians whom Paul was persecuting were suffering. And consider the marvelous passage in the vision of Isaiah of the Suffering Servant: "In all their affliction he was afflicted" (63:9).[46] That means that in all my affliction *he* is afflicted. He is my suffering Savior.

Yes, he bears our judgement on his heart continually. Yes, there is a real saving Connection with the Son of man, here and now! For you and me—just as we are, in the very moment of our next temptation, Today! Yes, he is able to save us fully now because he is interceding for us now. Will you let him in now, into that next temptation? The choice is ours; he is there waiting. (Study Rev. 3:20 in this light.)

**My End of the Bridge—Let Him In!**
This life-giving activity of Jesus is not some abstract principle; it is a real personal Presence—if the Spirit of Jesus really dwells in us (Romans 8:9). That's the Big If. Whether he dwells within us is our decision. What I'd like us to see is that the same instrumentality within us that enables interpersonal intercourse is now active with us and God. This may be hard to grasp; let me try to explain.

There is such a thing as actual spiritual oneness and union of persons. There's a "mechanism" between humans which mediates this; it's part of our design. Our design in the image of god enables person-to-person spiritual intercourse. We sexaholics abuse this when we cry, "Connect with me and make me whole." The point is that this same design feature in humans enabling us to have spiritual intercourse with one another, for good or bad, enables our spiritual intercourse with God (or the powers of evil!). We sex and relational *mis*connects should know; we're the experts on trying to fulfill that lack with all the substitutes. Listen to that old romantic ballad: "Drink to me only with thine eyes. . . ." We possessed the spirit of others and were possessed by the spirit of others.

## III—Real Victory in Christ

That same faculty we have between humans is how we possess *Jesus'* Spirit. Why should it be any different? We make too mystical and mysterious a deal out of such statements as "being filled with the Spirit," etc. There's no mystery to it at all. It's so simple. Union—real spiritual intercourse—with the risen Son of man can be just as natural as connecting with a friend. It is more natural. It's the natural movement of the heart to the Lover of our souls and to our heavenly Father. We *are* the dwelling place of God! (Isa. 57:15) Our bodies are the temple of his Holy Spirit (I Cor. 6:19). If, that is, the Spirit of Jesus really dwells in us.

In a context where he discusses sexual union and immorality, Paul says "he who is united to the Lord becomes one spirit with him" (1 Cor. 6:17). How can it be any clearer? We can become one spirit with the Friend of sinners, our Savior, intercessor, deliverer. In that next temptation! To think that my sin-controlled body, that your sin-controlled body, can actually become the temple of Jesus' Spirit! And our lustful and sinful natures are the continuing opportunity for us to realize this in our daily lives.

Thus, by Jesus' Spirit—by Jesus himself, his real presence—I can put to death the deeds of the body (Rom. 8:13). I *can*, through his presence. *I* don't have to do it; *he* is my Savior. Provided I suffer with him (v.17). Ah, there's the rub. I have to die to that temptation. I have to give it up and consciously bring him into it. There's no resurrection without crucifixion. How can I be raised with Christ in his resurrection power without following him in surrender? There's no union, no bonding, when there's anything in between; that's where Steps Four through Ten of the program come in . Those are the Steps designed to get the junk out of the way—SELF out of the way—so we're open for this new union, this improving of our conscious contact with God.

There is also great promise here: "Be faithful unto death," the Lord tells us, "and I will give you the crown of life" (Rev. 2:10). Life. Life in that temptation. "Be faithful

## Contact with Jesus Now

in dying to lust, and I will give you my life." That's what he's saying. This becomes a present reality, not just a far-distant hope. It can be real instantly, as instantly as the temptation itself. All I have to do to live free from the bondage of any of my sins is to suffer with him—that is, suffer the same way he did, in the obedience of faith. Suffer with him in letting him suffer for what I am tempted to do, instead of my doing it. And yes, I think he does actually suffer with us.[47] In obedience to God, I die to my lust and sin, upward to him, inward to him—to *him*. And he raises me from that death. Whenever I have done that, he has never failed to raise me.

Thus, my end of the Bridge is grounded in my sinfulness. There's no other point of identification between me and Christ! My sinfulness and temptation to sin is the only point where he can connect with me. That's difficult for some of us to accept, isn't it? But when you think about it, where else can he connect with us? In our righteousness? Where is our righteousness? Do we really have anything in our lustaholic resentaholic selves that is *holy*? That point of contact with the holy Savior is surely not any intrinsic righteousness of mine; I don't have any. (I used to think I did, before recovery.) It's not my belief; that's just knowledge about him. The Christ of God and I have but one meeting ground: sin—my sin and his relation to it.

The man who was accepted is the one who said, "God be merciful to me the *sinner*," not the man who said he was doing everything right and was religiously correct. (Luke 18). If we can but see this—our sin and Jesus' relation to it—*this* is what our leap of faith steps onto to bring us together. This brings about that real connection with us and the Savior inside ourselves in that moment of temptation. Jesus knows all about sin; he's been intimately connected with it. He has experienced my sin and your sin., so that's where we first meet and identify. It's just like it is in the program. We identify with one another, not on the basis of how great or holy we are, but we identify at the point of our weakness, our

## III—Real Victory in Christ

need. And that draws us together and makes us one. So it's the same with me and Jesus, only more powerfully, and with this great difference, that the union each time is Life-giving! Because *he* is the Life.

Therefore, on the one hand, the key is for me to see and acknowledge my sin and sinfulness. On the other hand, that honest look into myself—so devastating and despairing—forces me to look to Jesus and see his victory over sin and bearing my sin. It's the look of faith and hope. It's not my knowledge of who he is or what he's done that saves; it's the leap of faith, across the chasm of my insufficiency, that leap to him inside of myself in the moment of temptation. Thus, my connection with Jesus today is through sinfulness and faith: sinfulness, a fact; faith, the desperate leap away from sin onto the Saving One. That's why realizing my sinfulness is so fundamental to recovery; that's the essence of our First Step. We have to admit we're powerless over sin-in-us. This forces me away from SELF out onto a real connection with the sin-bearing Savior.

Thus, it turns out that this bridge between me and the Saving One, this bridge between you and the Saving One, is he himself. HE is the bridge. Speaking of his promised presence to his disciples, Jesus said that the Comforter, Jesus himself, dwells with you and will be *in* you (John 14:17). This was the promise of his Spirit being made available in a dimension bridging all time and space, for you and me today. The bridge is the indwelling presence of Jesus himself, his real presence. This is the connection we lustaholics sought in vain to make in all our *mis*-connections. This is the promise for our impossible joy—the real connection.

# 17

## The Real Connection

*What our Lord wants us to present to Him is not goodness, nor honesty, nor endeavor, but real solid sin; that is all He can take from us.*
                                             Oswald Chambers

Knowing all this truth about Jesus is one thing; knowing Jesus himself is quite another. The challenge, always, is to apprehend, lay hold of the person himself, as we are apprehended by him (Phil. 3:12 KJV).

**We Are Known**
This desire of Jesus to make our suffering his own, as we have seen in Hebrews, is based on the fact that he knows us. In Hebrews 4:12 we hear that the word of God is alive and active and piercing, discerning the thoughts and intentions of the heart, laying our souls bare, our deepest secrets exposed. What is that "word of God"? The believers to whom this letter was originally written had no Bible as we know it, so what is that "word of God" that knows our hearts? "Thou hast set our iniquities before thee, our secret sins in the light of thy countenance." (Psa.90:8) Christ is that Word. He is the one discerning the thoughts and intents of my heart! Jesus brings to light the hidden things of darkness and makes manifest the counsels of the heart (1 Cor 4:5). "All the churches shall know that I am he who searches mind and heart." (Rev. 2:23. See also 1 Cor. 13:12 and 14:25.)

I am known! You are known. Fully and completely. From the inside out. By the One who has actually lived in our sinful flesh and knows it from the inside out. I've always wanted desperately to be known for what I really was. Haven't you? Yes, I used to have to flee from it. But now I want to be known. Don't you? Being known for what we really are brings pain. But what comfort, what rest, to know that finally I am known. This is one aspect of the great "rest" the author is speaking of in Hebrews chapter 4. To be able to enter into this Sabbath rest, we must be open with the One who knows us and wants to take us to himself just as we are.

We are known! It's impossible to hide from him what we can so cleverly hide from ourselves. We are known by the only one who truly can know us and who is worthy to be our Judge. Wasn't this the Great Dread? But now it's the great attraction. (If it isn't, we're not walking in the light.) I was always trying to cover what I really was—inside, even from myself. Now, finally, in the light, I want to be known, as painful as it is. That's why I need "a safe haven where we could finally face ourselves," the precious sanctuary of a meeting where the Light is shining in our darkness.

When does he know me? Always. He either knows me in the very moment of temptation or he doesn't know me at all. He knows the sin in me. Because he has my human nature and "has been there." That's his mission. That very knowing brings my sin to the light, if I surrender my defenses and accept the awareness that the light brings. And that light, which is his very self, burns my sin away. "Our God is a consuming fire" (Hebrews 12:29). Like a laser beam flicking to and fro in the most secret recesses of my being. That fire is the love of God, revealing and burning away the sin. That's why we are invited to draw near with confidence and take mercy and grace to help in time of temptation. (The Greek verb in Heb. 4:16 may be more properly translated "take" than "receive.") So we're invited to draw near with boldness and *take* mercy and grace—in the time of temptation. Do you see why ours is called the program of action? I reach out to Jesus, give him my lust, resentment, or fear—in the very moment I'm being tempted—and take him into me, into that sin.

> The immanent God in us becomes wounded with us, suffers, struggles, hopes, and creates with us, shares every drop of our anger and sadness and joy [and lust, we would add]. The reality of God is so intimate as to be experientially inseparable from our own hearts. But that very same God is at once transcendent, the creating, sustaining, and redeeming Power over and above all things. We should not be dismayed that God's being surpasses understanding, for it is precisely through this mystery that God incarnate can both lovingly share our condition and powerfully deliver us from it.[48]

There is a sobering thought in all of this. This One who knows me and you from the inside out, first as the creating Word of God, then as assuming our fallen flesh, this is the One who "will judge the world in righteousness" (Acts 17:31). Yes, there will be a Day of wrath. Jesus is supremely suited for that task; there will be no getting around him. The Lord, in his vision to John in Revelation, in the seven letters to the groups in Asia Minor, again and again says, "I know your works . . ." He knows what's happening in us as individuals and he knows what's going on in our groups and fellowships. And it's because of this awesome fact that he calls us all to repentance.

Yes, we all are known, you and I—the thoughts and intents of our hearts—and we must all give account. So we might as well bring everything to the light today. Today, while we still hear his voice. In the very moment of temptation when we want to flee, when we're at our worst, that's when we're invited to come. Otherwise we are and will always remain as sick as our secrets.

*III—Real Victory in Christ*

**Union with Jesus**
In Rev. 3:20 the Lord says, "Behold, I stand at the door and knock; if any one hears my voice and opens the door, I will come in to him and dine with him, and he with me." That oft-quoted passage is used in evangelistic services. We've all heard it. But note that all seven of these mini-letters in Rev. 2 and 3 are written to believers! Years ago I began asking, "Lord, I don't hear your voice. When are you knocking on my door; when are you speaking to me?" Now for me I have an answer: He's knocking on my door and calling me in every temptation and trial. He wants to come into it! *He wants to embrace my sin and take it into himself.* He's saying, "Let go of it; I'll bear it for you. I have something better for you—myself. And you shall find rest unto your soul." And it works! It's real! He's real. The result promised in this passage always happens. He comes in to me, and I break bread with him! Yes, the holy God has allowed sin in his universe. But that's where we find him, where he finds us! That's the glory of our condition and impossible joy.

**Jesus the Sin Sink**
A heat sink in electronics is a metallic heat exchanger designed to absorb and dissipate heat from a device such as a diode or transistor. The device is bonded to a piece of metal known to conduct heat well, such as aluminum, copper, silver, or gold. Heat is conducted out of the device and "drains away" into the heat sink metal so the device itself, the diode, remains cool. For example, a silver spoon placed in a cup of hot coffee will cool the liquid faster than say a stainless steel or plastic spoon because silver is a better conductor of heat, a better heat sink, and it conducts heat out of the coffee better than steel or plastic.

    Jesus is my sin sink—the only sin-absorber there is. Do you want to keep absorbing your own? My sin is conducted into him when I bond with him in surrender and give my temptation to him. He's the only one in the universe designed to take sin away from me. I can dump all kinds of stuff on others, but I wind up still not free and clean. Jesus takes it by bearing the heat, taking on himself the death-effects that sin would cause if I drank. That's why my lust-transfer, my sin-transfer onto him, is such an awesome thing. I put my lust and sin onto him.

Look at what Aaron did on the Day of Atonement. Placing both hands on the head of the scapegoat, he confesses the sins of the people onto it, and then they drive the goat away into the wilderness never to return (Leviticus 16). That's a type of the Savior. I make Jesus bear the defilement and death of my sin—my lust-temptation, my hate-temptation, etc.—so I can be free and clean. And guess what? He takes it! "Behold the Lamb of God, who *takes away* the sin of the world" (John 1:29). This is the love of God. This is the present saving act of Christ—Today, now!

But look at what else Rev. 3:20 promises: He also breaks bread *with me*. Can it be—incredible!—that my brother, the Pioneer, my Savior gets something in fellowship with me in every surrendered lust and sin temptation where I open the door and ask him in? Think on it. Can it be that the loftiest moments in human relationship can be surpassed in such sin-transfers, such Connections with the Son of man? (I fear that in our Age of Entertainment isolation few have ever experienced the glory of even fleeting moments of the full realization of human intercourse and relationship.) You mean Christ gets something out of my bringing him into my temptation? It must be so. Look at it this way: Isn't that what we experience when we have true spiritual fellowship one with another?

Listen to John: "If we walk in the light, as he is in the light, we have fellowship with one another"—and cleansing from all sin. "That which we have seen and heard we proclaim also to you, so that you may have fellowship with us; and *our fellowship is with the Father and with his Son Jesus Christ.* And we are writing this that our joy may be complete" (I John 1:7,3-4 RSV). Can you believe that? This is not something religious, strange, or mystical. This is *fellowship* with the Father and the Son, and that fellowship has to do with cleansing from sin.

What I really wanted was not forgiveness; I begged for that again and again and again. I wanted release from the power of my sins. "Victory over them," as it says in the Third Step prayer.

Listen again to Jesus: "Inasmuch as ye have done it unto one of the least of these, my brethren, ye have done it unto me" (Mt 25:40). He identifies so fully with us that he not only suffers with our sin, hunger, thirst, alienation, nakedness, illness, and imprisonment, but is an actual co-partaker in our remedy and joy. Study this passage for yourself until the truth dawns on you. So simple, yet do profound. Let's take to heart and rejoice in what they said about him in derision: "This man receives sinners and eats with them!" He receives me; he sits at table and finds fulfillment in being with *me*. Thank God!

*My Lord, and my friend!*

**The Greatest Cure in the World for Low Self-Esteem**
Being known in this way by Jesus in successful sobriety and recovery is the greatest cure in the world for what is commonly called low self-esteem. (Many of us addicts use terms a lot stronger than low self-esteem when we begin to see it in ourselves, terms like self-hatred or self-loathing.) "Low self-esteem" is one of the most common buzz-words adrift on the ocean of modern psycho-babble. It is one of the easiest things in the world to diagnose, but one of the most impossible to overcome. The way the term is often thrown at us is that if we would only stop having low self esteem, we'd be okay! "Stop being down on yourself. Start saying you love yourself, over and over, preferably in front of a mirror."

I do not believe that sufferers from addictive low self-esteem, like me, can overcome it simply by bootstrapping ourselves up and out of it by some kind of affirmation. The cure for low self-esteem must be part of the cure of the whole person, from the inside out. And it begins with recognizing and dealing with our sinfulness.

*The cure for addictive self-hatred is knowing what we really are and being savingly known by the Son of man.*

Because he's the only one who knows and accepts us just as we really are. This is the real essence of First Step powerlessness. The cure for my low self esteem is coming to terms with my sinful nature as the grounds for Jesus' identification with it and his saving embrace of me in it. That truth of myself—my sinfully defective self in encounter with the real Son of man in temptation—that's the slow but sure cure, from the inside out. That is the whole message of this book. Once I know and am convinced that I am known by him, and once I know him, any grounds for inordinate self-contempt, so common with us addicts, slowly evaporate. True recovery, always, is from the inside out.

If you want to be cured from your addictive low self-esteem, get sober, stay sober, connect with the real Son of man in every revelation of sin and temptation, in fellowship with others doing the same, and get the focus off of your self and onto working with and giving to others. That's what the original Twelve Step program is all about. And that's the cure for low self-esteem.

## Jesus' Identification with Our Sinful Nature is Now Complete

The crowning expression of this glorious truth of our real connection with Jesus is summed up in Mary Magdalene's encounter with him at the mouth of the empty tomb (John 20:11-18). And how fitting that these words come to such a person as Mary. We lustaholics can identify with her. (Jesus cast seven evil spirits out of her, and she followed him and

*III—Real Victory in Christ*

ministered to his needs with others, Luke 8:2.)

Look at this scene at the tomb now. Peter and John have just left, and John, at least, leaves believing. But Mary hangs around. She just can't leave. Why? That empty tomb is her lost hope. Her healer, teacher, prophet, and master, this dear friend, is no longer in her life. She feels the loss, the emptiness and impossibility of it all. Being in all probability a recovering addict (perhaps sexually or relationally addicted or misconnected as we are), falling into despair, hopelessness, and depression comes naturally to her. As she insists on weeping, she stoops to look again into that tomb. It can't be that his body is not here, she says to herself. And if I cannot have him, I must at least have his body to mourn over and hang on to, even in death, for his death is my hopeless tragedy. How often we too would rather devolve into self-pity than trust the unseen God.

When she looks into the tomb this time, the two men in white are there, and they challenge her attitude: "Woman, why are you crying?" (Angels aren't people-pleasers. And how I look forward to that strength for myself!) "Because," she replies, "they have taken away my Lord and I don't know where they've put him." She then turns around and sees a man who also challengers her: "Woman, why are you crying? Whom do you seek?" "Sir," she replies, "if you have carried him away, tell me where you have laid him, and I will take him away. I don't want you messing around with my grief, self-pity, and depression. Just tell me where he is and I'll be on my way."

Blinded by self-obsession, she does not recognize the real Jesus. Mary was misconnected to an unreal Jesus too! Is it any wonder that so many of us are so misconnected that *we* do not recognize the real Jesus? Beware of the all-too-popular religious pseudo-connection with Jesus Christ! It will blind you to the real Son of man. She can't see him, but he breaks through to her. He calls her by name. He *knows* her. "Mary . . . ." She can't believe her good fortune. She recognizes the

## The Real Connection

voice. She has him again! She turns and leaps to embrace him.

But Jesus says, "Don't hang on to me!" (That's the literal translation.) "Don't hang on to me, for I have not yet ascended to the Father; but go to my brothers [the disciples] and say to them, I ascend to my Father and your Father, to my God and your God." That has to be the most amazing statement he ever made, if we can ever comprehend it. He's telling Mary, "There's something better than having me here, on the outside of your life as I have been. Hang on to that and you have nothing inside your self. Let go of *your* ('religious') Jesus, or you'll never have me within."

My prayer for us all today. Each of us must come to know a Jesus different from the one who did not save.

He is now and forever our brother-Savior. He has made himself one with us! In his life he encountered our very own human condition—Satan, sin, and death. And he overcame! Then on Golgotha, he opened himself to our very own sin and was overcome by it, under the curse, in lostness, death, and hell. But he was raised from that Death! By the love, mercy, and power of God. He lives. And who is he now? He is the one whose lifelong process of identification with us as sinners is now complete. *Jesus has now become like us even in experiencing sin.* He calls us brothers and sisters.

Listen to what he tells Mary Magdalene. This is a different Jesus than we have before Golgotha: "Tell my brothers—my disciples, my friends—that I'm going to my Father and your Father, to my God and your God." His words have a new ring to them; there is real intimacy with us here. He has broken through fully into our condition, having experienced our sin on the cross. He is one with us because he has experienced the Fall! He too fell, as the Great Sinner, by opening himself to my sin and yours. And now we can have the same relationship with his God and Father that he had. "Go tell them I ascend so they can have the same

## III—Real Victory in Christ

experience I have!" he says. "Don't you see? I had to do it by the obedience of faith too! You can too! Just follow me in dying to your next temptation, open the door, and let me in."

> He would come and dwell with us, if we would but open our chambers, our rooms, to receive him. But how shall we receive him if we hold this or that daub of authority or tradition hanging as pictures upon our walls as the real likeness of our Lord? Is it not possible that we may unwittingly close our doors against the Master himself as an impostor, because he doesn't look like the picture that hangs in our dwelling?[49]

But alas, this was my tragic condition—having religiously correct likenesses of Jesus hanging all over my mind, life, and ministry and shutting out the Lord himself. What about you? What we're trying to do in this book is to be in such a place that we too can hear him call us by name and discover, see like Mary, the real Son of man. Jesus stands before us today with the same plea as to Mary:

> "Don't hang on to your false conception of me, those of you who would trust in a church or a Book about me rather than me. False worship! That's a false Christ and false belief. I'm not a lifeless form, defeated, forever stuck on a cross, to be mourned over, a mere Son-of-God victim. Neither am I a halo-encircled Christ who does not know the personal power of sin-in-the-flesh. Stop your believism and mis-belief! I am Son of man/Son of God!
>
> "Don't be afraid. I am the First and the Last, the Living One. I became dead. Behold, I am alive for evermore. And I have the keys to your death and hell

## The Real Connection

because I've been all the way there and back. I'm the only one in the universe who longs to take you, *with your sin*, into myself, and set you free. That temptation you have right now. I want to come into it and take in onto myself. But you must give it to me. I'll take its death so you can be free and clean. Because I am the sin-taker, the death-taker. Come unto me, all you who labor and are heavy laden with lust, and I will give you rest."

*Even so, come quickly into our midst, Lord Jesus.*

# 18

### The "Obedience of Faith"

*Many a soul begins to come to God when he flings off being religious, because there is only one Master of the human heart, and that is not religion but Jesus Christ.*
                                                                    Oswald Chambers

The following pages are not easy. As we get into this topic, I'm going to challenge you with concepts which may be difficult to accept. I ask that you allow yourself the test by trying to see what I am experiencing and to believe only that I believe this is true for me, even though I may not always be expressing it well.

Real victory in Christ, the continuing theme of Part III, comes with a price: obedience, taking the *actions* of faith. A suitable introduction to this chapter would be to read again my "Bus Stop" experience in chapter 2.

### The Danger of Christian Knowledge

There is danger in all this Christian knowledge we've been talking about, that in knowing and believing this, we feel we have "the answer," that we don't have to go through the pain of working out the principles in our daily lives. I found out it doesn't work that way. It was working the Twelve Principles on my sins, beginning with my lust and resentment, that opened me so I could begin knowing the Son of man aright.

And for me, as someone powerless over lust, misconnection and other sins, knowledge *about* the real Jesus, even accepting his real humanity, is not the answer for my

## III—Real Victory in Christ

dilemma. The answer is not knowledge but present real *connection* with the actual living Person of the sin-bearer. How else can I have the sin borne without that actual connection? But the question is, How do I get that real connection? Following the twelve principles in fellowship brought me to the place where I could begin to enter this new experience. What works for me is (1) making those principles a way of life (2) in a fellowship of light (3) in continuing sobriety and recovery. This trilogy of actions was the precondition to beginning to discover what my lust was really looking for in the Savior. Why the Steps? How can they help predispose me, open me up, set me up for the Real Connection?

**The Twelve Steps**
Let's look at the Steps and see how they can set us up for this saving union:
**One:** Without in-depth acceptance of our powerlessness over temptation to lust (sin), no Connection is possible with the One whose relation to us is based *on* our sin. **Two:** Without the act of trust that he will restore, no Connection is possible. **Three:** Without an initial repentance toward God in sending away our lust and sins and thus turning our will and lives over to him, how can there be any motion away from Self toward the Savior? **Four through Ten:** Without dealing with all the wreckage of our past and present that's still destroying us on the inside—still holding on to wrongs—without all that stuff out of the way so we can be clean with others, how can there be any reaching out to or connecting with the Savior and his victory over temptation? We have to release all that stuff and be free of it so we can take hold on him. **Eleven:** Without practicing this conscious contact by actually resorting to him instead of lust *in the moment of temptation* (the essence of Step Eleven), how can we learn of this new way of deliverance from temptation? **Twelve:** And if these eleven principles are becoming a way of life, then our light will

break forth as the morning, and our lives will become part of the fountain of living waters going out to others.

**What About Faith?**
If working the Twelve Steps is so great, where does "faith" come in? This term, as used by many Christians in my experience, has proven to be the source of great confusion, even an obstacle.

The words "believe" and "faith" in the New Testament are most often translations of the Greek verb *pisteuein* and the noun *pistis*. The verb appears some ninety-four times in John and twenty-one times in Romans. The noun "faith" appears some forty times in Romans but never in John and only once in I John. "Of about twenty passages in the Gospels where *pistis* (faith) occurs as coming from Jesus lips, all but one conspicuously demand the sense of "reliance," or "trust."[50] But we tend to think of faith as mere belief. What I'm aiming toward here is to deepen our sense of what we call faith into what it truly represents in the life and teaching of Jesus and the rest of the New Testament. So let's now look at a phrase Paul uses which is very significant in discovering this deeper dimension of what we so glibly call faith.

**"The Obedience of Faith"**
The opening and closing of Romans, reputedly the great treatise on faith, give us a good clue as to what this letter of Paul—and faith—are all about. Look at the opening words: "Paul, a servant of Jesus Christ.... through whom we have received grace and apostleship *to bring about the obedience of faith* (1:1-5)." Now turn to the closing of Romans. We read: "Now to him who is able to strengthen you according to my gospel and the preaching of Jesus Christ ... *to bring about the obedience of faith*—" (16:26, emphases mine).

It looks as though Paul is telling me that the obedience of faith, whatever that is, is nothing less than the aim and end

## III—Real Victory in Christ

of the whole work of God in history as well as his own mission as an apostle. Thus, the entire thrust of the Good News as proclaimed in Romans, its whole claim on us, is, literally translated, "unto obedience of faith." The intent of the whole Gospel is to lead us to the obedience of faith. It's as though Paul is sandwiching his entire letter between these two identical flags to get our attention, to explain what the obedience of faith means. The Good News, which is the power of God unto salvation, has one purpose—bringing about the obedience of faith, which then becomes the key to my victory over the next temptation—lust, fear, resentment, or whatever.

Say those words out loud; look at them: **The obedience of faith.** What a powerful force they convey. They get my attention. Before I even try to understand the expression, something deep within tells me this what I'm learning to experience today and what I've always wanted. I thought I always had "faith" (belief), but knew I couldn't obey. Obey what? Obey the truth within me, the desires of my heart, the will of God, the law of God, what I knew to be right, to do what my heart truly wanted to do, and not to do what I did not want to do. So in me, faith and obedience were two separate ideas that simply never came together in my life. But they do come together! If we can accept it. To know God is to obey God. The Good News for me today is that the power of God is saving me from my lust. It saved me from my sin at the bus stop and the ice cream connection. And a thousand other misconnections. It's working where nothing worked before! *The difference today is that I'm surrendering to, dying to my lust; and that's obedience—the obedience of faith.*

"Obedience of faith"?—what a strange juxtaposition of terms for you, Paul! Aren't you called the apostle of faith? And isn't Romans supposed to be the great exposition of justification by faith? How can faith have anything to do with obedience? Much of the preaching I've done and heard would have me believe this expression is an oxymoron, it doesn't compute. All I know is that at the bus stop I obeyed a higher law than that of my own desire. I died to my lust, and this was *an act of obedience to God.* I was tempted to lust—right? But what was behind it? I was tempted by rebellion, rebellion against God. To have lusted would have been to consciously turn against God and exalt my own ego as Lord. Consider:

> My lust is always a conscious decision,
> driven by my ego in rebellion,
> to take what my ego demands,
> shut God out,
> to keep me from seeing the truth about myself.

That's the "anatomy," the "psychology" of sin, is it not?

It's taken me the better part of a lifetime to be able to discern that this is actually what's happening in my lust temptations. (The dynamics of other temptations to sin follow the same paradigm. We would do well to share at length and debate this with each other.) Lust is thus an act of *dis*-obedience. At the bus stop I was able to obey the will of God and do it through faith, not through my own power. That's where faith comes in. For me, obedience is the test of my faith, the expression of my faith. To obey is to have faith. Faith is obedience. A great many priests were "obedient to the faith." (Acts 6:7. See also Rom. 6:16f, 15:18; 2 Cor. 10:5; 1 Peter 1:22.)[51]

I need to interject something here. My faith to obey springs from knowing the love of Jesus for me and his relation to my sins. My faith springs from a true apprehension of who he is and what he's done for me. So this "faith" thing becomes very simple! I can get a handle on it now. That lone word "faith" kept me up in the air; I wasn't sure where I was. I always had this lingering doubt that I didn't have enough "faith," that I didn't "believe" enough.

## III—Real Victory in Christ

That kind of thinking alone should have tipped me off that my "faith" was simply another form of self and works—*trying*. The test of faith is always one's relation to sin, one's *response* to sin. The test of my faith is my response to a sin temptation.

My idea of that classic statement "justification by faith alone" was perverted. For me—and, I fear, many many others—"justification by faith" was taken in the sense that we presume to take it into our own hand to carry it through as the work of our own robust *believing*, and in that way *we* have a part in it and are certain of it.[52] This is salvation by works—which is no salvation at all!

Someone has said that we can reach the supreme expression of our sinful nature in religious self-sacrifice, which is the most perfect kind of self-glorification. This is where God is most completely impressed into serving us, and where he is most completely denied under cover of our most complete "faith." How insidious! The greatest enemy of the truth always seems to come under the guise of the very truth itself. Thus, the most false of all false gods is often today the god of the religious person, as it was with me. Jesus did not succumb to this temptation. He rejected that supreme satisfaction—the "high"—of religious believism, since that is the supreme form of sin.[53]

This throws some light on the classic "faith vs. works" problem theologians love to toss around. This solves the problem because there is no problem. Many (including Luther), have had trouble with the passages in James chapter 2 regarding "works," especially verse 22: "You see that faith was active along with his works and faith was completed by works . . . that a man is justified by works and not by faith alone." But now when we look at this word "works" in James as the obedience of faith, we would paraphrase this James passage as follows: "You see that faith was active along with his obedience, and faith was *completed* by obedience. That a man is justified by obedience and not by faith alone." So

## The "Obedience of Faith"

there's no contradiction between James and Paul—and Christ—when we see what Paul means by the obedience of faith. *Because the obedience of faith is what characterized the life of Jesus!* That's how he overcame sin. That was his life, *obeying* the Father. His faith found expression in his obedience.

This is good news! *This* is the Gospel. I no longer have to fear whether I am believing enough, whether I have enough faith. I just have to obey in surrendering that next temptation and trust God will raise me from that death.

### "What Happens When We Do Sin?"

The question might be asked here, What happens when we do sin? Before recovery, that question was uppermost in my mind. The mind-set from which such questions arise is symptomatic of the very kind of religious thinking I am trying to expose in myself and leave behind. Such questions reveal a low view of sin. I saw sinning as an anomaly, an accidental thing, something that just happened to me once in a while, like breaking one of the Ten Commandments. This is one of the key delusions I had which was keeping me from a faith that works.

The truth of the matter is that by nature I am sinful, whether I'm breaking one of the Ten Commandments or not. We saw this in Part II. I am sinful because the disposition of my flesh is sinful, because I want to sin; and that leads me to sin. Thus in me, that is in my flesh, there dwells no good thing (Romans 7). If I complete this day without "sinning," that means nothing as far as my righteousness is concerned. *Christ* is my righteousness; I have none of my own. If I feel I have not sinned today—a very dangerous perception on my part—it doesn't mean I'm not sinful; it doesn't mean that I am righteous. Where do my lust, resentment, and other temptations come from? From outer space? That other person out there is just the occasion for it. The temptations come from within, from my flesh, my sinful nature.

> *"For out of the heart come evil thoughts, murder, adultery, fornication, theft, false witness, slander. These are what defile a man."*
>
> (Matthew 15:19-20; see also James 1:14.)

Jesus is saving me from sins I would commit, saving from my sinfulness breaking out. He's saving me from the HIV of my spirit breaking out into full-blown AIDS. His righteousness is being revealed in me whenever I bring him in in the obedience of faith. But that doesn't change my basic nature. John tells us something that knocks us all to the ground: "whatsoever is not of faith is sin" and "if we say we have no sin we deceive ourselves, and the truth is not in us" (1 John 1:8). Do we need it any plainer? Just because I haven't broken one of the Big Ten today doesn't mean that I'm not a sinner. All of us constantly transgress here, whether we will see it or not, whether we feel it or not. I used to worry about whether I had sinned or not all the time because there was no salvation *from* sin in my life. Having One who comes into my sinfulness now releases me from the tyranny of that pernicious form of salvation by works.

Can you begin to see the release of joy this brings, this admission that I'm a sinner?

**The Righteousness of God**
We might better call this heading The Righteousness *From* God, since it's not God's righteousness we'll be talking about but righteousness from God to us. We'll be dealing with this word "righteousness" and its companion word "justification," which are so prominent in Paul.

The obedience of faith which we have discussed above is the first key phrase in the Good News of Romans. This brings us to what I see as the second key phrase: the righteousness of God. In the prologue to Paul's letter we read, "For in it [in the gospel] the righteousness of God is revealed through faith for faith; as it is written, 'He who through faith is righteous shall live'" (Rom 1:17 RSV).

Let's look at this statement as though we'd never heard it before, because from the King James version, we're used to hearing, "The just shall live by faith." A correct translation is very important to what we're talking about. Let me share with you my wrestlings over these terms, which have been wrestled with almost from the time they were first written. Note the word "revealed" here. (This will be examined again in Appendix 5 in connection with the wrath of God being revealed.) The righteousness of God is now revealed, disclosed, made manifest in the Good News. The emphasis here is that righteousness is revealed in the faith-encounter—*"through faith, for faith."* So, this righteousness from God is somehow connected with *my* faith.

Where am I today? Righteousness is being revealed in my life today. It's incredible, but it's happening. It's the righteousness from God, through the obedience-faith connection. I feel this now in reliving the bus stop sin-encounter, where I was tempted to lust. Overcoming the temptation to "have" that woman through a visual drink, overcoming it by my surrender and Jesus' bearing it for me, that was revelation of the righteousness from *God*. Because of my faith-death to that sinful impulse, I was loosed from it, and—lo and behold—righteousness prevailed instead of sin. So righteousness was revealed. Was it my righteousness that brought release? Absolutely not. My sinful nature was the window of opportunity for that lust. But righteousness was revealed, inside me. The righteousness from God, God enabling me to not obey sin and do right. What a marvelous feeling!

There's all the difference in the universe between any "righteousness" I may presume to claim by virtue of "not sinning" in any particular instance and the righteousness from God revealed when I see and die to that sin and am raised by God in newness of life because Jesus bears and is raised from that sin.[54] I am righteous? NO! Righteousness from God is being revealed in me? YES! Fantastic difference, if we can just begin to see and accept it.

I feel the force and truth of this righteousness-event, and I too, like Paul, say that I am not ashamed of this Gospel. And I can glory in this righteousness, because it is not mine, but the righteousness of God.

> *So that no human being might boast in the presence of God. He is the source of your life in Christ Jesus, whom God made our wisdom, our righteousness and sanctification and redemption; therefore, as it is written, 'Let him who boasts, boast in the Lord'"* (I Cor. 1:29-30).

In sobriety I wasn't making it; I was down for the count. I came to the point where I had to break through to righteousness somehow, not in the sense of some legal standing before God, some theological dogma which I used to try to have save me, but actually, to have victory over my sins—being loosed from them (Rev. 1:5). So the whole point is to know what we're talking about when we talk about being righteous through faith. This either is possible or it isn't. If it is not possible, if righteousness is only some theological or legal concept that people say exists in God's mind as he looks upon us in his mercy, that's one thing. But if righteousness can be a reality in a person's experience with his or her lusts here and now today, then this is what I've been searching for all my life.

*Being "considered" righteous by God without experiencing right-ness never worked for me! I need reality.*

The starting point here is not God, but me. Before I can see the truth about God, I must see the truth about myself. That's why the wrenching revelation of my sinful nature comes before experiencing Jesus' redeeming union with that

## The "Obedience of Faith"

nature. That's why Part II of this book comes before Part III; encountering the real me has to come before real victory in Christ. (Also, that's why Step One of our program has to come before Step Two.) Thus, the starting point in Romans, kicking off the whole letter, is to see how the righteousness of God is revealed. And to see how the righteousness of God is revealed, we must first see how our unrighteousness is revealed, in Romans chapters 1-7.

If we ever have any doubt about our unrighteousness, all we have to do is read Romans 1-7. And this is where my addiction comes in again. First seeing my utter powerlessness over lust, then, in recovery, seeing the progressive revelation of my defective (sinful) self (Steps 4-10), is all showing me what I really am, and through this, is preparing me for the Good News of the Son of man and righteousness that comes through faith. If I didn't have this impossible malady, lust-sex addiction, I probably never would have come through from death unto life. Now I can feel the force of the assertion, "He who through faith is righteous shall live." Let's stop relegating all this to some kind of heaven-saved-from-hell future. I was dead in sin, and today I live! The sin-death principle is still within me, but righteousness and Life are being revealed one temptation at a time!

*Thank you, my God and my Lord.*

**Repentance and Forgiveness**
The public confession of sins and righting of wrongs—repentance—which we see both in the Gospels and in the Acts, is the outward manifestation of Paul's concept of the obedience of faith. How could it be otherwise, that there are two Gospels? Otherwise, we have to submit to hyper-dispensationalism, which breaks up the New Testament into different "dispensations," where God treats people differently in the Gospels than he does in the Epistles, etc. Rather, the Good News is all of a piece—all of it! There's no difference between the message of John the Baptizer, Jesus, James, Paul,

## III—Real Victory in Christ

and John. Or Adam, Abraham, or Moses, for that matter! We simply see that the Good News as it developed historically over time in different places, circumstances, and peoples is one message.

God's forgiveness is not something deduced from an idea of God or his grace, but is experienced as his act in the continuing event of salvation within the individual. "Forgiveness renews the whole man, in whom sin was not just something isolated and occasional but the power which determined his whole being."[55] That's my story! This implies that to know forgiveness is first to know the power of sin in one's self. (How distant from so much of today's preaching and evangelism. And how fortunate are we, the lust-obsessed in recovery, who come to recognize that power of sin in us and flee for refuge in the Saving One!) Thus repentance and forgiveness are linked (Mark. 1:4 and parallels, Luke 24:47, Acts 2:38, 5:31, 8:22). Repentance and forgiveness are two aspects of the same event viewed from one perspective or the other. When I send away my sins, God sends them away! (For the concept of "sending away sins," which for me was a very crucial change in my understanding, see Appendix 3.)

Repentance is thus a process. I've come to rethink this whole concept in recovery. Yes, there's a one-time act of repentance, as there's a one-time decision in Step Three, but it is also a process. Today we seem controlled by the idea that the whole work of God takes place in that magical moment when we "accept Christ"—usually expressed as a belief formula. But repentance unto sending away of sin has a beginning but no end, since we continue to be tempted. Thus, when I am told to forgive others their wrongs, I'm being told, "Don't hold on to the sin of another—send it away! Send it forth, send it off, leave it alone, surrender it, release it, let it go!"

For me today, the whole question of the "assurance of salvation," "eternal life," "eternal security," or the like, has disappeared; it doesn't even enter my mind any more. Jesus is my salvation, my eternal life—today! I'm actually experiencing salvation and eternal life in my temptations.

Repentance unto the sending away of sins is the very essence of victory over lust and progress in recovery. And the call goes out to us today, as it does always: "Repent for the kingdom of heaven is *at hand*." The moment of decision for you and me is the next temptation to lust or fear or resentment. Today! That's where we can begin to find the true God. In the desperation of our hell!

**Faith in Action**
When I am tempted with any wrong which I become conscious of, I never think of "sin" as I used to; I just feel the wrong inside. It gets my attention. The sin-feeling comes before any conscious light goes on saying, "Oh, this is a sin." What a joy not to be bound to such legal hairsplitting servitude! Now when I am tempted, I can first acknowledge the Lord's presence in revealing that to me: I can see that I am being tempted, that I feel the power of wrongness. Thus, I know the Revealer is there within, lighting my darkness so I can see and name it. He's the Light. This takes the denial, fear, and guilt out of my temptations. He's there! So then, I can bring him into the temptation on the spot, and he can deal with it, and he does.

Look at it from his perspective: First, he himself tasted that temptation to sin and felt its power in the days of his visible presence. When tempted, he overcame it through the power of the Father. Then, he absorbed its blow when he opened himself to it on Golgotha, drank it, bearing its spiritual death and lostness. And finally, he was raised victorious over its death and power. And he now stands in the service of God to deliver us from that very temptation. So, when I give it to him, he takes it onto himself, suffering its death, and I am released from my sin—on the spot! That's the righteousness of God being revealed in me.

## III—Real Victory in Christ

This way, I don't have to "do it." I don't have to make my victory happen. I don't have to deny my sinfulness, and I don't have to try to stop the sin or fight it—ineffective and deadly for us addicts. I just bring him into it. He's the sin-bearer, the sin sink. I invite him into my temptation. I ask him to bear the consequences of that sin so I won't have to. I tell him I don't want to suffer the result of that lust or bad feeling any more; it kills the Life in me. I want it to kill him instead! Yes, it must be that personal! He is my sin offering now. His death and resurrection are operating for me now. I have to kill my sacrificial lamb now, as each household had to do in the Passover. We have to make personal contact and make that sacrifice and kill that sacrificial Lamb. In this way we make contact with the Lamb of God in each temptation and have that sin slay him so we can be free and clean.

He bears the death of my lust now, and he is raised from that death now. And I am raised together with him now because I have joined myself to his death now. Can you see how the death and resurrection of Jesus are a continuing reality in our experience with sin? I am set free from my sin—on the spot. I am tempted to sin, out of my sinfulness, but I don't have to sin! Like the incident at the bus stop. And righteousness is being revealed. *"He who through faith is righteous shall live!"*

Finally, I have a faith that works. Jesus is saving me from my sins! Now! This is the impossible joy.

• • •

I'd like to add some afterthoughts here. You can probably guess that I've been wrestling for a long time with terms such as "justification," "righteousness," "forgiveness," and "faith." Wrestling with these terms is an ongoing process. I don't subscribe to any particular school of theology; I have to make all of this real for me. It has to ring true in my own life, not in my head. I see these terms today as simply reflecting different aspects of being loosed from the power of sin. The theological concept of justification was abstract for me; I could never quite connect. This and other related concepts were merely ideas, even truths if you will, treated again and again in the systematic theologies of various writers throughout church history, writers who were also wrestling with their meaning. I would try to understand them and even believe them, much as if I were to answer questions on a final exam, but I had no idea then that that's all they were—ideas, and not my own personal experience. It was all ideological, instead of experiential, talk instead of walk.

Paul and the other New Testament writers must have recognized the difficulty of mere words describing spiritual experience and reality. That's why I use John, the Synoptic Gospels, and Acts to help interpret Paul. If all I had was Paul, I'd have a one-sided representation of the Gospel, getting only his perspective, through his experience and vocabulary. On the other hand, John's entire Greek vocabulary consisted of something like only five hundred words, simple words from everyday life. Paul, the learned scholar, used a very "educated" vocabulary. John the fisherman was not Paul the intellectual. And James was James, not John or Paul. And Luke the historian was not Paul or John. God in his wisdom saw to it that spiritual truth was refracted through the facets of different personalities and vocabularies, much as light is refracted uniquely from each facet of a diamond. Thus the word of God suits all our needs, whoever we are, wherever we are, emotional, intellectual, and spiritual. And thus the never-ending wonder of revelation as we read and ponder these writers year after year as each was trying to convey what words can never adequately convey—the Person and work of the Son of God/Son of man.

We've got to make sure that the truth of God resonates with real human experience. *Our* experience. And we lustaholics are forced to make these concepts real in our lives. Doctrines or concepts, even right concepts, don't give us

*III—Real Victory in Christ*

power over lust. Right thinking never led us to right acting. Rather, it is right actions which lead us to right thinking. We've got to have reality. Because nothing but reality will save us in that next temptation and give us what our lust was really looking for.

# 19

## Victory over Temptation

When all is said and done, the whole matter of recovery for a lust/sex addict comes down to one instant in time, the point of the next temptation. Typically its's the temptation to take the visual or fantasy "drink." If we have no real victory at that instant, we have no victory, even if we may be technically sexually "sober." That instant is the action-point of our spiritual disease. In that instant is the revelation of the thoughts and intents of our heart. We have either died to lust, or we have not. If we have not, we're still under the power of lust. False recovery is very widespread in the sex addiction recovery movement. False because without recovery from lust, there is no recovery. The length of time of our not acting out sexually may even blind us to our real condition.

**The Solution**
Let's summarize what I've been sharing up to now by putting it in terms of a practical approach to victory over temptation:

**1. Get Sober.** Nothing happens for recovery for us without an initial putting down of the drug—lust and acting out, of whatever form—and surrender to God. That putting down and surrender is the beginning of sobriety. We can come into the program for all sorts of reasons, but unless we are personally ready and willing to stop, forget it. "Until we had been driven to the point of despair, until we really wanted to

## III—Real Victory in Christ

stop but could not, we did not give ourselves to this program of recovery." Though we may try to avoid it, this truth is hammered home in our individual and collective experience again and again. That's our story. I don't think anyone or anything written—surely not this book—can make us want to stop. We do it when we do it. The program can come into play only when we make that initial surrender.

Thus, the first prerequisite for making the truths of this book effective in your life is experiencing the reality of Steps One through Three. And this comes about in fellowship. We may not even know what those Steps are (Appendix 4), but we must have experienced surrender of our malady and surrender to God out of our powerlessness. How can we know the Savior from *lust* if we have never died the impossible death to that next lust temptation? How can we know the resurrection from our lust without having experienced the surrender of crucifixion?

The other prerequisite for someone wanting to appropriate the truths of this book is an initial working of the principles of Steps Four through Ten—in fellowship. That's what I had to do. One must be willing to clear out the wreckage of the past and actually start cleaning house before one can begin to know the true Savior and begin experiencing salvation from that next lust temptation, salvation *in* that next lust temptation. That's what repentance is all about—sending away our wrongs.

There's a price to pay for knowing the real Saving One and release from lust. The price is not merely attending Twelve Step meetings. Neither is the price "belief," confession to a wife or anyone else, "trying to stop," total honesty in describing our inner lives and failures, or discovering our dysfunctional past or how much we were victimized. The price for knowing the Saving One is a change of attitude, a change of heart—nothing less than repentance in action, an ongoing process. We stop doing our own will and start obeying the will of our Father who is in heaven. But sobriety is just the beginning. (The how-to steps of initial sobriety are covered in basic form in such books as *Alcoholics Anonymous* and *Twelve Steps and Twelve Traditions*.) So, number one, to know the Lord, *this* Lord, you've got to break through into initial sobriety, even if it's done in blind faith, or even lack of faith.

**2. Know What You Are.** Let's put this self-awareness in terms of what we really are today. Speaking for myself, I know that I, in my flesh, am captive to lust and misconnection. I am also a fearful person, a resentful person, one who easily has bad feelings toward others, one who is judgmental, unforgiving, self-glorifying. . . . I am a sinner. That is, I have a nature inclined to sin, which leads me into sin, and which cannot save itself. In the beginning, all we are usually aware of is that we are powerless over the addiction, but more self-awareness follows in time. It must, if we are in real recovery. Progressive revelation of our defective self is a sign of true recovery.

This initial affirmation of the real self is the beginning; the full meaning of the First Step grows with time. This is also the reason why so many in our programs do not progress in recovery. Recovery for me did not work without the in-depth realization of powerlessness and ego-deflation. I don't know anybody who "takes" or "works" the First Step. Powerlessness and unmanageability are not actions or decisions; they're an admission of existing fact. The First Step takes us, and only when we finally accept defeat and give in, do we see the open door of grace. Admitting powerlessness in time of temptation is using the principle of the First Step on a continuing basis. So, know what you really are. Come to terms with it.

**3. Know That You Are Going to Be Tempted. Make Peace with Temptation.** Because I have a sinful human nature, I'm going to be tempted. Because the neurons of my

*III—Real Victory in Christ*

brain are programmed to lust, I'm going to be tempted with lust.[56] Being tempted is not only unavoidable, it's part of the Plan. Yes, if we can see it. It was God's plan for Jesus to be tempted, how could it be otherwise with us? Right up to the End. As he is, so are we in this world (John 4:17). Jesus said, "It is necessary that temptations come" (Mt. 18:7). Expect it. Own the temptation. Make peace with it. Accept what it tells you about yourself. Temptation surrendered is the way to God. That's the amazing grace I'm discovering.

**4. Know That You're Powerless Over Being Tempted.** Know that you have no control over whatever temptation happens to knock on the door or appear in the window of your mind. What we have done and thought may have created the situation in which the temptation appears, but regardless, the memory, trigger, fantasy, or dream can pop into consciousness without our direct control. The window through which temptations appear in consciousness is our sinful nature, and we certainly have no direct control over that. This is why, as soon as I'm aware of it, I own the temptation: "Lord, you know that I want to lust after this person right now." We thus can slowly overcome the fear of lust. We need to recognize that in many of us there is a deep fear of lust, of being overcome, of losing control and letting the Darkness back in.

**5. Know Who He Is.** Well, who is he? He's the one we've been trying so imperfectly to see in this book. Let's try to recap:

- He had my sinful nature in the days of his flesh.
- He acknowledged his powerlessness over those human impulses and his total dependence on the Father. I think he acknowledged his powerlessness over those human impulses *because* he was totally dependent on the Father. His dependence on the

Father shows me that in his humanity, he was powerless over that nature he shares with us. "Of myself I can do nothing . . . . the Father does the works."[57]

- He surrendered those impulses to sin to the Father.
- He overcame temptation by relying on the Father.
- On Golgotha, he bore the spiritual death of my sins, taking the full consequence of "sinning" my sins.
- He thus knows sin, from the inside out—my sin, your sin.
- He was raised from that Death; he survives sin. That's why he can take mine today. He *is* the resurrection and the life today.
- Having suffered in temptation as we do, and thus being the discerner of the thoughts and intents of our heart, he now knows what's transpiring in my mind and heart and yours. He knows.
- He *is* the sin bearer. That's why I can make the great transference onto him, the sin-exchange, and let him embrace my sin and take its death onto himself away from me.

That's who he is. Can you accept it?

**6. Bring Him In and Make the Transfer.** Accepting who I am and who he is, I can then say, "Lord, you know I want to lust after this person right now," or, "I'm afraid, and here's my fear. Come in and bear my lust and fear so I won't have to. I put it onto you. I want you to bear and overcome its death so I won't have to bear it. I receive your presence. Come in, Lord Jesus." Then I pray for the object of my temptation until I feel fully free and clean.

To know and accept these six principles is what this book is all about.

## III—Real Victory in Christ

**7. Count It All Joy.** The final principle in victory over temptation is to count it all joy (James 1:2-4). When these six principles we've been discussing are active in my life, I discover that my sobriety, instead of being fear-driven, self-driven, wife-driven, even program-driven and religion-driven, is joy-driven. Fear-driven sobriety shuts God out; the joy response brings him in. "Whenever I 'count it all joy,' I have joy! What a gift."[58]

**Summary**
In the moment of temptation I have thus acknowledged my sinfulness and powerlessness. I send away that sin to him and die to it; I die to what I want to do. I take the contrary action. In that act I am embraced by Jesus, and in that bond, my sin drains away into him, is burned by the consuming fire of the love of God. Jesus is my sin-sink. He is the one and only sin-bearer. That's his whole reason for being. He takes it as he has always taken it, onto himself. He takes *me* to himself. He is the Lamb of God who takes away sin—from *me*.

But he is also the Resurrection and the Life, so I am raised with him from that death. Whenever I surrender with him, I am raised with him. Yes, it works! I am loosed from that sin-temptation and made alive with him. I don't get relief until I make the transference; but as soon as I do, I'm loosed. And this new life is *his* life. I have received the life-connection again! I have received his Life. I have received *him*! This is the Real Connection. His presence *is* the overcoming. I don't have to do it any more! Bringing Jesus into me at the time of temptation is practicing the presence of God. And it does take practice, again, and again, and again. But what a payoff—life!

Listen to George MacDonald: "He gave himself . . . to his father's children . . . to transfuse the life-redeeming energy of his spirit into theirs."[59] When I was a child, I had a series of blood transfusions which saved my physical life. I can see it now, lying on that cold stainless steel table in the

Children's Hospital operating room. And my mother or another relative would be on the adjacent table. I see the nurses walking over to me with a bowl of blood in their hands. And they bring that bowl over to my table. This was in the days they didn't have prepackaged blood; they had to draw it out and transfuse it on the spot. They make an incision in my arm or ankle and inject the blood directly into me. In those days a blood transfusion was very very personal and immediate.

Can you see MacDonald's statement in this light? When we bring him in, Jesus transfuses the life-redeeming energy of his spirit into ours. His spiritual life actually comes into our spiritual bloodstream. We get a spiritual transfusion of Life every time we die to sin, upward, to him and bring him in. That's why each temptation can become the occasion of receiving grace—a sacrament instead of a sin!

**The Scapegoat.** The title of this whole chapter is "Victory over Temptation." We either have victory or we don't. Let me say again that the solution I've found and am continuing to discover is that the real victory over our temptations as lustaholics is not in ourselves, but in the One "who loved us and gave himself for us"—our Scapegoat. God had to present this to the human race in very graphic and tangible terms relevant to the culture, so we can see and do it:

> .... Aaron shall lay both his hands upon the head of the live goat, and confess over him all the iniquities of the people of Israel, and all their transgressions, all their sins; and he shall put them upon the head of the goat, and send him away into the wilderness. . . . The goat shall bear all their iniquities upon him. . . .
> (Leviticus 16:20-22)

## III—Real Victory in Christ

Imagine the scene. The people of Israel have confessed their sins to the priests in their various tribes, and eventually somehow these sins all come up to Aaron the high priest. And Aaron puts his two hands on the head of that goat and confesses all the people's sins. And then, they send the goat away into the wilderness and make sure he never comes back. There's a remedy for sin which is being typified here in this sacramental religious ritual of ancient Israel.

So, what does this mean for me, in my culture today? The dictionary definition of sacrament goes something like this: "a formal religious act as a sign of a spiritual reality." And as you know, various churches refer to different sacraments: baptism, the Eucharist, etc. I'd like to circumvent the whole discussion of sacraments and refer to the simple fact that I need sacramental reality on the *inside* of me every time I'm tempted. Regardless of what I may resort to in my religious rituals, I need the efficacious reality of sacrament inside, where my lust, resentment, and fear appear. And I need it *when* they appear, in the instant of temptation. If I have to wait to perform the religious ritual itself, I'm lost.

Thus, the sacramental ritual of the scapegoat on the Day of Atonement is what I actually do often in sending away my lust and other temptations. Often, especially in severe temptation, I will put out both of my hands onto the imaginary head of the Savior and so make that transference of my lust/fear/sin onto him. Note that most of the sacrifices in Leviticus require that the person place his hand on the head of the animal *as it is sacrificed*. What does that signify? It signifies identification, that we are consciously transferring the death of our sin into the death of that which is being sacrificed. So put your hand on Jesus' head! This is salvation. This is putting your sin onto him. This is the sacrament. This is partaking of the efficacy of his body and blood. (How precious it would be if those actually experiencing this victory over lust could someday break bread in Communion together in praise and thanksgiving.)

## Victory Over Temptation

**Easter Every Day.** Bringing Jesus in and making the sin-transfer is now the key to the whole victory process for me. It is so crucial, yet so difficult to communicate, that I'd like to try another tack. If none of this makes sense to you, don't worry about it; I'm not that clear on it myself. I sense there's something of great promise here, so I'll try to put it into words.

What happens in this transfer? What happens when Jesus takes my sin now, in any given temptation today? I notice that after the transfer, I don't have that sin temptation any more; it has left me. I will be tempted again, of course, but the current temptation is actually gone. Can we not say that the same kind of thing happens now that happened on that first Easter morn? If Jesus was raised from sin's death then, must he not be raised—that is, somehow released—from its death-effects now? Is not the same God and Father who overcame sin and death in Christ by raising him from the dead dealing with sin and death the same way he always has? He is the Overcomer of Sin and Death.

I believe the resurrection-power of the Author of life is eternally active whenever we die with Christ to temptation. Thus, I can expect that the very same thing which happened to Jesus will happen to me spiritually—now, today, in that next temptation. When I die to a temptation with Christ, I shall be raised, just as he was. Raised together with him! (Eph 2:5,6) There's life after lust! After resentment. After fear. If I die to it with him. That's what we call surrender.

But sorry, there's no resurrection without crucifixion! So try dying. God is faithful. It works. If he raised Jesus from the death of the whole world's sins, he will surely raise you and me from our death in the next sin temptation. And we can trust him, because Jesus did, having our very same human nature. This is the confidence we have, that we too will be raised—the empty tomb! Incidentally, being raised from my sin-death time after time after time seems to give me the hope Paul speaks of when he cries,

## III—Real Victory in Christ

*"O Death, where is thy victory; O Death, where is thy sting?"* My physical death will be a victory, just as my every sin-death is!

**Let the Surrenderer In.** Here's another beautiful thought to consider: Does not letting Jesus into me when I am tempted let in to me the will to surrender? Jesus always willed surrender to the Father, at any cost. He died to his own self. So, when we let Jesus in, we are letting in the spirit of the Surrenderer, so his surrender becomes ours. I don't know what's really going on, but this is how it seems to work for me. When that impossible temptation strikes, instead of trying to summon the courage or will to surrender it, I ask him into it; I *take* him in! The reason I am inclined to believe that *he* is my will to surrender is that the will to surrender comes whenever I let the Surrenderer in. So the will to surrender, the actual dying to the sin and resurrection, all come with Jesus—once I let him in *before* I have drunk or acted on the temptation. Isn't this infinitely better than trying to handle these impossible temptations ourselves? The stupid arrogance of trying to do it ourselves!

Look at what Paul says in Philippians 3:8-11:

> Indeed, I count everything as loss because of the surpassing worth of knowing Christ Jesus my Lord. For his sake I have suffered the loss of all things, and count them as refuse, in order that I may gain Christ and be found in him, not having a righteousness of my own . . . but that which is through faith in Christ, the righteousness from God that depends on faith; that I may know him and the power of his resurrection, and may share his sufferings, becoming like him in his death, that if possible I may attain the resurrection from the dead.

Paul uses this whole passage to show how true believers worship by the Spirit of God, rejoice in Christ, and put no confidence in the flesh (verse 3). They stop trying!

Let me paraphrase this passage to show how I apply this passage to myself, putting all the confidence in him:

> For the value of actually knowing and experiencing my Lord, I consider all my own belief, ritual, and striving meaningless and ineffective—a total waste. That's why I gladly let it all go to gain Christ himself; there is no righteousness of my own. But there is righteousness! It comes from God, and I connect with it through the obedience of faith in Jesus. Thus, my aim in temptations to sin is that I may know Jesus in the power of his resurrection. But that means I must also surrender to the suffering of death—dying to that temptation. Patterning my responses to sin after his own—becoming like him in his death—is what never fails to bring about my resurrection out from that death.

I understand the last words "attain the resurrection from the dead" as referring not to some future resurrection or privileged status, but to the deliverance here and now from the sin, and connection with his life as the result.[60] That's why Paul can say in another place, "I am crucified with Christ, nevertheless I live. . . ." (Gal. 2:20). In other words, Paul lives in resurrection power by experiencing resurrection from the dead. Praise God!

Jesus' real presence within me is the answer to all my life's needs, if I can but see it at the time of need and invite him in.

## My Morning and Evening Surrender

My morning and evening quiet times have evolved over the years into periods of spiritual nourishment, meditation, and prayer. They're still evolving and never stay the same. This

## III—Real Victory in Christ

is what I find myself doing today: Each morning, as soon as I arise, I get alone and have my quiet time of devotional or scripture reading, meditation, and prayer. I close the prayer time with something like the following. The words vary from day to day, and year to year, of course, as needs arise. They've got to stay real or else they're meaningless and turn into some sort of pseudo-religious exercise. And I share this only to show what I was doing at the time this was written and to encourage others to put their daily surrender and requests for sobriety in their own terms in their own way every day.

"Thank you, Lord, for keeping me sober last night. I'm powerless over my lust, my sex, my sexuality, my orientation, and misconnection with others." (In the evening I would add that I'm powerless over fear of acting out in my sleep, and, at that time, fear of earthquakes [after the big one of January 1994, when we thought it was the end].)

"I want you to keep me sober from *every* lust today—conscious, subconscious, active, passive, and from every misconnection with others. I want you to bear it and overcome it for me. I want you to bear its death. Also I ask that you keep me sober from unlove, fear, anxiety, and care.

"I ask you to guard and shield me from the lust, sin, evil, and dysfunction of others and from every power and influence of the adversary.

"I take refuge in you. Come in, Lord Jesus. I receive your presence. I take your presence. You are my Strength. You are my Resurrection and my Life." I thank him for his presence and promise, "I will not leave you desolate; I will come to you" (John 14:18; Rev. 3:20). I take him at his word in this, even when I don't feel like it.

> "Father, take my will and life and health and marriage and family and Fellowship and time today and do and build with me as you will. Relieve me of the bondage of self today. Take away my defects, and give me what I need to do your will today. Show me what I can do for the suffering and needy today. Thy will, not mine be done."

This quiet time is usually the best part of my day; without it, I feel like only half a person, missing the Life-connection. Then I go out, take my walk or whatever, break my fast, and go about the business of the day.

> CAUTION: Repeating formula prayers is not saving union with the Son of man. Such union issues from the repeated obedience of faith in times of actual temptation and trial.

**Adversary Temptations**
There have been times when temptations to lust, act out sexually, or go negative in bad feelings of resentment, anger, or fear have been so unusually intense that I was forced to take drastic action. For example, just this morning, I found myself experiencing a thrusting shaft of evil in anger temptation, where the intensity of the feeling was enormously disproportionate to my average day-to-day temptations. Without getting dogmatic on this sensitive subject, I can at least say that there appears to be something different than the usual in such instances. Often, I only wake up to that fact after it really gets my attention and hits me between the eyes. This doesn't happen that often, but it does happen. At such times there seems to be a component of the temptation that comes from outside of me. Most of my temptations probably come from within my own disordered nature, my sexaholism. But on such occasions I wonder if something has come in through the window of that nature from the outside. That's

## III—Real Victory in Christ

when I sense it may be from the adversary. Jesus may have experienced this delayed reaction too (as we saw in his Wilderness temptations in chapter 5).

> *Be sober, be watchful. Your adversary the devil prowls around like a roaring lion, seeking some one to devour* (I Pet. 5:8).

In such times, as soon as I suspect this may be the case, I resort to the same defense the Son of man used. In his Wilderness encounter with the adversary, Jesus commanded him to be gone and made three assertions, resorting to the word of God and not his own strength in each case. And this is how I use them (here again, words will vary with the occasion):

> I command aloud, "Begone in Jesus' authority!" Then I say, "It is written, thou shalt not tempt the Lord thy God. It is written, thou shalt worship the Lord thy God and him only shalt thou serve. It is written, man shall live by every word from God."

This is how I do what Peter suggests when he goes on to say, "Resist him, firm in your faith, knowing that the same experience of suffering is required of your brotherhood throughout the world" (5:9). Whenever I have done this, it has never failed me. When I say "Begone," that's what Jesus said (Mat. 4:10). When I say "In Jesus' authority," I'm asserting that I am doing this not in any power or authority of my own, but in his authority and presence. (I feel many of us grossly misunderstand and misuse the "in Jesus' name" formula.) And in the three utterances themselves, I am speaking of myself as much as of or to the adversary. Not only is he not to tempt the Lord God, but *I* am not to tempt him by obeying the temptation, by letting the temptation take me. Not only is the enemy to worship the Lord God, but that is *my* job in that moment too, to worship God in surrender and obedience instead of nourishing and getting a hit off that sin. And when I assert that man shall not live by bread alone but by every word from God, I'm asserting and confessing that *I* shall not live by the sustenance, the "bread" which this temptation promises so seductively. I will live not by indulging in that sin—the enemy's lie—but by the obedience of faith in the word of God.

I notice that in his own personal life, Jesus did not use the "binding Satan" formula referred to in connection with his apostles' ministry. Rather than trying to exercise some such gift, whatever it may be, I think I'm safer doing what Jesus did for himself in his own temptations.

(Here's a bit of conjecture: In this connection, when we are still close to evil in our addiction as when we first try for sobriety, I wonder if some of us may be unable to see that we are openly vulnerable to adversary temptation from without and thus have no defense against it yet. Can that be another reason why so many cannot get or stay sexually sober? I don't know. But if that is true, it is all the more reason we must have a spiritually close-knit fellowship of brothers-in-arms, bearing one another's burdens in our common warfare (see Part IV and Ephesians 6 ). Something else we could talk about is the related question, What does it mean to be possessed with lust? What have we let into our lives—our souls!—when we came under the tyranny of being powerless over lust?)

# 20

## Temptation Flagrante

I'd like to share something that happened to me when I was several years into my current sobriety. It was one of the most flagrant episodes in my recovery. Only a lustaholic can appreciate this story; it may seem silly to others. I had gone to the Post Office to mail some program packages, only to find a long line of people waiting for service at the counter. As I came to the end of the line, I saw that the young woman in front of me was not only a trigger image in appearance and dress, but was actively scanning about for a connection (the "double-whammy" for a sex drunk like me!). It was summertime, and she was clad in a flimsy see-through garment. This was an extremely unusual case. Attractive women can know that they are attractive and still refrain from putting it out there on a silver platter. This poor lass seemed obsessed with having to get someone—anyone—to misconnect with her. Often, we're not really certain whether the lust object is in pursuit mode trying to connect with us; we realize our lust may be reading that into the situation. Not in this case!

For me, this was the moment of truth. And utter powerlessness! It can strike sheer terror into the heart of a sex addict who wants recovery. It certainly did mine. Fear of being overcome? How would you describe the fear?

I began praying and surrendering, all the while feeling the overpowering pull of desire to take that visual drink standing right there in front of me only inches away, filling most of my field of vision. I had passed victorious through

## III—Real Victory in Christ

deep waters before, but this was deep deep. I kept my eyes closed or averted and kept reaching out, upward, for sustenance. And, thanks be to God, I didn't have to drink.

Then, the worst possible happened. I dropped my keys. They fell to the floor in front of me, only inches behind her. My heart stopped. There was no way I could retrieve those keys without seeing what would be there inches in front of my eyeballs. An impossible trigger! I was gone! I just stood there, catatonic. Webster defines catatonic as a psychomotor disturbance that may involve stupor, rigidity, and inappropriate or bizarre posturing. And you should have seen me there—rigid, in a stupor, and bizarre. It's humorous now, to look back upon it all.

Well, I just kept standing there, frozen, terrified at what I would have to see, knowing that merely taking in that visual image, I would be utterly defenseless against *drinking*. This is the action-point of our malady, isn't it? That's what was going on in that

> ...titanic warfare, doing battle against unseen principalities and powers.... Anguish filled his being. In the subjective darkness there was eerie cynical laughter. Huge distorted peals, twisting through his being. And rippling across that warped darkness the image of a face. Now seductive beauty; now demonic malevolence. All his inner senses reeled under the assault as he was hurled into the fiery black abyss, the whirlpool of burning waters pulling him down, down, down...[61]

Looking back on that incident, I realize I didn't have it. Several years sober and totally involved in carrying the message to others, I simply did not have it. I had no defense against *that*. So where was my recovery? All my sobriety and program work was not enough.

Fearing she and others were wondering why I didn't pick up my keys—I was standing there for an eternity—I became greatly distraught, knowing I would have to do something. I was even surreptitiously nudging the keys along with my shoe. Finally, unable to stand it any longer, in utter desperation, I cried out in my spirit—that telegram without words—"HELP!!!" I had been praying ever since I had got in line, but this was different. It was a desperate cry of hopeless drowning. And I went down after my keys.

I can't explain what happened. All I know is that I bent over, crouched down, reached out my hand, got my keys, and straightened up again. With my eyes open. But I did not see her. My eyes were open, but I did not see *her*. As I went down, I sensed a Presence between me and that death-threatening image (again, only a lustaholic understands). As though a shield was in front of me. There was a lightness, gladness, and joy about this that took away all fear, dread, conflict, and anxiety. It was a gladsome presence, and I knew I was safe and free. I feel now that it was the very Presence of my saving One, there between her and me, absorbing all the lust onto himself, shielding me, saving me from my lust and hers. The love—and suffering—of the Son of man. His real presence.

I breathed easy, and for the rest of the time in line was rejoicing, praying for her with love and gladness in my heart.

*And may the Lord bless you even now, dear troubled heart, wherever you are, and give you his peace. I bless you and pray you well.*

• • •

This was the beginning for me. A new beginning, but *the* beginning of what would eventually lead to a new kind of victory over temptation. I had been praying to know him better, what his death meant for me here and now, and this

## III—Real Victory in Christ

was how it actually started—where this book actually got started! Not in the Bible study or quiet time, not during meditation or where the prayers were offered, but in the white heat of temptation and survival in the real world out there. I knew the Presence of the Friend of sinners!

Now, several years later, in the writing of this text, things have quieted down. The temptations themselves are usually not as intense and fearful, and his presence is "in quietness and confidence . . . in returning and rest." The Lord himself is my shield. The Lord *is* my Shepherd, I shall not want. Nevertheless, I know I am not immune; not recovered, only recovering. I can be back in that Post Office experience in the blink of an eye, and just as vulnerable. Because I am just as powerless over lust now, in myself, as I was then. That's why I can't trust in myself and have to put *all* my trust in the Guardian of my soul (I Peter 2:25).

• • •

Why such fear in these encounters? We should talk more about this too. Part of the intensity of this abnormal fear may well be the fact that we have let an evil presence into our being when we crossed a line in our lusting. We let the spirit of lust in—a spirit which may well be demonic. Whatever it is, it is a *super*-natural force, super-powerful, the negative god. It can kill. It offers the promise of life, but it is spiritual death. So for someone who is sober and in recovery and who is experiencing progressive victory over lust, to be confronted like that, the fear is fear of spiritual death, fear of being overcome, not just by Woman but by that evil force. This is why lustaholism is ultimately so different and has little if anything to do directly with the mere biology or psychology of sex addiction. Is the only Remedy for some of us to know the real presence of the saving Son of man? I don't know, but I would wish this Remedy upon all. *He* is the impossible joy.

# 21

## Joy in the Impossible

*". . . Deliver all those who through fear of death were subject to lifelong bondage."*

**The Luster's Fear of Dying**
This passage, as is true of the entire context of Hebrews 2:8-18 which we studied in a previous chapter, reveals much about our condition as lustaholics, and I'd like to pursue it further. I've often been puzzled by why "fear of death" in this verse is connected with "lifelong bondage," that is, addiction. I could never connect fear of death with addiction, even though it struck a note. I think such puzzlement arose because I restricted the expression "fear of death" to fear of dying physically. But I think the author's concept of death is larger than the merely physical, just as the true meaning of Jesus' death is much larger than the physical. What if the reference to death here also refers to the feeling we addicts experience when tempted, where our whole system screams out that we're going to die if we don't take that "drink"? Isn't that what made my Post Office experience in the previous chapter so terrifying—the fear that I would *have* to drink, that I would die if I didn't?

In our particular case, then, we could paraphrase the passage to read, ". . . . deliver all those who, through fear that not lusting or not misconnecting will kill them, remain in bondage to an impossible addiction."

## III—Real Victory in Christ

For the typical lust addict, our whole system does scream out that we're going to die if we don't take that "drink." It's too fearful *not* to drink. Lust is our spiritual life-support system. Yes, the fear is that real. So, we wind up drinking. We're hooked on it and remain a slave. It's the fear of this kind of death that keeps us in bondage and forces us to keep slipping with lust.

The sad fact today is that so very many in the sex addiction recovery movement and in the church remain in bondage to lust, sex, and relational misconnection because of this very threat of death. They are unable or unwilling to connect with the Life-giver instead. We can't break through this death-barrier; we shrink back at the death-threat of not lusting or misconnecting with someone. Because that attitude and behavior has taken the place of the real connection with our Maker.

It's so unnatural for us *not* to lust or misconnect that it carries the actual threat of death when we are faced with surrendering the temptation. Ours is the compulsion of the look, the fantasy, or the misconnection, which when denied, is the very threat of death. But eventually we learn the hard way that for us to *drink* is to die. So recovery is learning to act against the fear—to lean into the fear—and go ahead and die. So we can live. The amazing paradox of our program.

This is why the decisive action-point of our malady is the instant of temptation, typically in the look, the memory, or the fantasy. That's where we face the feeling of death each time. And that fear drives us to resort to that drug again and again and again. That's why we feel we *have* to drink—so we won't die!

We've used and heard all kinds of formulas on how to deal with a lust temptation. Some are foolish or frantic, such as the three-second rule: "If you look for over three seconds, you're lusting." Variations on such formulas are ingenious. What's yours? As though lust had anything to do with duration. Lust has nothing to do with duration and everything

*Joy in the Impossible*

to do with *intent*. If the intent is to snatch a quick drink, does it really matter how long it is, or even what we see? No. The intent is what we *are*. We need salvation from the intent, the disposition of our heart. And repentance via the Steps, together with a true apprehension of the real Savior, will give us that intent.

Most of us initially feel it's something *we* must do to get out of it. "I shouldn't be doing this!" we say to ourselves, as we go ahead and take the drink. This tells me that we don't fully understand the nature of what we're dealing with and that we underestimate the strategies of spiritual blindness and denial. This is "works of the law" instead of the love of God, which we can discover in the saving presence of the Savior. We don't comprehend that lust is a disposition of the heart, an *attitude*. We rely on our own efforts—even our prayerful efforts—to save us. (Who says religious exercises can't support the illness?)

This is why so many of us—so-called sober from "acting out"—do not recover from acting *in*. Mere sexual sobriety just deals with externals. Sober is not well. The tragedy in such lust-avoidance or lust-distraction technique is that we can still "feel better about ourselves" by going to meetings—or church—and getting tacit support there for our sin-sickness.

### Is Victory over Lust Progressive?

True sobriety includes progressive victory over lust. How can there be any argument with that? We know of no instant cures from lust yet (though we keep an open, if skeptical, mind). But our relation to this concept of progressive victory may be too shallow. We can abuse it. We can misuse it. We can hide in it. So let's examine the question: ***Is there such a thing as progressive victory over lust?*** There are two ways of looking at it.

## III—Real Victory in Christ

On the one hand, I came slowly to see in my own progressive recovery what lust is and the many ways I denied and blinded myself to what was really going on. Apparently it takes a certain amount of recovery to *begin* to see lust for what it is, and continuing growth to see it better. I didn't discover lust as the underlying pathology until I stayed sexually sober. The overt "drool," which many of us connect with raw lusting, is merely one of the more obvious forms. What about addiction to Woman or Man, the "wandering *heart*" or "appreciating" beauty? Ours is preeminently the malady of the *misconnection,* as we hear in the cry, "Connect with me and make me whole!" What about lust in the marriage? Lust is cunning, baffling, and powerful, and more gets revealed. In this sense, victory over lust is progressive.

On the other hand, *in the instant of temptation*, there is absolutely no such thing as progressive victory over lust. Any rationalizations we have notwithstanding, whenever that image, that fantasy, or that memory hits, we either lust or we don't. We either drink or we don't. The intent is either there or it isn't. There's nothing progressive about it. There's no in-between. Suppressing it through will power might be considered kind of an in-between, but not really.

Suppression or repression—will-powering it—is just another avoidance technique which may be worse than consciously going ahead and lusting. Worse because in that forced ascetic denial, we think we're making it. But the lust is still there inside, building up steam. It's like saying I really want to lust, but for whatever reason, *I* will put it away. That's really not surrendering it to God. It's locking it in a cage deep within. It's another form of will power or "white-knuckling it." That's not *victory* over lust; it's merely trying to put a bridle on it, putting lust on hold. There's no freedom in suppression, only more fear. And it all lodges in the subconscious, storing up energy, only to bust out later in dreams or get expressed in other forms, such as resentment (or even self-loathing) or cross over into other addictions,

## Joy in the Impossible

such as food or TV. For the lustaholic, there's no way out of our awesome dilemma. Except the Program way of surrender to God, dying to it, and being released from it in that moment of temptation.

In AA we hear the expression, "Resentment is the number-one killer of alcoholics." With us, the killer is conning ourselves to disguise lust. Of course resentment and self-pity take a close second. (Some of us come to see that resentment is just another form of lust.) Lust is a killer in the sense that disguised or tolerated, it is responsible for failure to achieve sobriety and/or true recovery—*spiritual* death. We don't see that *"Lust kills the spirit . . .Lust kills me."*

Too often this idea that victory over lust is progressive becomes the excuse for aborting true recovery. "I'm sober so many years" equates to "I'm okay now." As though calendar sexual sobriety is the "real" sobriety. Or, as we hear so often, "Well, I'm dealing with lust the best I can; it's a goal to aim toward." Incredible justification for our status quo. As though the physical act of sexual sobriety was in itself recovery, when it's only the prerequisite for recovery—being loosed from that next temptation in freedom and joy. More often, we hear nothing at all about member lust temptations. The person who calls himself technically sober is still drinking. Missing out on true recovery. This is tragic and damages group and Fellowship unity. Continuing sexual sobriety is only the prerequisite for recovery. The recovery which our program promises is being saved *in* that next temptation, being released from its power. Instead of being self-driven or fear-driven, recovery is the victory of impossible joy.

Therefore, the first and only line of defense in a lust temptation must be a changed attitude of the mind and heart, before we even move an eyelash. *Recovery from the intent.* That's where Jesus met and overcame, and that's where victory over lust is *not* progressive. If one's attitude is a decision to give up lusting in surrender and reliance on God, that attitude will be in place before we're even tempted. Then, when hit with the image, in that first blink of an eyelash, the Shield of his presence is already in place, and we don't have to *do* anything. Victory over lust is where you *are*, where you are in your attitude with your Lust-bearer, not what you *do*. If the Shield is already in place, you don't have to *do* anything. That's where we are either saved from it or not. Victory over lust begins with the daily *decision* to give up lust to God. Deliverance in the moment of temptation follows as a consequence. (Morning and evening, I ask him to keep me sober from *every* lust. I also ask him to keep me sober *in* every lust.) We *can* do it—by not *trying* to—and bringing him into it.

**Real Recovery**
We may have this whole idea of sex addiction sobriety backwards. We need to consider and talk about this very seriously. Victory over lust is the real recovery, and continued sobriety from acting out sexually flows from that. There is no true recovery if all we're doing is not acting out. Merely not acting out only minimizes the real problem, which is *acting in*. Question: Should the persistent practice of acting in be considered sober? People are saying No. What would the Master say? *"But I say to you that every one who looks at a woman lustfully has already committed adultery with her in his heart."*

On coming into the program, most of us are mainly concerned with stopping the acting out. That's because our sobriety historically started there. That's what we thought was killing us. But once sober, we begin to see the real problem. Remember that the Program is aligned with the AA model of *not drinking*, but ours is an *internal* drug, the alcohol of the spirit. Think about it. We need to get down to the nitty-gritty basics and stop shortchanging the basic principle of recovery, *being set free from having to lust*.

## Joy in the Impossible

The Calendar Sobriety Syndrome is deadly. Someone has called it "smoke-alarm" sobriety or "so_dry_ety." I laud those who are beginning to set their dates back with a decision to stop deliberately acting in. Let's encourage and support one another in breaking through the Lust Barrier. Maybe that's our equivalent of AA's statement of "separating the men from the boys."

### It's Impossible

This is where we'll discover that true sobriety from lust by our own doing is *impossible*. This is where we're up against our real powerlessness and have no recourse but to One who can restore us to sanity in the very temptation. I wonder if it would not be better to challenge people right up front with the fact that *recovery* is impossible without victory over lust. Once we discover we're powerless over lust, let's challenge each other so we don't hide it. Let's keep bringing it into the light.

For myself today, I am absolutely powerless over lust in some form or other. But there is One, who himself is my victory over it, whenever I go through that fear of death, die to the temptation, upward to him, and bring him in, personally, savingly. *He* works! I don't have to lust.

The temptation in the sex addiction recovery movement is to open up the attitude toward sobriety, to broaden it so it isn't so "impossible." (I believe all the sex addiction recovery fellowships may be beginning to realize just how impossible true recovery is.) And opening up sobriety makes us appear to be more democratic, tolerant, and politically correct. I feel it should be the other way around, that we should make it more "impossible," so people will be forced to find their Saving connection before settling into either the Slipper Syndrome or the Calendar Sobriety Syndrome or shifting from acting out to acting in. Why not state the nature of this problem as it really is, right up front: True *recovery*—joyous victory *over* lust—is utterly

## III—Real Victory in Christ

impossible without finding God, cleaning house, and working with others. That is the distilled essence of the original Twelve Step program. Have you found God *in your lust?*

Our old-timer friend who wrote this Epistle to the Hebrews was right: Fear of dying to lust does hold us in bondage to the slavery of impossible addiction. And the longer we're in the fellowship of recovery, the clearer we see the true spiritual nature of our addiction and our utter dependence on him who *is* the Resurrection and the Life. But in each temptation—over and over again—we, you and I, must be willing to go through that fear of death *with him* that we may be raised with him out of that very temptation and discover that there really is *life after lust*

• • •

The whole point here is that **we don't have to lust at all.** We can and will be tempted—by triggers, memories, and fantasies—but we don't have to drink at all. We can have total victory over lust *in that next temptation*, which is all we ever need. **There is no victory over lust before the fact!** No silver bullet that makes us immune. The victory is in the prior attitude, before we're ever tempted, in the intents and disposition of our heart. We either have it or we don't. And it's our choice, either to serve the god of Self, the god of Lust, the lower darkness, or embrace the One who is eager and able to save us. The choice is ours. Today! The choice either to drink or to give up, die to self, die *in* that next temptation. Thus, victory over lust, our Great Impossible, becomes The Great Possible! We *can* discover and experience the expulsive power of a new affection. This is our calling, our hope, and our great joy in fellowship.

# 22

## The Personal Sacrament

We have come full-circle to the fulfillment of joy in personal recovery. He bids us take, eat, and drink of himself. As a lustaholic I must have the real sacramental presence of the living Son of man, any time, anywhere, every time, everywhere. I believe this is what our Lord was offering in John chapter 6, where he talks about eating his flesh and drinking his blood. Follow along, if you will, in your Harmony of the Gospels, where it's easier to see the scene in context.

The feeding of the five thousand is described in all four gospels. The next day, related in John 6, after they have crossed back over the lake again, everyone winds up at Capernaum, and we hear Jesus' interaction with people in the synagogue (6:59). Seeing the mass frenetic excitements of the multitudes which had finally caught up with him again, thinking they had lost him after the miraculous feeding, he tells them, "You seek me, not because you saw signs, but because you ate of the loaves and were filled." Note the word "filled." Their physical hunger was completely *satisfied*. By this lone solitary man! Here, for the first time, the miracles strike home *personally* to the basic human survival instinct of the mass—physical hunger. This has the effect of attaching the crowds to him and their wanting to stay with him in a frenzied personal kind of way. So he sets about revealing what he has to offer in our true spiritual connection with him.

He tells them, "Don't get so excited about going after physical food and satisfying your physical hunger, which will

## III—Real Victory in Christ

end; but work for, go after the food which abides unto eternal life. ***This*** is the kind of food I can give unto you. Strive to obtain it." Without hesitation they jump to ask, "What do we have to do?" "***Believe*** on me," he says. And here we get one of the keys to interpreting the New Testament Greek words *pisteuo* and *pistis*, "to believe" and "faith," words so crucial in unraveling the mess of today's religious addiction predicament. We'll see that rather than implying intellectual assent and belief as we know it today, he means something entirely different, something so non-religious, so personal and real that most of his hearers will not be able to receive it.

When he makes the condition by which eternal life is obtained to be such a direct and personal connection with himself, they ask for a sign from him such as Moses gave when he produced manna from heaven. "What are *you* going to do for us?" And he replies, "My Father gives you the true bread, which comes down out of heaven and gives *life* to men." What a promise! They respond immediately, with genuine sincerity in their plea. They sense he offers something more than they can even conceive. They've seen enough of his miracles to know that he really delivers. Intuitively, greedily, expectantly—remembering how he fed them yesterday—they cry out, "Lord, always give us this bread! Yes, something that will fix us! Just like manna from the skies. Here, kneeling at the altar right before you, we open our mouths wide. Give it to us! Give it to us ***Lord!***"

And how we identify. A religious ritual, administered by someone in authority. And we passively, submissively, receiving it. Just like he gave us the bread and fish. Yes, Yes, give it to us! Something tangible we can relate to! (If it were only that easy, and don't we sometimes act as though it were that easy?). Then he delivers the bombshell: **"*I* am the bread of life. He who comes to *me* shall not hunger, and he who believes on *me* shall never thirst. I'm not a miracle worker or just another leader like Moses; *I* am the source of life. Not physical life—*Life!* Eternal life."** The life of the

## The Personal Sacrament

spirit. The soul's life. The very life of God. The very Spirit of Life itself.

Now we get a glimpse into what "belief" really is, what being a "Christian" really is, what being a member of the body of Christ really is: "Believing in me is *coming* to me" (v.35). A movement of the spirit from self to *me*. The words "believing in me" are literally "believing *into* me." A change in direction, plus actual spiritual intercourse with the *Person*. He says, "This is the will of my Father, that everyone beholding the Son and believing into him may have life eternal, and I will raise him up at the last day." (v.40)

Now it begins to dawn on the people that something is amiss here. "He says, *he* is the bread which came down from heaven? What gives? We know his father and mother!" But they will not understand. They cannot. For "having the form of godliness" denies the power thereof. You cannot put new wine into old wineskins. Religious addiction: The ritual form of religion so conditions us that we are blind to what constitutes the real Life-Connection

So all he can do is say it again, "I am the bread of life. Eat of this bread for your spiritual life." They still can't get it. They *won't* get it. Because they don't want to even think that real life, spiritual life, life eternal, salvation, must come through personal intercourse with a person. "This can't be right; it goes against the concept of religious ritual, against our religious duty and belief. Why can't you just *do* it to us?"

So he gives it to them in a way only his true followers, the childlike pure in heart, will perceive. To others, such as those with whom he is arguing, his outlandish statements serve to "make the heart of this people dull and their ears heavy so they *cannot* hear." His words are bizarre and weird in the extreme. He says, "The bread I give is my *flesh* for the life of the world." (v. 52ff)

This really sets them off: "How can this man give us his flesh to eat?" So he does them one better: "Unless you eat the flesh of the Son of man and drink his blood, you do not

201

## III—Real Victory in Christ

have life in yourselves, you do not have the Source of life. For my flesh is true food and my blood is true drink." That does it! Many turn away. "This is a hard saying; who can hear it?"

Even his disciples murmur at this, so he explains, "It is the *spirit* that gives live; the flesh profits nothing." This is Jesus' own interpretation of what eating his flesh and drinking his blood is all about. "This is all in a spiritual sense, not physical. The Spirit gives life, my Spirit. Of course you cannot eat my flesh and drink my blood. But you can eat and drink of *me*, just as you do your lust objects. Only with this difference: I *give* you Life, and they take it from you. You must appropriate me and ingest me just like you appropriate and ingest food and drink and lover."

And who better than the lustaholic can know what it means to "drink" in a person? It's the very essence and expression of the lustaholic perversion. But in trying to be the substitute for the Real, our perversion has perverted the real. And he says, "*I* am the real." This goes along with what he says in verse 56: The "eating" and "drinking" are "abiding in me." "To eat my flesh and drink my blood means to **abide in me**—your conscious deliberate act of taking me in. It is being **personally satisfied and filled**, spiritually, just as you were satisfied and filled physically with the loaves and fishes, only infinitely more." (Remember, this was said long before the Upper Room Last Supper.)

His disciples murmur, but the Twelve seem to get it; they somehow aren't offended and understand. Peter says, "To whom shall we go; you have the words of eternal life." He understands: It is the spirit, personal union, that mediates life; the flesh is of no avail (v.63).

The point for us is that the lustaholic *must* have the real bread, the real flesh, must drink the real lifeblood of the Son-of-man-Son-of-God, the spiritual life-Source, his very own Presence. Any time, anywhere; every time, everywhere. The lustaholic's disease has created a god-hunger such that nothing but real spiritual intercourse, union, assimilation, experiencing, abiding personal Presence will satisfy. ***Satisfy! Fill!*** We are the lucky ones! We ***must*** be filled!

      Study Gal. 2:20, Rev. 3:20, and Col. 1:27 in this new light. Then pray to experience that reality.

# Part IV

# REAL FELLOWSHIP

# 23

## The Fellowship of Light

*"That which we have seen and heard we proclaim also to you, so that you may have fellowship with us; and our fellowship is with the Father and with his Son Jesus Christ. And we are writing this that our joy may be complete. . . . if we walk in the light, as he is in the light, we have fellowship with one another, and the blood of Jesus his son cleanses us from all sin."*
I John 1:3-4

John's joy was incomplete without co-fellowship with others experiencing the Father and the Son in cleansing from sin. That's another reason why I'm writing this book, so that my own joy may be fulfilled in such fellowship.

The Big Book of AA tells us that God "will show you how to create the fellowship you crave" (page 164). What fellowship do you crave?

The problem of lust/sex addiction is well described as being physical, emotional, and spiritual, and that healing has to come about in all three areas. We overlook the fact that the malady is also cultural, interpersonal and social, and that recovery must include healing here too. Recovery is not solitary; it is collective, a mutual undertaking. And increasing awareness of the self and the Savior must lead to a deeper fellowship of the Spirit. The fellowship of walking in the Light. We may or may not have this in our church or Twelve Step meetings today. I venture to say that most of us do not.

## IV—Real Fellowship

If we have it, it is a precious gift to be guarded, nourished, and passed on.[62]

Today we live in a world where our culture is the media. Just look at the amount of time we spend working alone; on the computer, reading the paper, magazines, and books; watching the news, TV, and movies; listening to radio or audio; driving, or being otherwise diverted or entertained; versus the amount of time we are sitting face-to-face talking with each other in quiet human intercourse. (This may be one reason why merely going to Twelve Step meetings, even without sobriety or recovery, is such a good feeling for so many today.) We who were obsessed with sexual intercourse have lost true intercourse of *person*. It has vanished from our world. Isolated and alone—alone in the crowd or in our own homes—we don't relate at the level of normal human intimacy.

However, with our overpowering need as the impossibly lust-addicted and misconnected, in recovery, we have the best possible opportunity for having such a fellowship as John describes:

> *That which we have seen and heard we proclaim also to you, so that you may have fellowship with us; and our fellowship is with the Father and with his Son Jesus Christ.*

Such a fellowship, with those in real Connection, is something few of us have known today. But it is there for us whenever we fulfill the conditions for its realization. This is what our souls really crave. Without it we resort to all the proliferating substitutes and means of escape, including religion, therapy, and self-help programs. Sobriety is the foundation for this; without sobriety no true fellowship is possible. We can have sociability or solidarity, maybe; unity, maybe; but can we have *fellowship* without sobriety? No. But once in sobriety, progressive recovery should awaken us to

## The Fellowship of Light

our primal need—fellowship with the Friend of sinners and with one another.

*The fellowship of light is the fellowship of sinners.* Sinners in union with the Saving One, overcoming the sin within. A fellowship of overcomers, carrying in their defective vessels the real presence of the Light of the world into our own groups and homes first, then into the lost and needy world in which we live.

**What Kind of Fellowship Do You Crave?**
Do you want a fellowship in name only, where people get together each week to "let it all hang out," where there are no clear concepts of either lust, sexual sobriety, or recovery? Is it meetings where focus of the group is inward, and self-ism and victimology are the order of the day? Is it meetings where sobriety principles may be subscribed to but are not experienced? Where people count calendar sobriety as an end in itself and are still captive to lust? Where we smile and say, "Keep coming back!" and keep supporting the illness? Is it meetings where personalities are put before principles? Or, do you want a fellowship where we walk in the Light, are sober and surrendered to God and the common good, with progressive awareness of and victory over lust and the defective self? A fellowship where the focus of the group is not inward but outward, where there is the natural impulse to carry our light to those still in bondage so the captives can be set free?

Today, we in the Christian community and also those of us in the Twelve Step addiction recovery movement, especially sex addiction recovery, need to examine—inventory, if you will—the movement itself. We need to assess the effectiveness of what we're doing and how we're doing it. We need to face the reality of failure in sex addiction recovery and work and pray together for a new beginning. We need to discover ways of improving meeting quality and safeguarding the sanctity of meetings and making

## IV—Real Fellowship

sure all of us, not just the newcomer, can have the fellowship we crave and find what our lust was really looking for.

Above all, we need to discover that real Connection, where we are no longer fear- or self-driven but moved by joy, the joy that God has forever entered our sinful human condition, has taken our sins upon himself, and now eagerly awaits, in every temptation, to embrace us in our sinfulness, take our lust upon himself, and set us free in that moment. This joy is possible, here and now, today.

# 24

## The Fellowship of Cleansing

During Jesus' last meal with his disciples (John 13:1-20), and just prior to his institution of the holy communion, he rose from supper, laid aside his garments, and girded himself with a towel. He then poured water into a basin and began to wash the disciples' feet. When he had finished and taken his garments, he resumed his place and made this incredible statement: "If I then, your Lord and Teacher, have washed your feet, you also ought to wash one another's feet. For I have given you an example, that you also should do as I have done to you." What does this mean?

Although some throughout church history have taken this rite literally, some even calling it a sacrament, it is not commonly practiced, nor has it ever gained the same status as, for example, baptism and the Eucharist. We have no New Testament evidence that foot washing was ever a ritual in the apostolic church, and most churches throughout history have made no place for it in their liturgy. There's no question as to why we should do it; it's a direct injunction of our Lord. The question is, What does it mean and how are *we* to do it?

### Is This for Us Today?
If we read the text carefully, we'll see that rather than this being some obscure practice irrelevant to us today, it represents the inner sanctum of true fellowship of those walking in the Light, without which there is no fellowship intimacy in the body of Christ.

## IV—Real Fellowship

First, we learn that the experience is a manifestation of the love of Christ: "Having loved his own who were in the world, he loved them to the end" (13:1). This experience was a love manifestation, a parable of love, a metaphor for love, an acting out of love.

Secondly, we see that this is for some kind of personal cleansing. Jesus tells Peter that if one has bathed (I take this to mean the washing of regeneration, Titus 3:5), one need only to wash his feet.

Thirdly, this washing of feet is how we serve one another, because this is how our Lord and Teacher served us (13:13-17).

Fourthly, the practice brings special blessing: "Blessed are you if you do them" (13:17).

Fifthly, the experience creates something very special—true union with one another: "If I do not wash you, you have no part in me" (13:8). That means if we do not wash one another, we have no part in each other.

And finally, no one of us is above another in this experience of cleansing and union (13:13-17). The leader is servant, and we thus become servants of one another.

This is fellowship of the most profound sort. Compared with this, look at what substitutes for it today—attending a religious "service" or attending a Twelve-step meeting, for example.

So, what is this washing which we can and should do with one another? Its inner meaning must refer not to the physical, but to cleansing of the spiritual being. Jesus made that very clear with his response to Peter. But how can one wash another's spiritual being? Let me offer my feelings on this subject by way of presenting a challenge toward deeper fellowship. There is something in what Jesus is telling us to do that is largely lost to us today. Whatever else this passage tells us, I think this washing of feet is something we can experience in fellowship. We can experience it when we identify with and take upon ourselves in love, the defects,

## The Fellowship of Cleansing

sins, and shortcomings of one another with a view to helping one another see and overcome them.

**A Sacred Responsibility**

A passage in John looks at this from another perspective:

> *"If anyone sees his brother committing what is not a mortal sin [literally "sin unto death"], he will ask, and he will give him life. . . ."* I John 5:16

Some versions read *"God* will give him life," but "God" is not in the original; the translators assumed it must be God who gives the life, but that weakens the force of the original. Avoiding the question of what is or is not mortal sin, the point here is that if we see that our brother is involved in sin, we can ask and the brother (or sister) will receive life. And this privilege and duty of ours is put in the context of the confidence we have when we pray according to God's will (verse 14). (Also, see James 5:19-20.)

> The boldness of access to God, which finds expression in prayer, finds its most characteristic expression in intercessory prayer. Fellowship with God involves fellowship with man (1:3). The energy of Christian life is from the first social. Hence St John passes naturally from the general thought of prayer to that of prayer for the brethren. And in doing this he fixes attention on the failures of Christians. These are the sorest trial of faith.
> 
> The prevailing power of intercession corresponds with the Christian revelation of the unity of the Body of Christ. When this power is exercised for others it is exercised in a true sense for ourselves, and not, arbitrarily as it were, for those apart from us. *Apostolic teaching recognizes a mysterious dependence of man upon man in the spiritual order like that which is now being shown to exist in the physical order. . .* .(emphasis mine)[63]

## IV—Real Fellowship

Yes, in the Twelve Step movement we've made a breakthrough start at rediscovering this "mysterious dependence of man upon man." And what an amazing thing this scripture teaches: by dealing specifically with another's sin, we can actually help a brother or sister. What we do can become a means of grace for another. And for ourselves! And what better context for praying for another than doing it in fellowship? The whole message of I John is set in the context of the deepest and most real of true Christian fellowship.

In the traditional Twelve Step programs, we "live and let live," being careful not to "take the inventory" of others. By this we mean we do not judge others in a rejecting way. But some seem to interpret this slogan as meaning total irresponsibility toward any shortcomings of others in the group. The Twelve Step fellowship is not the fellowship of the first epistle of John. True fellowship in the Saving One is deeper, and must be so, and thus it must deal with sin, individual sin. "If we walk in the light as he is in the light, we have fellowship with one another and the blood of Jesus his son is cleansing us from all sin" (I John 1:7). Cleansing is part of the fellowship! Walking in the light brings true fellowship, and true fellowship brings awareness and cleansing of sin.

**Real Connection**
*When we wash another's feet, we are making contact with that person at the point of their defects and sins, for that's where Jesus makes contact with us.*

When we wash one another's feet in a spiritual fellowship in our Lord's presence, we're making contact with that person at the lowest dirtiest part of them, the same place *we* need spiritual work done. We hold the feet which have trudged through the dirt and dust and muck, the very point of their defects and sins where they walk daily, because that's where Jesus makes contact with us.

## The Fellowship of Cleansing

Often, I can't see my shortcomings, but others can and do. Do they have a responsibility to me? Yes, in *fellowship*. But instead of *telling* another member their wrongs, we are to wash their feet in that matter. We make love contact with them by taking on their sin, into our hands, taking it on ourselves as though that sin is ours. That's the meaning of taking another's soiled feet in our hands. In this context, everyone's sin is mine. And we can say, "Lord, this person's sin is my sin, and I want you to forgive and cleanse this person from it." That's the attitude of love, which is the prerequisite for washing another.

If tempted to resent or reject the person, we take contrary action; we take actions *against* our feelings. We spiritually embrace the person *in* that sin of theirs, as Jesus embraces us in ours. Impossible, isn't it? But we can do it if we take the action against our feeling in the spirit of our Lord. We take their dirtiness in our hands, upon our spirits. We open ourselves to their defect. Whereas telling someone what's wrong with them alienates us, making contact with their defect or shortcoming in this way draws us together. *We identify*, and it makes us one. The power of love is born and realized when we identify and unite with another's sin. This is a calling, a high calling. But it's the prerequisite for the real fellowship we must have.

"If I do not wash you, you have no part in me." These words are some of the most profound our Lord ever spoke. If I do not serve you in cleansing, by embracing and confronting in you what I have been given to see, or if you do not so serve me, we have no part in each other. We can be friends, fellow-workers, even husband and wife, but yet have no part *in* each other. Having a part in each other is the "real connection" we talk about. It is true fellowship, the deepest possible intercourse of persons. Not easy, and loaded with the liabilities of our egos!

## IV—Real Fellowship

We can't bathe the whole person; only the Lord can do that. But we can be true to what we see in the defiling walk of one another and bring that to the Light for washing. Otherwise, his or her defilement can defile or compromise our fellowship, for light cannot fellowship with darkness. This experience is largely lost to us today because we've lost the consciousness of sin in ourselves and the imperative of cleansing in fellowship. "Bear one another's burdens and so fulfill the law of Christ." Yes, we—you and I—are to fulfill the work of Christ, the Christ principle, in fellowship! An incredible challenge for us today.

But such a fellowship as Jesus enjoins can only be experienced among persons who are already bathed, people who have already made the saving connection with the Son of man. "For what partnership have righteousness and iniquity? Or what fellowship has light with darkness" (2 Cor. 6:14). That's why we seldom have such fellowship in traditional Twelve Step meetings (or in church), because this requires more than mere sobriety. It requires willingness to *recover* and longing for real fellowship with others hungering after righteousness and real connection with the Son of man.

And note that Jesus' washing of his disciples' feet came *before* they actually partook together of the Lord's Supper. Very important. John makes a special point of this in 13:1: "Now before the feast of the Passover...." We need to take heed, lest we partake of that Communion unworthily and drink judgment upon ourselves (I Cor. 11:27-32). We need to look seriously at the connection between these two sacraments. We're missing something here.

**Real Servanthood**

By the time of this supper, Jesus had come to full realization of his identity and authority (13:3). Fully realizing his lordship status, Jesus kneels before each disciple and performs the service of a slave, washing the dirt from their very feet. Yes, there is something lacking or "left over" to us

## The Fellowship of Cleansing

in Christ's work for his body (Col. 1:24). Jesus is no longer here to do it in person; are not we, the members of his Body, the only ones left to serve one another as he did in this?

What did Jesus feel as he took their feet in his hands, knowing in himself what he was really doing, taking their sin and incompleteness onto himself? He was identifying, drawing out his soul to each, opening himself to the weakest and lowest in them. Taking them into himself, just as they were.

I find that I can better make contact with this love of Christ toward another if I too make some gentle contact, such as touching the arm while looking into their eyes. Saying something at a distance seems to kill rather than build up. For me, touching the person breaks the unreality in my mind, breaks the barrier between me and seeing their defects, breaks down my resistance to what I'm seeing. And that touch triggers the love which I do not have. In that way I can take them in.

When the Lord comes up to Simon Peter and tries to do this, Peter recoils: "Hey! You'll never wash my feet!" Did he pull away from the physical touch, or did he sense there was something deeper going on? Peter's is the same reaction I have when persons confront me with my defects. My immediate instinct is to recoil defensively. Don't touch *me*! But when I get past that initial stage of shock at having to look in the mirror of truth and sense there may be something I haven't seen before, as from the Lord but coming from another sinner, I can surrender to the willingness to see the truth about myself, especially if that person gives me the touch of identification and kindness.

### Nobody Said It Would Be Easy

This is never easy! Most often, I get such encounters from those I would never have chosen. Never. Perhaps that's why our Lord says what he does in 13:20: "Truly, truly I say to you, he who receives any one whom I send receives me; and

## IV—Real Fellowship

he who receives me receives him who sent me." Now that is heavy. You won't believe some of the people he's sent to me to help me see myself! That's how this apparently disconnected statement of Jesus connects with the foot washing scene. It's not to be our choice who deals with us in this washing; we accept it as though Jesus were there kneeling before us. And, wonder of wonders, when we do so receive this love-connection from another, we discover that we are receiving Jesus himself! "As ye have done it unto one of the least of these, ye have done it unto me." Incredible!

We will not do this perfectly, especially at first. And of course such a practice is fraught with danger, especially with recovering addicts and our load of emotional and spiritual liabilities. This is definitely not for everyone! Unsober, unsurrendered egos, not open to the Spirit and love of Jesus, would wreak havoc here. That's the beauty of doing this together, in fellowship. One-on-one, our own defects and motivations are suspect and can come into play destructively, especially since we are so self-obsessed. But when we are within that circle and are all open to the Light, there's a moderating influence present so that we are safeguarded from what otherwise might be tendencies toward resentment, judgmentalism, rejection, and an unforgiving or punishing spirit.

The size of such a group is an important factor in the quality of meetings. Experience has shown that when a group gets larger than perhaps a dozen, the dynamic changes, and intimacy begins to be compromised. Another important factor is regular attendance. There can be no spiritual unity such as we long for where members are not committed to one another and the group. If you're not there, you're not *a part of*. If you show up only occasionally, you can be a divisive factor. Your spirit is not one with the group.

I find it very striking—and this will knock you over—that Judas Iscariot, the man who betrayed him, was still with the disciples when Jesus washed their feet (John 13).

## The Fellowship of Cleansing

Jesus must have washed his too! However, Judas is not present during the memorial breaking of bread and drinking of the cup, which follows. Satan enters Judas during that meal, and he leaves to betray Jesus after Jesus had washed his feet. There's a very powerful lesson here—frightening. We can expect that there are and probably always will be those in our fellowship who are not one with our Lord, yet our Lord is touching them too. But for them it becomes a judgement instead of a fellowship of cleansing. Does this mean we are to wash their feet too? Apparently. We are responsible for taking right actions toward one another; we are not responsible for their condition and their wrongs. Not easy! It takes the grace of God and the love of God in a fellowship of light.

To sum up this idea of a cleansing, helping fellowship, we can do no better than affirm this passage from God's word to his people:

> Brethren, if a man is overtaken in any trespass, you who are spiritual should restore him in a spirit of gentleness. Look to yourself, lest you too be tempted. Bear one another's burdens, and so fulfill the law of Christ. For if any one thinks he is something, when he is nothing, he deceives himself. But let each one test his own work. . . .
>
> Galatians 6:1-4

*This* is washing one another's feet.

Finally, a caution: There can be no cleansing fellowship as Jesus instituted if the majority of members have not experienced the bathing of regeneration which brings them into real union with the Body of Christ. Such a situation would be fraught with all sorts of problems. And of course, it goes without saying that sobriety is a given.

*IV—Real Fellowship*

Such cleansing fellowship as Jesus intended brings joy because it is actually helping us and others. It is exposing and healing. And the Lord is actually there! Isn't that what we've always wanted, the fellowship our hearts crave?

And yet there is more. Such a fellowship of cleansing is what truly prepares us for bearing joyous witness to the resurrection in the fellowship of harvest.

# 25

## The Fellowship of Harvest

There is no *fulfillment* of our joy if it does not flow outward to others.

While writing chapters 23 and 24 (I believe that was 1992), I opened the little book, *My Utmost for His Highest*, to the October 16th reading and was struck with the utter timeliness of the text, as though I were being guided: *"Pray ye therefore the Lord of the harvest, that He will send forth labourers into His harvest"* (KJV). I read again this marvelous passage in Matthew 9:35-38, one which has been arresting me for quite some time. When Jesus saw the people gathering about to see and hear him, "he had compassion for them, because they were harassed and helpless, like sheep without a shepherd." The connotation is of sheep lying about prostrate, helpless, and vulnerable, with no one to lead them. That's the condition of the multitudes drawing forth our Lord's compassion in the days of his flesh. How he must be feeling about our situation now! Is there any personal, familial, social, or cultural pain and anguish greater than that which is felt by and from the multitudes in lust/sex slavery today, even among our own members?

How our Lord must suffer seeing the multitudes in the religious institutions and in the sex addiction and other recovery organizations "prostrate and helpless." With their deeper hunger for God going unfulfilled. The message keeps coming through that lust and sex addiction are in epidemic proportions in the *Christian* community, and in the clergy. In the recovery movement, what very low percentages of men and women are staying sexually sober, and how few among these are gaining victory over lust and misconnection! Where

## IV—Real Fellowship

is the promised recovery?! Our unwitting support of the illness cries out for remedy. Where is the remedy? What do we do? What would the Master say?

Our Lord's response today is as simple and clear as it was then. We don't engage in any great enterprises or new movements. We don't try to "make it happen." We simply do what he told us to do: We pray to the Lord of harvest that he send laborers into his harvest. That was his command then; it must be his command now, as always. But he says "pray *ye* ." Plural! That means we pray together!

I am more convinced than ever that we sober ones in true recovery who are called to follow this Son of man must obey him even in this. That we get together and take actions of obedience to our Lord's injunction. That for and out of our own continued recovery we follow him for the needs of the broken and bound still out there. This means that we not cease attending our own program meetings lest we separate ourselves from where the front-line action is, where sinners like us are coming in, and where God is meeting us in power, victory, and life—if indeed that be so. But it also means that we shift the focus outward, away from contemplating our navels in self-centered individual and group narcissism and shift focus out onto those still suffering and needy. And pray the Lord of harvest that *he* send laborers into his harvest. And then actually follow him out there and do it!

But there can be no *fellowship* of harvest ingathering as our Lord sees it without a *fellowship* of victory over lust in the inner person, a *fellowship* of mutual cleansing, and a *fellowship* of union together in him. Proof of the real spiritual awakening as the result of the Steps automatically brings with it the impulse of life from within going out to others in need. We either have it or we don't. If we have it, nothing can stop that message of our redeemed life from flowing out to the lost. But if we don't have that awakening, no amount Program or writing or organization can save us or our world from lust. But if his life is manifest in fellowship in victory

*The Fellowship of Harvest*

over lust and self and mutual cleansing, then nothing can prevent such a harvest. That's a big IF.

Where is this Life manifest among us today? If and when it comes about, it will be focused not inward on the self, but outward, flowing out to the lost, because that's where He will be doing what he came to do and has always been doing, seeking and saving the lost. If and when this happens, we'll know it because we can't make it happen from the outside in. It will happen from the inside out and nothing can prevent it. Such an awakening will be the outward manifestation, the evidence of real recovery, a recovery which glorifies the risen Son of man.

I look forward in hope to such a time of blessing and joy, of God's power in our midst, enabling us to prevail for others in fellowship what we seem incapable of now. It would make Christ's work our work, and once again we would have the power of his presence in seeking and saving the lost—our lost. Only a short time after Jesus came again to his disciples in that powerful upper room experience (Acts 2:4), we see them in that glorious harvest time of ingathering, in their testimony, and in the breaking of bread together in their homes with glad and generous hearts (Acts 2:46). And in prevailing and seeking and saving the lost. This was their new beginning. Pray God it will be ours.

*Even so, come soon into our midst, Lord Jesus.*

# APPENDIXES

# Appendix 1

# Notes on Jesus' Identification with our Fallen Human Nature

> *Everything in the world is more or less misunderstood at first: we have to learn what it is, and come at length to see that it must be so, that it could not be otherwise. Then we know it; and we never know a thing really until we know it thus.*
> The opening lines to George MacDonald's sermon, "Salvation from Sin"

The first author I happened across who supported the view of Jesus' humanity as I have come to see it was the late Swiss theologian Karl Barth (1886-1968), who, though a contemporary and controversial in some areas, has already been ranked with Augustine, Aquinas, and Calvin. (I don't believe in arbitrarily limiting one's sources to those belonging to one school or another. If everyone in church history had believed and taught exactly the same, there would have been no progress in understanding revelation. We continue to learn through the many-faceted experiences and ideas of those who have gone before.) Barth also cites certain nineteenth and twentieth century reformed theologians before him who held this view, men "pilloried for considering Christ as adopting a fallen nature."[64] Such men challenged the traditional reluctance on this issue: Gottfried Menken, (1812), Edward Irving (1827), H.F. Kohlbrugge (1844), J.C.K. v. Hofmann (1852), Edward Bohl (1887), H. Bezzel (1925), and others. Excerpts from Barth and some of these

## Appendix 1

others quoted in Barth follow. (See his *Church Dogmatics* I/2 pages 132-171 for a full discussion of the theology and history of the doctrine of Jesus' identification with our fallen human nature, especially pages 147-158.) Quoting these and other authors here does not imply endorsement for everything they say; they should be read critically.

"The deeper we can fetch Christ into the flesh, the better it is" (p. 149).

"He is a man as we are, equal to us as a creature, as a human individual, but also equal to us in the state and condition into which our disobedience has brought us" (p. 151).

"The 'Word' is not only the eternal Word of God but 'flesh' as well, i.e., all that we are and exactly like us even in our opposition to Him. It is because of this that He makes contact with us and is accessible for us" (p. 151).

"He bore innocently what Adam and all of us in Adam have been guilty of. Freely He entered into solidarity and necessary association with our lost existence" (p. 152).

". . . It was a human nature such as was in Adam after the Fall and is in all his successors" (p.154, Gottfried Menken, 1812).

"God has adopted a lost humanity, sinful men and women. . . . Hence it is a God-deriding enterprise of the flesh to aim at raising itself up to God by its own power and wisdom and righteousness . . ." (p.154, H.F. Kohlbrugge, 1844).

"Either the Son of God brings salvation to pass under conditions of life like ours or else everyone has to start all over again and to fulfill independently God's claims upon us" (p. 155, Edward Bohl, 1887).

"Our unholy human existence, assumed and adopted by the Word of God, is a hallowed and therefore a sinless human existence; in our unholy human existence the eternal Word draws near to us" (p. 156).

"The point is that . . . Jesus did not run away from the state and situation of fallen man, but took it upon Himself, lived it and bore it Himself as the eternal Son of God. How could He have done so, if in His human existence He had not been exposed to real inward temptation and trial, if like other men He had not trodden an inner path, if He had not cried to God and wrestled with God in real inward need? It was in this wrestling, in which He was in solidarity with us to the uttermost, that there was done that which is not done by us, the will of God" (p. 158).

• • •

The following comments are from Vincent P. Branick's article, "The Sinful Flesh of the Son of God (Rom 8:3): A Key Image of Pauline Theology," *Catholic Biblical Quarterly*, 47, 1985, pages 246 - 262:

"Contemporary christology has shown great interest in the humanity of Jesus. . . ." (p. 246).

"If Christ comes [in the likeness of sinful flesh], he comes as the full expression of that sinful flesh. He manifests it for what it is" (p. 250).

"When Paul speaks of Christ's 'sinful flesh,' he is thus pointing to a dimension which is more 'cosmic' than ethical, expressing especially the *situation* of Christ" (p. 251).

"The intensity of the anti-God aspect of [flesh] in Romans 8 is clear. . . . This is the sinful flesh of which Christ is the full manifestation. This is the sinful flesh that unites him with humanity in its sinfulness" (p. 252).

"For our theological perspective, we see sin as an action of the created person contradicting the law and love of God. We ask if such sin could be said of Christ, the incarnate Son of God, and we conclude with the rest of the NT that Jesus was absolutely sinless" (p. 256-7).

"But flesh, sin, and death are more than the individual's personal problems. They reflect and are part of

*Appendix 1*

a cosmic . . . perversion. For Paul, the individual [and hence presumably Christ] is affected as being part of this perversion" (p. 257). "As related to Christ, the terms [sin and flesh] express above all the objective, larger-than-human, the corrupting, anti-God power-sphere of unredeemed existence . . . . This cosmic sense of [sin and flesh] thus leaves room for the affirmation of Christ as sinless in an ethical, personal sense" (p. 261).

"Paul is making the point that Jesus was really subject to the power of sin and died 'for its sake,' 'under its claim'" (p. 259).

"It is the resurrection, then, that makes palatable the image of Christ as an expression of sinful flesh or as sin itself" (p. 259).

"Above all we see a Jesus who began his ministry by undergoing the rite of baptism. The beloved Son of the Father appears first of all in this ritual for sinners. He was not like the recognized pure and pious people of his day" (p. 261).

• • •

The following comments are from Florence Morgan Gillman's article, "Another Look at Romans 8:3: 'In the Likeness of Sinful Flesh,'" *Catholic Biblical Quarterly*, 49, 1987, pages 597 - 604:

"For Paul to intimate full congruence between Christ and sinful flesh, therefore, is to focus not on Christ in terms of personal sin but on his full sharing in human existence. . . . Thus, while one may speak of Christ's involvement in humanity's unredeemed existence, room is left for affirming Christ as sinless in a personal sense" (pp. 602-3).

"[Sinful flesh] does not signify *guilty* man, but man in his *fallenness*—man subject to temptation, to human appetites and desires, to death" (p. 603).

"[Paul's statement of Christ being in the form of sinful flesh affirms] that Christ was involved in the same power sphere of unredeemed existence as other humans, that he bore the identical sin-prone flesh that all humans have" (p. 604).

• • •

The following is from James D.G. Dunn's commentary on Romans in *Word Biblical Commentary*:
". . . God achieved his purpose for man not by scrapping the first effort [Adam and his Fall] and starting again, but by working through man in his fallenness, letting sin and death exhaust themselves in this man's flesh, and remaking him beyond death as a progenitor and enabler of a life [according to the Spirit]. Hence whatever the precise force of the [likeness], it must include the thought of Jesus' complete identification with 'sinful flesh' (cf. NEB: 'the same human nature as any sinner'). . . ." (Word Books, 1988, vol. 38, p. 421).

I add here a statement of F. J. A. Hort (of the historic Greek New Testament team of Westcott and Hort) from his *The Way the Truth the Life:* "His [Jesus'] own nature must be so inwardly at one with the nature of man, and of every world in which man can move. . . ." (p. 53). And I ask, How can Christ can be the Vine and we sinners the branches (John 15) is if he does not have our same sin-controlled nature?

• • •

An examination of the creeds of Christendom not only shows little testimony against this view of the nature of Jesus' humanity, but I think goes a long way in supporting it. Of the scores of creedal statements of every sort, from earliest to modern times, I find only the Irish Articles of Religion of 1615 (and possibly the Confession of the Free-Will Baptists of 1868) specifically contrary: "Christ, in the truth of our nature, was made like unto us in all things—sin only excepted—from which he was clearly void, both in his life

*Appendix 1*

and in his nature."[65] (One might ask what is the "truth" of our human nature if it is void of sinfulness?)

I see the following as supporting the view I have taken in this book: Origen of Alexandria (AD 230) said Jesus "took a body like our body, *differing in this point only*, that it was born of the Virgin and the Holy Ghost."[66] The Symbol of Chalcedon of 451 states Jesus was "consubstantial with us according to the manhood; *in all things like unto us*, without sin. . . ."[67] The Athanasian creed has the interesting statement, "Equal to the Father, as touching his Godhead: and *inferior to the Father as touching his Manhood*."[68] (Emphases mine.)

Question 16 in the historic reformed Heidelberg Catechism of 1563 deals with the nature of Jesus and asks the dual question why he must be both true and sinless man. The answer to why Jesus must be "true man" reads, "Because the justice of God requires that *the same human nature which has sinned should make satisfaction for sin*" (emphasis mine).

A survey of other creedal formulations reveals the following key expressions:

- The Augsburg Confession, Luther's Small Catechism, and the Formula of Concord: "man's nature," "true man," "our brother"[69]
- The French Confession of Faith, 1559: "has put on our flesh" . . . man, like unto us, capable of suffering in body and soul . . . the true seed of Abraham and David"[70]
- The Scotch Confession of Faith, 1560: "very God and very man . . . . the veritie of his humaine nature"[71]
- The Thirty-Nine Articles of the Church of England, 1571 and 1801: "took man's nature . . . of her [Mary's] substance . . . . very God, and very man"[72]
- The Canons of the Synod of Dort, 1619: "really man"[73]
- The Westminster Confession of Faith, 1647: "take

- upon him man's nature, with all the essential properties and common infirmities thereof"[74]
- Congregational Union of England and Wales, 1833: "partaking fully and truly of human nature"[75]
- Easter Litany of the Moravian Church, 1749: "was tempted in all points like as we are"[76]
- Methodist Articles of Religion, 1784: "took man's nature . . . very God and very man"[77]
- Articles of Religion of the Reformed Episcopal Churches in America, 1875: "took man's nature . . . very God and very man"[78]
- The Second Helvetic Confession, 1566: "The flesh of Christ, therefore, was neither flesh in show only, nor yet flesh brought from heaven . . . . the same substance with us, and 'in all points tempted like as we are, yet without sin'"[79]
- American Congregational Statement of Faith, 1883: "who was tempted like other men"[80]
- The Presbyterian Church of England, 1890: "became man by taking to Himself a true body and soul"[81]
- Brief Statement of the Reformed Faith, 1902: "became truly man"[82]
- The Basis of Union of the United Church of Canada, 1925: "became truly man."[83]

It should be noted that in most of these statements, such expressions of true humanity were followed by a qualification such as "without sin," which obviously refers to the fact that even being "very man," Jesus did not sin, which is the view I have taken.

The only Christian ecclesiastical body I am aware of which makes Jesus' fallen human nature an explicit article of faith is the Catholic Apostolic Church, also called Irvingites. Edward Irving (1792-1834), former Presbyterian minister of Scotch Calvinistic persuasion, was the pioneer of this body, which apparently still exists today. Irving made special

*Appendix 1*

account of the incarnation and humanity of Jesus (published in 1830), "maintaining that he assumed our *fallen*, i.e., temptable, mortal, corruptible nature, yet without sin itself, into complete fellowship with his divine person." The body of Christians who call themselves the Catholic Apostolic Church teach that "by being born of a mother of the fallen race, he [Jesus] took the common nature of man, with all its infirmities, burdens, and liabilities, so that he could be tempted in all points like as we are, and be dealt with in all things by the Father as the representative of mankind."[84]

• • •

Thus, as Brooke Foss Westcott says, "Scripture is wholly free from that Docetism—that teaching of an illusory manhood of Christ—which, both within the church and without it, tends to destroy the historic character of the Gospel."[85]

I hope there is indeed "great interest in the humanity of Jesus" today (Branick, above). It is no accident that such interest is relatively recent, considering this is the period when the industrial, scientific, and reality revolutions were escalating in earnest, inaugurating our modern predicament (see my *Lust Virus*). And now, with the advent of our addictive culture, it is not only appropriate but evidence of the marvel of God's grace and love, that we lust and sex addicts and relational misconnects can and *must* have a personal Savior who can identify with and actually come into our sin and take it onto himself so we can be free and clean.

## Appendix 2

## Parable for a Lustaholic

The following is taken from George MacDonald's story of the captive, found in his *Gifts of the Child Christ*, vol 1, pages 10ff (William B. Eerdmans, Grand Rapids, 1973). Originally written in 1878, the story recounts how a runaway boy, taken into the home of a wise old man, comes upon a marvelous scene in that enchanted place:

... [I]n the middle of [the dungeon] upon the floor, sat a prisoner, with fetters to his feet, and manacles to his hands; an iron collar was round his neck, and a chain from the collar had its last link in an iron staple deep-fixed in the stone floor. His head was sunk on his bosom, and he sat abject and despairing.

... [T]he man lifted his head, and his look caught and held him [the boy]. For he saw a pale, worn, fierce countenance, which, somehow, through all the added years, and all the dirt that defiled it, he recognized as his own. For a moment the prisoner gazed at him mournfully; then a wild passion of rage and despair seized him; he dragged and tore at his chains, raved and shrieked, and dashed himself on the ground like one mad with imprisonment. For a time he lay exhausted, then half rose and sat as before, gazing helplessly upon the ground.

By and by a spider came creeping along the bar of his fetters. He put out his hand, and, with the manacle on his wrist, crushed it, and smiled. Instantly through the gloom came a strong, clear, yet strangely sweet voice—and the very sweetness had in it something that made the boy think of fire. And the voice said:

## Appendix 2

"So! in the midst of misery, thou takest delight in destruction! Is it not well thou are chained? If thou was free, thou wouldst in time destroy the world. Tame thy wild beast, or sit there till I tame him."

The prisoner peered and stared through the dusk, but could see no one; he fell into another fit of furious raving, but not a hair-breadth would one link of chain yield to his wildest endeavor.

"Oh, my mother!" he cried, as he sank again into the grave of exhaustion.

"Thy mother is gone from thee," said the voice, "outworn by thine evil ways. Thou didst choose to have thyself and not thy mother, and there thou hast thyself, and she is gone. I only am left to care for thee—not with kisses and sweet words, but with a dungeon. Unawares to thyself, thou has forged thine own chains and riveted them upon thy limbs. Not Hercules could free thee or himself from such imprisonment."

The man burst out weeping, and cried with sobs: "What then am I to do, for the burden of them is intolerable?"

"What I will tell thee," said the voice; "for so shall thy chains fall from thee."

"I will do it," said the man.

"Thy prison is foul," said the voice.

"It is," answered the prisoner.

"Cleanse it then."

"How can I cleanse it when I cannot move?"

"Cannot move! Thy hands were upon thy face a moment gone—and now they are upon the floor! Near one of those hands lies a dead mouse; yonder is an open window. Cast the dead thing out into the furnace of life, that it may speedily make an end thereof."

With sudden obedient resolve the prisoner made the endeavor to reach it. The chain pulled the collar hard, and the manacle wrenched his wrist; but he caught the dead thing by the tail, and with a fierce effort threw it; out of the window it flew and fell—and the air of his dungeon seemed already clearer.

After a silence, came the voice again:

"Behind thee lies a broom," it said; "reach forth and take it, and sweep around thee as far as thy chains will yield thee scope."

The man obeyed, and, as he swept, at every stroke he reached farther. At length—how it came he could not tell, for his chains hung heavy upon him still—he found himself sweeping the very foot of the walls.

A moment more, and he stood at the open window, looking out into the world. A dove perched upon the window-sill, and walked inquiringly in; he caught it in his hands, and looked how to close the window, that he might secure its company. Then came the voice:

"Wilt thou, a prisoner, make of thyself a jailer?"

He opened his hands, and the dove darted into the sunlight. There it fluttered and flashed for a moment, like a bird of snow; then reentered, and flew into his very hands. He stroked and kissed it. The bird went and came, and was his companion.

Still, his chains hung about him, and he sighed and groaned under their weight.

"Set thee down," said the voice, "and polish thine irons."

He obeyed, rubbing link against link busily with his hands. And thus he labored—as it seemed to the boy in the vision—day after day, until at last every portion within his reach, of fetter, and chain, and collar, glittered with brightness.

"Go to the window," then said the voice, "and lay thee down in the sunshine."

He went and lay down, and fell asleep. When he awoke, he began to raise himself heavily; but, lo! the sun had melted all the burnished parts of his bonds, the rest dropped from him, and he sprang to his feet. For very joy of lightness, he ran about the room like a frolicking child.

Then said the voice once more:

"Now carve thee out of the wall the figure of a man, as perfect as thou canst think and make it."

*Appendix 2*

"Alas!" said the prisoner to himself, "I know not how to carve or fashion the image of anything."

But as he said it, he turned with a sigh to find among the fragments of his fetters what piece of iron might best serve him for a chisel. To work he set, and many and weary were the hours he wrought, for his attempts appeared to him nothing better than those of a child, and again and ever again as he carved, he had to change his purpose, and cut away what he had carved; for the thing he wrought would not conform itself to the thing he thought, and it seemed he made no progress in the task that was set him. But he did not know that it was because his thought was not good enough to give strength and skill to his hand, that it seemed too good for his hand to follow.

One night he wrought hard by the glimmer of his wretched lamp, until, overwearied, he fell fast asleep, and slept like one dead. When he awoke, lo! a man of light, lovely and grand, who stood where he had been so wearily carving the unresponsive stone! He rose and drew nigh. Behold, it was an opening in the wall, through which his freedom shone! The man of light was the door into the universe. And he darted through the wall.

• • •

Each of us can translate this parable for ourselves, it is so apt an illustration of our work with the Steps. Does painfully burnishing each link of the chain sound familiar? Everywhere in this marvelous story I see intimations and reflections of our own journey into recovery and freedom. Especially since ours is a program of *action*, and that action is the key, the magic chisel that carves away the prison wall of our stony hearts. That action is the obedience of faith, obedience to the One who loved us and gave himself up for us.

## Appendix 3

## "The Remission of Sins," by George MacDonald

I can think of no author who has helped reveal a greater consciousness of the love of God to me than George MacDonald. See his *The Hope of the Gospel*, first published in 1892, and his *Unspoken Sermons* (Series One, Two, and Three). That consciousness is reflected in the spirit of MacDonald himself, which comes through in his writings. C. S. Lewis has said, "I know hardly any other writer who seems to be closer, or more continually close, to the Spirit of Christ Himself." (From the Preface to *George MacDonald: An Anthology*.) If this book does nothing more than introduce the reader to MacDonald, I will give thanks to God.

I would like to share with you a passage from MacDonald that was very helpful to me. First published in its original form in 1892 in his *The Hope of the Gospel*, this is a condensation of Chapter 2 of that book, "The Remission of Sins," edited by Rolland Hein and published in 1974 by Harold Shaw Publishers, Wheaton, Illinois, under the title *Life Essential*.

Reprinted by permission of the publisher

[Note: MacDonald understands "repentance for the forgiveness of sins" to mean, literally, "repentance unto the *sending away* of sins." The Greek word translated "forgiveness" can have both connotations.]

*Appendix 3*

## The Remission of Sins

*"John the baptizer appeared in the wilderness, preaching a baptism of repentance for the forgiveness of sins."*

Mark 1:4

God and man must combine for salvation from sin, and the same word, here and elsewhere translated *remission* [i.e., in the KJV; forgiveness in the RSV], seems to be employed in the New Testament for the share of both in the great deliverance. Both God and man send away sins, but in the one case God sends away the sins of the man, and in the other the man sends away his own sins. That the phrase here intends repentance unto the ceasing from sin, the giving up of what is wrong, I will try to show at least probable.

**Prepare the Way of the Lord**
In the first place, the user of the phrase either defines the change of mind he means as one that has for its object the pardon of God, or as one that reaches to a new life: the latter seems to me the more natural interpretation by far. The kind and scope of the repentance or change, and not any end to be gained by it, appears intended. The change must be one of will and conduct—a radical change of life on the part of the man: he must repent—that is, change his mind—not to a different opinion, not even to a mere betterment of his conduct—not to anything less than a sending away of sins.

Next, in St. Matthew's gospel, the Baptist's buttressing argument, or imminent motive for the change he is pressing upon the people, is that the kingdom of heaven is at hand: "Because the King of heaven is coming, you must give up your sinning." The same argument for immediate action lies in his quotation from Isaiah: "Prepare ye the way of the Lord; make straight in the desert a highway for your God." The only true, the only possible preparation for the coming Lord, is to cease from doing evil, and begin to do well—to send away sin.

## "The Remission of Sins"

Again, observe that, when the Pharisees came to John, he said to them, "Bear fruits that befit repentance": is not this the same as, "Repent unto the sending away of your sins"?

Note also, that, when the multitudes came to the prophet, and all—along with the classes most obnoxious to the rest, the publicans and the soldiers—asked what he would have them do, his instruction was throughout in the same direction: they must send away their sins, and each must begin with the fault that lay next to him. The kingdom of heaven was at hand; they must prepare the way of the Lord by beginning to do as must be done in His kingdom.

They could not rid themselves of their sins, but they could set about sending them away; they could quarrel with them, and proceed to turn them out of the house: the Lord was on His way to do His part in their final banishment. Those who had repented to the sending away of their sins, He would baptize with a holy power to send them away indeed. The operant will to get rid of them would be baptized with a fire that should burn them up.

I think, then, that the part of the repentant man, and not the part of God, in sending away of sins, is intended here. It is the man's one preparation for receiving the power to overcome them, the baptism of fire.

**Real Existence**
Not seldom, what comes in the name of the gospel of Jesus Christ must seem, even to one not far from the kingdom of heaven, no good news at all. It does not draw him; it wakes in him not a single hope. He has no desire after what it offers him as redemption. The God it gives him news of is not one to whom he would draw nearer. But when such a man comes to see that the very God must be his life, the heart of his consciousness; when he perceives that, rousing himself to put from him what is evil, and do the duty that lies at his door, he may fearlessly claim the help of Him who "loved him into being," then his will immediately sides with his conscience; he begins to try to be; and—first thing toward being—to rid himself of what is antagonistic to all

*Appendix 3*

being, namely, *wrong*.

Multitudes will not even approach the appalling task, the labor and pain of being. God is doing His part, is undergoing the mighty toil of an age-long creation, endowing men with power to be; but few as yet are those who take up their part, who respond to the call of God, who will to be, who put forth a divine effort after real existence. To the many the spirit of the prophet cries, "Turn ye, and change your way! The kingdom of heaven is near you. Let your King possess His own. Let God throne Himself in you, that His liberty be your life, and you free men. That He may enter, clear the house for Him. Send away the bad things out of it. Depart from evil, and do good. The duty that lieth at thy door, do it, be it great or small."

For indeed in this region there is no great or small. "Be content with your wages," said the Baptist to the soldiers. To many people now, the word would be, "Rule your temper"; or "Be courteous to all"; or, "Let each hold the other better than himself", or, "Be just to your neighbor that you may love him." We must bestir ourselves in the very spot on which we stand.

[*Author:* This bestiring of ourselves in the very spot we stand is what the man in the dungeon had to do before he could go free. And for lustaholics, what does repentance unto the sending away of sin mean? For you and me—today? Will we send away sin in that next lust, resentment, and fear temptation? We send it away by bringing him into it.]

**Understanding Christ's Baptism**
We shall now, perhaps, be able to understand the relation of the Lord Himself to the baptism of John.

He came to John to be baptized; and most would say John's baptism was of repentance for the remission or pardon of sins. But the Lord could not be baptized for the remission of sins, for He had never done a selfish, an untrue, or an unfair thing. He needed no forgiveness; there was nothing to forgive. No more could He be baptized for repentance: in Him repentance would have been to turn to

## "The Remission of Sins"

evil! Where, then, was the propriety of His coming to be baptized by John, and insisting on being by him baptized? It must lie elsewhere.

If we take the words of John to mean "the baptism of repentance unto the sending away of sins"; and if we bear in mind that in His case repentance could not be, inasmuch as what repentance is necessary to bring about in man was already existent in Jesus; then, altering the words to fit the case, and saying, "the baptism of willed devotion to the sending away of sin," we shall see at once how the baptism of Jesus was a thing right and fit.

That he had no sin to repent of, was not because He was so constituted that He could not sin if He would; it was because, of His own will and judgement, He sent sin away from Him—sent it from Him with the full choice and energy of His nature. God knows good and evil [Gen. 3:22], and, blessed be His name, chooses good. Never will His righteous anger make Him unfair to us, make Him forget that we are dust. Like Him, His Son also chose good, and in that choice resisted all temptation to help His fellows otherwise than as their and His Father would.

Instead of crushing the power of evil by divine force; instead of compelling justice and destroying the wicked; instead of making peace on earth by rule of a perfect prince; instead of gathering the children of Jerusalem under His wings whether they would or not, and saving them from the horrors that anguished His prophetic soul—He let evil work its will while it lived; He contented himself with the slow unencouraging ways of help essential; making men good; casting out, not merely controlling Satan; carrying to their perfect issue on earth the old primeval principles because of which the Father honored Him: "You love righteousness and hate wickedness. Therefore God, your God, has anointed you with the oil of gladness above your fellows."

To love righteousness is to make it grow, not to avenge it; and to win for righteousness the true victory, He, as well as His brethren, had to send away evil. Throughout His life on earth, He resisted every impulse to work more

*Appendix 3*

rapidly for a lower good—strong, perhaps, when He saw old age and innocence and righteousness trodden under foot.

What but this gives any worth of reality to the temptation in the wilderness, to the devil's departing from Him for a season, to his coming again to experience a like failure: Ever and ever, in the whole attitude of His being, in His heart always lifted up, in His unfailing readiness to pull with the Father's yoke, He was repelling, driving away sin—away from Himself, and, as Lord of men, and their savior, away from others also, bringing them to abjure it like Himself.

No man, least of all any lord of men, can be good without willing to be good, without setting himself against evil, without sending away sin. . . . Therefore is the stand against sin common to the Captain of salvation and the soldiers under Him.

**The Holy War**
What did Jesus come into the world to do? The will of God in saving His people from their sins—not from the punishment of their sins, that blessed aid to repentance, but from their sins themselves, the paltry as well as the heinous, the venial as well as the loathsome. His whole work was and is to send away sin—to banish it from the earth, yea, to cast it into the abyss of non-existence behind the back of God. His was the holy war; He came carrying it into our world; He resisted unto blood; the soldiers that followed Him He taught and trained to resist also unto blood, striving against sin; so He became the Captain of their salvation, and they, freed themselves, fought and suffered for others.

Such, then, as were baptized by John, were initiated into the company of those whose work was to send sin out of the world, and first, by sending it out of themselves, by having done with it. Their earliest endeavor in this direction would, as I have said, open the door for that help to enter without which a man could never succeed in the divinely arduous task—could not, because the region in which the work has to be wrought lies in the very roots of his own being, where, knowing nothing of the secrets of his essential existence, he can immediately do nothing, where the Maker of him alone is potent, alone is consciously present.

The change that must pass in him more than equals a new creation, inasmuch as it is a higher creation. But its necessity is involved in a former creation; and thence we have a right to ask help of our Creator, for He requires of us what He has created us unable to effect without Him. . . . All that the children want is their Father.

The one true end of all speech concerning holy things is—the persuading of the individual man to cease to do evil, to set himself to do well, to look to the Lord of his life to be on his side in the new struggle. Supposing the suggestions I have made correct, I do not care that my reader should understand them, except it be to turn against the evil in him, and begin to cast it out. If this be not the result, it is of no smallest consequence whether he agree with my interpretation or not. If he do thus repent, it is of equally little consequence; for, setting himself to do the truth, he is on the way to know all things. Real knowledge has begun to grow possible for him.

# Appendix 4

# The Twelve Steps and Twelve Traditions

## The Twelve Steps of Alcoholics Anonymous

1. We admitted that we were powerless over alcohol—that our lives had become unmanageable.
2. Came to believe that a Power greater than ourselves could restore us to sanity.
3. Made a decision to turn our will and our lives over to the care of God *as we understood Him.*
4. Made a searching and fearless moral inventory of ourselves.
5. Admitted to God, to ourselves, and to another human being the exact nature of our wrongs.
6. Were entirely ready to have God remove all these defects of character.
7. Humbly asked Him to remove our shortcomings.
8. Made a list of all persons we had harmed, and became willing to make amends to them all.
9. Made direct amends to such people wherever possible, except when to do so would injure them or others.
10. Continued to take personal inventory and when we were wrong promptly admitted it.
11. Sought through prayer and meditation to improve our conscious contact with God *as we understood Him,* praying only for knowledge of His will for us and the power to carry that out.
12. Having had a spiritual awakening as the result of these Steps, we tried to carry this message to alcoholics, and to practice these principles in all our affairs.

*Appendix 4*

The Twelve Steps and Twelve Traditions are reprinted with permission of Alcoholics Anonymous World Services, Inc. Permission to reprint the Twelve Steps and Twelve Traditions does not mean that AA has reviewed or approved the contents of this publication, or that AA agrees with the views expressed herein. AA is a program of recovery from alcoholism only. Use of the Twelve Steps and Traditions in connection with programs and activities which are patterned after AA, but which address other problems, or in any other non-AA context, does not imply otherwise.

**The Twelve Traditions of Alcoholics Anonymous**

1. Our common welfare should come first; personal recovery depends on AA unity.
2. For our group purpose there is but one ultimate authority—a loving God as He may express Himself in our group conscience. Our leaders are but trusted servants; they do not govern.
3. The only requirement for AA membership is a desire to stop drinking.
4. Each group should be autonomous except in matters affecting other groups or AA as a whole.
5. Each group has but one primary purpose—to carry its message to the alcoholic who still suffers.
6. An AA group ought never endorse, finance, or lend the AA name to any related facility or outside enterprise, lest problems of money, property, and prestige divert us from our primary purpose.
7. Every AA group ought to be fully self-supporting, declining outside contributions.
8. Alcoholics Anonymous should remain forever nonprofessional, but our service centers may employ special workers.
9. AA, as such, ought never be organized; but we may create service boards or committees directly responsible to those they serve.
10. Alcoholics Anonymous has no opinion on outside issues; hence the AA name ought never be drawn into public controversy.

11. Our public relations policy is based on attraction rather than promotion; we need always maintain personal anonymity at the level of press, radio, and films.
12. Anonymity is the spiritual foundation of all our traditions, ever reminding us to place principles before personalities.

**Differences in Wording in Step One and Tradition Three**
The following differences in wording of Step One and Tradition Three between the sex addiction fellowships are noted for those unfamiliar with these programs:

The wording of Step One for Sexaholics Anonymous reads "We admitted that we were powerless over lust—that our lives had become unmanageable;" for Sex Addicts Anonymous it reads "powerless over our sexual addiction" or "powerless over our compulsive sexual behavior;" for Sex and Love Addicts Anonymous it reads "powerless over sex and love addiction;" and for Homosexuals Anonymous it reads "powerless over our homosexuality and that our emotional lives were unmanageable."

The wording of Tradition Three for Sexaholics Anonymous reads "The only requirement for membership is a desire to stop lusting and become sexually sober;" for Sex Addicts Anonymous it reads "a desire to stop compulsive behavior;" and for Sex and Love Addicts Anonymous it reads "the desire to stop living out a pattern of sex and love addiction."

## Appendix 5

## The Wrath Connection

*When I acted out in the red light district the last time, I knew exactly what was happening. The consequences were right there in front of me. It was a conscious decision of my will turning against God in rebellion; it was an ego-demand to lust; it was a perversion. And I knew the price I'd be paying for it was destruction inside <u>myself</u>.*

A chronic "slipper"

The man who related this experience, a practicing Christian, has been in a sex addiction recovery program for years but had been unable to regain the sobriety he had initially. He is beginning to feel the consequences of lust for what they really are, within himself. We can thus ask the question, Do the consequences of sin within us change just because we happen to be believers? A very important question.

If I or the man above give in to sin today, are we somehow exempt from its automatic consequences within us? The answer is no. This may be difficult for some of us to see. I could never have seen this before recovery. I see that the automatic consequences of lust (sin) are always the same, whether taking place before we were "believers" or afterward. The consequences are always there within us—immediate, natural forces issuing from the nature of sin itself. The Hebrew idea of sin included its consequences within us. We seem to separate the act of sin from its immediate consequences. We seem to consider the consequences of sin

*Appendix 5*

as something *outside* us, or taking place at some future time. More often, we fail to see any consequences at all, superstitious that God will somehow take care of everything.

Another way of saying this is that sin reveals the wrath of God. Failure to realize this wrath mechanism robs us of the motivation to see, surrender, and be saved from our lust and other sins. I use the term "wrath mechanism" because I believe it is just as innate a human characteristic as any other human trait.

Paul's analysis of this sin-wrath process appears in Romans 1, verses 18-32.

> For the wrath of God is revealed from heaven against all ungodliness and wickedness of men who by their wickedness suppress the truth. For what can be known about God is plain to them, because God has shown it to them. . . . so they are without excuse; for although they knew God they did not honor him as God or give thanks to him, but they became futile in their thinking and their senseless minds were darkened. Claiming to be wise, they became fools, and exchanged the glory of the immortal God for images resembling mortal man. . . .
>
> Therefore God gave them up in the lusts of their hearts to impurity, to the dishonoring of their bodies among themselves, because they exchanged the truth about God for a lie and worshiped and served the creature rather than the Creator. . . .
>
> For this reason God gave them up to dishonorable passions. Their women exchanged natural relations for unnatural, and the men likewise gave up natural relations with women and were consumed with passion for one another, men committing shameless acts with men and receiving in their own persons the due penalty for their error.
>
> And since they did not see fit to acknowledge God, God gave them up to a base mind and to improper conduct. They were filled with all manner of wickedness, evil covetousness, malice. Full of envy, murder, strife, deceit, malignity, they are gossips, slanderers, haters of god, insolent, haughty, boastful, inventors of evil, disobedient to parents, foolish, faithless, heartless, ruthless. Though they know god's decree that those who do such things deserve to die, they not only do them but approve those who practice them.

## The Wrath Connection

This classic passage at the opening of Paul's great letter to the Romans has been interpreted as describing the heathen, the non-Christian; it's easy to see why. But its truth is much larger than that if we consider the whole context.

> So we understand these verses as the revelation of the gospel's judgement of all men, which lays bare not only the idolatry of ancient and modern paganism, but also the idolatry ensconced in Israel, in the Church, and in the life of each believer.[86]

Note the reference in this quote to *idolatry as ensconced in the life of each believer*. We miss the force of this truth to our own peril.

Try as I might to dismiss this passage and push it onto the non-Christian—surely this can't be talking about me!—it always returns to haunt me. It confronts me even now; I can't escape it. It holds up a mirror and forces me to look at myself. Something deep inside has me identifying with it powerfully. In this description there seem to be universal principles at work, and these laws never sleep. They describe the effects of the sin-process in each of us. They reveal the wrath of God.

I would like to show how the wrath of God is revealed even now, in us, against ungodliness and unrighteousness. This may help jar us out of our comfortably low view of sin which is so prevalent today and bring us into powerful saving union with the Christ we could otherwise never know.

### Wrath the Automatic Consequence of Sin

> *God's wrath is being revealed from heaven against every kind of ungodliness and unrighteousness of men who suppress the truth by their unrighteousness.* (Rom. 1:18)

*Appendix 5*

All revelation is characterized by apparent paradox, as is the spiritual life itself. There is God's perspective, and there is man's, and man can never fully resolve the paradox because we can never put ourselves in God's position. Thus, I see two aspects of God's wrath: that which we create ourselves and that which reflects God's response to it.[87] Even though in some ultimate sense these may be one and the same, I will be laying emphasis on the wrath we ourselves create—the human perspective. However, a few words are in order on God's wrath as response to sin lest we thereby dismiss this more traditional aspect of the wrath of God.

While I was persisting in sin, God was in the right against me, but I would not allow that. I hid within my Christian belief system and thought I was immune, that only the "godless out there" were under wrath. I tried to maintain my own rightness with God—as a "Christian"!—instead of allowing that *God was in the right against me in my sinning.* I did not realize that it was this very wrath, God's being against what I was doing, that would lead me to repentance. That's the key we fail to see: the purpose of the wrath of God is so we can finally embrace the love of God.

Grace would not be grace if God did not oppose man's opposition to himself.[88] And the Old Testament gives abundant evidence of the principle and outworking of God's wrath in opposing man's opposition to himself. We see it from Adam, Cain, and what happened to the worlds of Noah, Sodom, and Egypt to the whole history of the people of Israel. One passage sums it up:

> The Lord, the Lord, a God merciful and gracious, slow to anger, and abounding in steadfast love and faithfulness, keeping steadfast love for thousands, forgiving iniquity and transgression and sin, but who will by no means clear the guilty, visiting the iniquity of the fathers upon the children and the

children's children, to the third and the fourth generation. (Exodus 34:6f)

Coupled with this, we should remember that there is no wrath of God that can be anything other than the redemptive fire of his love. The consuming fire that is God (Hebrews 12:29) is the fire that exposes and burns away sin *because* God is love. Our modern concept of love is too shallow. True love must embrace the fire that leads us back to him. The ultimate expression of this is that he did not spare his own Son from that wrath. The death of Jesus the Christ on the cross is the revelation of God's wrath from heaven against sin.[89] The reality of the wrath of God is only truly known when it is seen in its revelation upon the person and within the person in Gethsemane and on Golgotha, when he let himself be overcome by sin.[90] Jesus opened himself to wrath when he let himself be overcome by Sin.

**The Wrath Is Self-Induced**
Now to that aspect of wrath we unleash within ourselves. In the passage quoted above, note that Paul says the wrath of God is being *revealed*, made manifest. And note the continuous present tense. Somehow, in the realm of our ungodliness, wrath is revealed; that is, it becomes apparent. My experience helps me see what this means.

I connect with wrath whenever I start practicing unrighteousness in any form, because that's when I suppress the truth of God in me. Wrath goes into effect immediately, inside me, whether I realize it or not. In order to lust or resent, I have to suppress the truth of God—the reality of God as Lord—and act on my own. Self rules. To lust or resent, I have to shut out and thus turn against God.

I'm sure my chemistry is altered whenever I give in to lust or resentment. The wrath produced by sin has direct physical and spiritual consequences within me. Some say they can feel the "rush" produced during lust or resentment,

## Appendix 5

which is merely a physical (chemical) symptom what's happening spiritually inside. What is happening inside is *dis*connection—I've cut myself off from God—and *mis*connection; I've connected with the negative force. Unfortunately, we usually cannot detect these sin-wrath effects unless we have known prior victory over lust and resentment in recovery. Example: You don't know you've lost your serenity until you've had some. We usually aren't aware of the connection between our lust and the wrath it produces.

The wrath also comes into place automatically because I suppress the truth about my self—that I am not my own independent source of life. Instead of surrendering my will and created being to the Creator, in the act of lust I become god of my life. "I want what I want when I want it!"— whether it be thought, attitude, word, or deed.

So the wrath process goes to work inside me automatically, regardless of whether I am (as I was) a preacher "preaching Christ" or a pagan. I think one reason I may have had for kicking myself out of the ministry was to escape this growing feeling that wrong was coming back on my own head, that what I was doing was destroying *me*. The wrath-process is simply a law of the spiritual realm that can no more be set aside than the law of gravity. "What goes around comes around." The fact that we continue to exist physically and religiously while experiencing wrath—a situation typical of our condition today—deceives us into thinking we must be okay. I'll never forget the first adultery and wondering why lightning did not strike. But it did strike—inside. I was changed by that adultery. This is one reason why we need a proliferating horde of addictions to escape feeling this human wrath process going on inside ourselves. The consumer-oriented culture and the entertainment and media revolutions are tailor-made to pander to this need. (See my *Lust Virus*.)

**Wrath in Action**

It's interesting to note that most recovering sex addicts I know eventually see the negative force which is underlying their addiction come to the surface and break out—anger; rage; hatred; resentment; hostility; a judging, condemning, or unforgiving spirit; etc. And once they come off their "drugs" of whatever sort and get into recovery—watch out!. Call it ego-force or whatever. This negative force—wrath—seems to be one of the common "fringe benefits" of addiction and is often directed outward, against people, places, and things.

In the early 1980s I went to my first gay and lesbian meeting. As I came into the meeting someone took me aside and asked, "Ron, have you ever heard of gay rage?" I said, "No, never heard of it." And he said, "Well, you'll see." And see I did. But self-induced rage is not limited to those in same-sex addiction. Look at the self-loathing and self-hatred many of us so-called heterosexual lust addicts have let into our lives and the rage we thrust into our homes.

It is more difficult to see that wrath is also directed against the self in things like guilt, shame, self-hatred, masochism, depression, psychosomatic illnesses, and death-fear (death-expectancy). Lust and resentment are acts of violence within the perpetrator, violence against the self. Perversion of reality is the most damaging kind of violence to one's own spiritual being. It makes everything go haywire. What unleashes the negative force within me is that I have turned against the Light in order to practice sin. That's what makes lust and bad feelings toward others increasingly painful in recovery. At the same time, resentment and lust become increasingly toxic. I can tolerate them less and less; so if I continue in them, I must resort to yet other "drugs."

Ask the recovering lustaholic about his or her anger and resentment. Ask how many have more than a nodding acquaintance with rage. There seems to be no negative force that we, the lust and sex-addicted, have not unleashed within ourselves. And against others. These are the spiritual

## Appendix 5

addictions which underlie the physical and destroy the soul. Thus, from my personal human perspective, the physical, emotional, and spiritual consequences within me of my sinning *are* the wrath of God. Wrath is self-produced, and such wrath can only expect judgment. God has no choice but to oppose our opposition to ourselves and deliver us up to our own negative choices. In this sense, the wrath of God is man-made. We can stop blaming God for being the fearful breather of fire and brimstone when we see this reflexive aspect of our own sin.

I witnessed the life of a Christian lust/sex addict who had tried to stay sober for years in the program but couldn't make it for any considerable period. He finally dropped out, only to reappear a few years later at a meeting. The change in this man was very apparent. The anger he had pretty much kept in check earlier was now in the open. He admitted it himself. One could feel it in his voice and demeanor. We could see it in his face. The change was frightening. That negative force was now in complete control. On the same evening when I saw this man come back, I heard a relative newcomer with three months sexual sobriety sharing. His anger was beginning to surface, though he did not know what was going on and felt confused by it all. This man, who had previously sounded very "Christian" in meetings and gave the appearance of being kind and gentle, was "itching to do violence to someone," waiting for anyone to cross him so he could "light into him." In both cases the rage, once covered, was breaking out into the open. Rage is the screaming out of the soul against its own self-destruction.

At this point, the "adult child" school may interject that the rage is merely a symptom of the victimization we have suffered. Of course, there is truth in this, but I try to avoid descending into the current pop-psychology trap of focusing on the wrong others have done to me. The key factor in what has made me what I am is not what "they" did to me but my attitude *toward* them and what happened.

## The Wrath Connection

Newton's Third Law of Motion states that for every action, there is an equal and opposite reaction. I think the corollary of this is true for each of us in the spiritual realm: For every unrighteous action I put into motion, there's an automatic and immediate negative reaction within me. The wrath of God revealed—self-induced. It's a law of our nature. Unfortunately, that negative reaction—that self-pollution and damage—is also felt in those around us and in the world in which we live and move and have our being. We make our world what it is.

**Wrath in the Culture**
There could very well be a connection between lust and violence (see my *Lust Virus*). Most of us seem to keep the wrath force directed inwardly, against ourselves, although we may not realize that. But when that negative force does come out, it can reveal itself in many ways. I sense a huge negative force building up in our culture, requiring all the addictive "drugs" at our disposal to keep it at bay. It is mostly under the surface, but is beginning to break out more and more. Note the new phenomenon of freeway shootings, where irate motorists blast away with something stronger than their car horns. Note the new phenomenon of church burnings. Years ago I remember predicting that churches would be torched—such the rage of some against the failure of their advertised ability to save. Note the unusually shrill wrath expressed around certain sexual political issues. Increasingly, the wrath is breaking out.

Lust is violence (see "Anatomy of a Look" in chapter 14), and our world is promoting lust in virtually every aspect of our lives today. Because our relation to the media is actually a form of spiritual intercourse, our connection with lust is more immediate and pervasive than at any other time in human history. An overlooked solution to the drug and violence problems is to mitigate lust-pollution. And the only way to mitigate lust-pollution is to mitigate it in the lives of individuals, beginning with me and you.

The wrath of self-hatred points up what may be a missing link in the pornography question—whether there is any connection between pornography and violence. (The reason this connection is missed is because the culture does not view pornography as the spiritual issue which it really is.) A single act of lust in my heart is, I believe, an act of violence against another, even though the object of that lust may not know or feel a thing. Isn't it interesting, however, that when a good woman does happen to catch a man lusting after her, she feels violated; and the man, when caught looking, reacts as though he were caught actually violating that person. If you've ever observed someone in the raw act of lusting after another, you know what I mean.

I'd like to add that a single act of lust in my heart is not only an act of violence against another, but is preeminently an act of violence against *myself*. In it, the wrath of God is being revealed in me. If we can but see it.

**Wrath Means Being Delivered up to the Sin-Process**

> *"For this reason, God gave them up . . ."*
> (Romans 1:24,26,28)

Note the three stages of the "giving up" in this passage. The natural and inevitable effect of the sin-process is that in giving myself up to it, I automatically separate from God. I give up God. Worse yet, this cuts God off from me! He gives *me* up—to myself! Horrible thought! Abandoned to myself? No wonder the darkness, depression, and hangover symptoms following drinking bouts with lust/sex described by so many. Even in my late teens I remember often taking ten or fifteen vitamin B1 capsules at a time after masturbating. I quickly graduated to giving myself hypodermic injections of pure thiamine. Anything for false energy to try and dispel the darkness of losing my self, shutting God out, and being seduced again by Lust. The aftermath of masturbation actually felt like losing part of my spirit, as though part of my spirit had drained away. We know so little about this physical-spiritual aspect of sex and sexuality.

How pathetic, now that I look back on it. But I didn't know what was happening then. In later years, it was the wife and children who also suffered. That conscious cutting off from God has such terrible side effects, producing an inner rage of self-hatred for what I am doing to myself. Self-loss. And to prevent the wrath from destroying me in depression or insanity, I lashed out toward those closest to me. If my writing can help serve, even in some small way, as an indirect amends for those destructive years, I would be most grateful.

God delivers me up to the sin-process because I give myself up. I have the godlike freedom of choosing my destiny because I am made in the image of God. This is my God-given attribute, free choice as a human being. I have choice over my destiny simply by my attitude. And God lets me do it. He gives me up to myself. How can he do anything else? This is a very important way of looking at this concept of the wrath of God.

Being given up by God means being cut off from the real me and having no choice but to misconnect with myself or others, seeking the endless train of vain and empty substitutes.

## Summary: The Laws of the Sin-Process in Romans 1

I have touched on the basic principle of the immediate consequences of sin within us. If we were to go through the whole passage of Romans 1:18-32, as I have done elsewhere, we would see that what Paul has presented there is nothing less than the laws of the sin-process at work in human experience—in you and me.

Let's summarize these now. Note the progression of the sin-wrath process, and how this also describes the addictive process:

*Appendix 5*

1. Wrong attitudes and actions (unrighteousness) suppress the truth of God in one's life (verse 18).
2. This conscious decision shuts God out (verse 18).
3. This results in wrath, futile thinking, and distortion of reality (verse 21).
4. We compensate by asserting our own understanding instead of the truth (verse 21).
5. Denying the true knowledge of our self and God and substituting a false reality, we become fools (verse 22).
6. Loss of the true God must be counteracted by connecting with false gods—the most immediate, appealing, and gratifying of which are images that can be possessed via the senses or fantasy. How apropos for today's image-driven lustaholic. We now unwittingly serve false gods, regardless of any religious convictions or practices we may engage in (verse 23).
7. Abandoning the true God, we are given over to the sin-process (verse 24).
8. Exchanging the truth about God in the Lie creates a loss at the core of our being which *must* be filled. Lust fills the void through impurity (verse 24).
9. The Lie in this exchange is the false worship of creature and self, image-likenesses instead of the real Presence of God (verse 25).
10. The intolerable loss produced by the Great Abandonment forces lust to push against all bounds, seeking ever more potent forms of expression and possession. Sexual lust offers one of the most palpable substitutes for personal union with our Source. Dishonorable sexual passions lead to sexual perversion, which is expressed both heterosexually and homosexually (verses 26, 27). We fail to see the sex perversion in our so-called heterosexuality today. Is increasing heterosexual perversion in a culture a

11. contributing factor in the rise of homosexuality? (See my *Lust Virus*.)
11. Continuing to abandon God, we are shut up to our diseased mental processes, so corrupted as to be untrustworthy guides in moral decisions (verse 28).
12. This leads to all manner of sinful judgment and expression (verses 28-31).
13. The rage of feeling the abysmal loss in the Abandonment, and knowing we are the ones responsible, creates self-hatred and generates a death-expectancy (verse 32).
14. The negative force behind this rage and wrath seeks expression and validation by finding others doing the same, by pushing itself onto others and pulling others down with us, by promoting itself, and by trying to convert others—even the world, if it can—to the Lie (verse 32).[91]

• • •

This Romans passage, which reveals the wrath of God, not only describes the sinful nature but the sinful *process*. These principles are universal laws which you and I cannot get around, in effect in everyone. Whenever lust (sin) is practiced, the natural consequences follow within the individual, as surely as the law of gravity is maintained. And just as there is "no distinction" in the operation of physical laws between Christian and non-Christian—apples fall on all heads alike—so there is no distinction among persons regarding these spiritual principles of the sin-process. That is the whole thrust of Romans chapter 2, if we can see it. There Paul looks at the religious person in his pride and says, "Hey, you're guilty of the same."

The sin-principles are in effect for believer and non-believer alike. Whenever I start practicing any sin, these laws kick in automatically, and the wrath-process starts anew. I

## Appendix 5

testify to this from my own experience. The wages of sin *is* death. There is no escaping the wrath of God *because it originates in me.* But thank God, it is that very wrath of God which leads me to repentance. Whenever I stop practicing sin in the obedience of faith, the righteousness-process starts anew.

**Behind God's Anger**
I'd like to share an incident in a program meeting I attended recently that has helped me see the wrath of God in a new light. It was a newcomer sex addict's second meeting. He had slipped since the prior week's meeting and was now only two day's sober from sexual acting out—still on a "full stomach," as we say. Gone were the conviction and signs of repentance we had witnessed in him the previous week. He said he was feeling better and was not "beating himself up about it" (his slip), and would we mind if he read a passage of Scripture to us (he brought his large Bible along for the occasion)? We never saw him again.

Most of the others in the meeting were chronic slippers, there being only one regular attendee who had more than a couple of months of sobriety. I felt myself getting upset. I wanted to say what I had felt for a long time, that if I ever heard another member say they were not beating themselves up for acting out, I was going to puke. Over the years, I heard this so many times that I came to see it was signifying that coming to meetings was actually helping the person feel better about themselves, even though they were still acting out their addiction! It had become obvious to me that such persons (and their groups) were using the program meetings to support the illness rather than recovery. This is a devastating indictment of much of the so-called Twelve Step program of today. That program was originally based on principles and "tough love" instead of pseudo-democratic weakness catering to personality.

## The Wrath Connection

As I left the meeting and started driving home, I asked myself, What was *I* angry about? I realized that I actually feel the insobriety of others. I don't understand this; call it empathy if you like. To feel another who is remaining comfortable in lust wounds me. I hurt with it. And this hurt produces anger. Group unity and any hope for true fellowship are compromised. And I need true spiritual fellowship, so I am directly threatened. We should start getting less tolerant with lust in meetings.

Then the thought dawned on me: *God* is the one who preeminently feels our sin and hurts with it. And the result is God's righteous anger, God's wrath. Look at that first chapter of Romans again. The righteousness of God is revealed (v. 17) *because* his wrath is revealed (v.18). And finally, the love of Christ is revealed (8:35). Do you see the sequence? Before righteousness and love can be revealed in us, wrath must be revealed! And I bear witness to this sequence. It was the wrath process at work in me that brought me to my knees in surrender. Nothing else did it—not belief in Christ, not religious devotion, not prayer, not counseling. Nothing. My recovery began with the wrath being revealed in me as a natural part of the sin process. There was no righteousness or love of God without it.

We need to take a serious look today at the real meaning and consequences of sin within us and face up to the wrath of God that is being revealed in our lives, our culture, and in our fellowship today. Can the *church* face the fact that wrath is being revealed in the church today?

• • •

Yes, there is "idolatry ensconced in the Church and in the life of each believer"—in you and me. Idolatry. And yes, this means we must be willing to face how the sin-process works wrath within us. Now, today. *There is no other way to encounter and know the real Jesus.*

So, do I want the sin-process and its wrath at work in my life?  Do you?  If we continue in addiction, lust, resentment, unforgiveness, etc., we reap the consequences within us immediately, whether we see it or not. How many times have I seen sex addicts return, after having gone back out there into lust, only to be shocked at their physical and spiritual disfigurement and demonic defilement that manifests itself as never before. How many more times—countless, it seems—have I let myself descend into resentment or unforgiveness and felt the results within me. Wrath is revealed; we are being delivered up to the consequences of sin; and given over to futile thinking, a darkened mind, and perversion. No wonder that today we have so many psychosomatic ailments. And so many addictions to cover them up!

By his grace, let us be willing to surrender now. Let us behold the saving Son of man as he is for us today, in our very sinfulness and wrath, so his righteousness can be revealed in us. The righteousness of the Son of man, who loves us and gives himself up for us.

## Acknowledgments

Harper & Row, *A Harmony of the Gospels for Students of the Life of Christ*, by A.T. Robertson, 1950. *The Word of God and the Word of Man*, by Karl Barth, 1957.
Harper & Brothers: *The Creeds of Christendom*, by Philip Schaff, 6th ed., three vols., 1931.
Harper San Francisco: *Addiction and Grace*, by Gerald May, 1988.
William B. Eerdmans: *The Gifts of the Child Christ* by George MacDonald, 1973. *Theological Dictionary of the New Testament*, edited by Gerhard Kittel, translated by Geoffrey W. Bromiley, 1964, also the edition abridged in one volume by Geoffrey W. Bromiley, 1985. *The Gospel According to St Mark, the Greek Text with Introduction Notes and Indices,* by Henry Barclay Swete, 1952. *Commentaries on the Epistle of Paul the Apostle to the Hebrews*, by John Calvin, 1948. Calvin, *Institutes of the Christian Religion,* 1953. *The International Standard Bible Encyclopaedia*, ed. by James Orr, 1939. *Psychology as Religion, the Cult of Self-Worship*, by Paul C. Vitz, 1977.
SA Literature: *Sexaholics Anonymous*, 1989. *Recovery Continues*, 1990. *Discovering the Principles, Our Growing Experience with the Traditions*, 1991.
Thomas Nelson: *The Holy Bible*, Revised Standard Version, 1959.
T. & T. Clark: *A Critical and Exegetical Commentary on the Epistle to the Romans,* vol 1, by C. E. B. Cranfield, 1975. *Church Dogmatics*, by Karl Barth, 1975. *Critical and Exegetical Commentary on the New Testament (Matthew)*, by Heinrich August Wilhelm Meyer, 1883.
J. J. Flynn: *The Hope of the Gospel*, by George MacDonald, 1988 (originally published by Ward, Lock, Bowden and Co., London, 1892). *Unspoken Sermons*, Series One, by George MacDonald, 1987 (originally published by Alexander Strahan, London, 1867).

Oxford University Press: *The Epistle to the Romans*, by Karl Barth, translated from the 6th ed. by Edwyn C. Hoskyns, 1933. *The New English Bible*, 1970.
Macmillan and Co.: *The Epistles of St John: The Greek Text with Notes and Essays*, by Brooke Foss Westcott, 1883. *The Epistle to the Hebrews*, by Brooke Foss Westcott, 1889.
The University of Chicago Press: *A Greek-English Lexicon of the New Testament and Other Early Christian Literature*, ed. by William F. Arndt and F. Wilbur Gingrich, 1979.
Baker Book House: *Word Pictures in the New Testament*, by Archibald Thomas Robertson, 1930.
Word Books: *Word Biblical Commentary*, volume 38, *Romans* 1-8, by James D. G. Dunn, 1988.
Discovery House Publishers: *My Utmost for His Highest*, by Oswald Chambers, 1963.
Alcoholics Anonymous World Services: *Alcoholics Anonymous*, 1955.
*Catholic Biblical Quarterly*: "The Sinful Flesh of the Son of God" (Rom 8:3), 47:1985 and "In the Likeness of Sinful Flesh", 49:1987.
Scribners: *History of the Christian Church*, by Philip Schaff, vol. 1, 1887.
SCM Press LTD: *A Shorter Commentary on Romans*, by Karl Barth, 1959.
Doubleday: *Catechism of the Catholic Church*, 1995.

# Notes

1. George MacDonald, *The Hope of the Gospel*, p.78f.

2. C.E.B. Cranfield, *A Critical and Exegetical Commentary on the Epistle to the Romans*, vol 1, p. 381f. See this section of Cranfield for an excellent capsule summary of the issue of Jesus' humanity, including analysis of the more popular view.

3. C.K. Barrett, *A Commentary on the Epistle to the Romans* (Black's NY Commentaries), London, 1957, as quoted in Cranfield, op. cit., p. 381. See also B.F. Westcott, *The Historic Faith,* London, Macmillan, 1890, p. 64.

4. Karl Barth, *The Epistle to the Romans*, 1968 (sixth ed. of the 1919 original), p. 277. See also appendix 1 for some crucial passages from his Church Dogmatics and from other theologians. At first glance, this concept may put us off, but these passages represent some very bold and original thinking.

5. Karl Barth, *Church Dogmatics*, I,2, p.153f.

6. Mary, Martha, Mary Magdalene, and a host of others for example. See Mk 15:40f, Lk 23:49, and Mt 27:55f.

7. See Luke 4:23-24; John 6:42; 7:12, 16, 20, 27, 28, 41.

8. Barth, *Church Dogmatics*, IV, I, p. 263.

9. George MacDonald, *Unspoken Sermons* (Series One), p. 133.

10. Oswald Chambers, *My Utmost for His Highest*, p. 75.

11. Kurt Aland, et al, *The Greek New Testament*, 3rd corrected edition, 1983. For example, Nestle's Greek New Testament of 1953 shows a colon, whereas the Nestle-Aland of 1953 shows a question mark. Apparently, the manuscript evidence is inconclusive.

12. George MacDonald, *Unspoken Sermons*, Series Three, p.73.

13. H.B. Swete, *The Gospel According to St Mark, the Greek Text with Introduction, Notes and Indices,* 3rd ed., 1951, p. 342, and A.T. Robertson, *Word Pictures in the New Testament,* 1930, vol. 1, p. 212.

14. The words for these expressions in the Greek text are *thambeo, ademonein,* and *perilupos . . . heos thanatou.*

15. John Calvin, *Epistle of Paul the Apostle to the Hebrews*, p. 123, and his *Institutes of the Christian Religion,* II:xvi:10, p.443.

16. H.A.W. Meyer, *Critical and Exegetical Handbook to the Gospel of Matthew*, 1881, vol. 2, p.271f.

17. H. A. W. Meyer.

18. John Calvin, *Institutes of the Christian Religion,* II:xvi:10, (p. 443).

19. Meyer, op. cit., p. 275.

20. See also Leviticus 19:17 and 22:9,16, where the sense of bearing sin is illustrated.

21. John 14:3, 18, 23, 28; 16:7; Rev. 3:20.

22. Barth, *Church Dogmatics*, IV, 1, p. 504.

23. *My Utmost for His Highest*, p. 97, April 6.

24. Cranfield, *Romans*, vol. 1, p.360. Also see James D. G. Dunn, Word Biblical Commentary, vol. 38, Romans 1-8, vol. 1, pages 411-412.

25. Ibid., vol. 1, p. 366.

26. Dunn, *Romans*, vol. 1, p. 407.

27. Cranfield, *Romans*, vol. 1, p.358.

28. As to the sins of men, Christ makes propitiation for them (Heb. 2:17); he forgives them (Matt 9:2ff, Col 2:13); he takes them away by bearing them (I John 3:5, John 1:29, Heb. 10:4,11); he looses men from them (Rev. 1:5, comp. Rom. 6:22); he cleanses men from all sin (I John 1:7); he saves from sins (Matt 1:21). (B.F.Westcott, *The Epistles of St. John*, p. 37-40)

29. Oswald Chambers, *My Utmost for His Highest*, p. 87.

30. See Romans chapter 16 and Cranfield, *Romans*, vol. 1, p. 21.

31. Cheryl Russell, as reported in *Time* magazine, November 16, 1992, p. 58.

32. B.F. Westcott, *The Epistle to the Hebrews*: The Greek Text with Notes and Essays, 1889, p. 424 and p.33. The nine passages referred to are: 2:9, 3:1, 6:20, 7:22, 10:19, 12:2, 12:24, 13:12, and 13:20.

33. *Theological Dictionary of the New Testament*, (TDNT), ed. by Gerhard Kittle, trans. by Geoffrey Bromiley, 1976, I:487-488.

34. The passages are: 2:10ff, 5:ff, 7:28, 2:17, 4:15, and 12:2. See Westcott's fine analysis of *teleiosis*, Hebrews, pages 63-67.

35. Westcott, *Hebrews*, p. 66.

36. Arndt and Gingrich, *A Greek-English Lexicon of the New Testament*, 2nd ed., 1979.

37. B. F. Westcott, *The Epistles of St. John: The Greek Text with Notes and Essays*, 1883, p. 85.

38. *Theological Dictionary of the New Testament*, 1:628.

39. The First Step reads, "We admitted that we were powerless over (------------)—that our lives had become unmanageable."

40. Westcott, *Hebrews*, p. 107.

41. Arthur M., personal communication.

42. Cranfield, *Romans*, vol. 1, p. 388.

43. *Theological Dictionary of the New Testament (one-vol. ed.,*Bromiley), p. 1163.

44. Barth, *Church Dogmatics*, IV, 1, p. 313-318.

45. Karl Barth, *The Word of God and the Word of Man*, Harper and Row, 1957, p. 48.

46. For the continuing action of Christ's sacrifice, see also I John 1:7, Heb. 9:12, and I Peter 1:2.

47. I realize there is an apparent contradiction here. On the one hand, we read in Hebrews 9:25-28, "Nor was it to offer himself repeatedly . . . for then he would have had to suffer repeatedly since the foundation of the world. But as it is,

he has appeared once for all at the end of the age to put away sin by the sacrifice of himself. And just as it is appointed for men to die once... so Christ, having been offered once to bear the sins of many...." On the other hand, we read that Christ has appeared as a high priest, entering once for all time into the Holy Place of the heavenly sanctuary, taking his own blood, and thus securing an eternal redemption (9:12). With all due discretion, I resolve the apparent contradiction by holding that although the sacrifice on Golgotha was a one-time event, the principle of that event—the bearing of sin—is eternal. How else can he bear *my* sins; he died two thousand years ago? The action of his blood is effective now, in the heavenly sanctuary. See quotes from Barth in preceding pages of this chapter. Does Jesus take my sin now without feeling its pain and death? I don't know. But if God chose to suffer the consequences of sin, I tend to think he feels every sin and that it is his love for me that burns it away. Remember, the realm of God
(the kingdom of heaven, kingdom of God) transcends space-time-matter. See Acts 9:5. Love hurts!


48. Gerald May, *Addiction and Grace*, p.124.

49. George MacDonald, *Unspoken Sermons*, Series One, pp. 69-70.

50. Handly Dunelm, article on "Faith" in *The International Standard Bible Encyclopedia*, Grand Rapids, 1946, vol. I, p. 1088.

51. See Cranfield, *Romans*, vol. 1, p. 66f for the equivalence for Paul of faith in God and obedience to him. Also see Barth, *Church Dogmatics*, II:1 p. 37.

52. Karl Barth, *Church Dogmatics*, IV, 1, p.263

53. Idem., IV,I, p. 263,4.

54. The Death-Resurrection event of Jesus is the act intersecting time and the eternal, thus transcending time and space. This is how I can be raised *with Christ* (Eph. 2:6). This also makes me wonder whether there can be righteousness in this sense without temptation via my sinful nature? Could this be one aspect of a possible solution to the problem of evil?

55. *Theological Dictionary of the New Testament*, 1, p.512.

56. See Gerald May's revealing chapter on "The Neurological Nature of Addiction" in his book *Addiction and Grace*.

57. John 5:30 and 8:28 (Greek), John 7:17f, 7:28, 14:10, 15:4. I note with sadness that Dr. Bob and Bill W., the co-founders of AA, misquoted Jesus by saying, "Of myself I *am nothing.*" Jesus never said he was nothing!

58. The experience of a recovering lust/sex addict can be found in "The Joy Response" in *Recovery Continues*, SA literature, 1990.

59. *The Hope of the Gospel*, p. 197.

60. The word for resurrection in this final clause is *exanastasis*, the only instance of its use in the New Testament. The usual word and that occurring elsewhere in this passage is *anastasis*. I reject making the two words equivalent as some interpreters do. Why would Paul use the two words in the same passage if he intended no difference? Addition of the *ex* prefix to the usual *anastasis* should be taken literally: I want to be like him in his death—by dying to temptation—so I can be raised *out of* the death that sin would cause.

61. *Genesis Interface*, an historical novel of the future.

62. For a description of good twelve Step meeting quality, see *Discovering the Principles, Our Growing Experience with the Traditions,* p. 12, SA Literature.

63. Westcott, *The Epistles of St. John*, p. 181f.

64. Vincent P. Branick, "The Sinful Flesh of the Son of God (Rom 8:3): A Key Image of Pauline Theology," *Catholic Biblical Quarterly*, 47, 1985, p. 246.

65. Philip Schaff, *The Creeds of Christendom*, with a History and Critical Notes, vol. III, p. 531.

66. Origen, *De Principiis*, in Schaff, *Creeds*, vol. II, p. 23.

67. Schaff, *Creeds*, Vol. II, p. 62.

68. Schaff, vol. II, p. 69.

69. Idem., vol. III, pp. 9, 79, 99.

70. Idem, p. 367f.

71. Idem, p. 444.

72. Idem, p. 488.

73. Idem, p. 586.

74. Idem, p. 619.

75. Idem, p. 731.

76. Idem, p. 800.

77. Idem, p. 807.

78. Idem, p. 814.

79. Idem, p. 851.

80. Idem, p. 914.

81. Idem, p. 917.

82. Idem, p. 923.

83. Idem, p. 936.

84. Schaff, *Creeds*, vol. I, pp. 906, 912.

85. Westcott, *John*, vol. 1, p. 101.

86. Cranfield, *Romans*, vol. 1, page 106.

87. The subject of the wrath of God is much broader and deeper than I indicate here for the immediate purpose of this book. For example, see Karl Barth, *Church Dogmatics*, II:1, 393ff.

88. Barth, *Church Dogmatics*, IV,1, p. 490.

89. Karl Barth, *Church Dogmatics*, IV, 1, p. 541f, and *A Shorter Commentary on Romans*, p. 26.

90. Cranfield, *Romans*, vol. I, p. 110.

91. For another perspective, read the chapter in *Sexaholics Anonymous* titled "The Spiritual Basis of Addiction," pages 45-58.